PROJECT PLANNING, SCHEDULING, AND CONTROL

Fourth Edition

PROJECT PLANNING, SCHEDULING, AND CONTROL
A Hands-On Guide to Bringing Projects in on Time and on Budget

JAMES P. LEWIS

McGraw-Hill

New York   Chicago   San Francisco   Lisbon   London
Madrid   Mexico City   Milan   New Delhi   San Juan
Seoul   Singapore   Sydney   Toronto

The *McGraw-Hill* Companies

1 2 3 4 5 6 7 8 9 0 DOC/DOC 0 9 8 7 6 5

ISBN 0-07-146037-3

McGraw-Hill books are available at special quantity discounts to use as premiums and sales promotions, or for use in corporate training programs. For more information, please write to the Director of Special Sales, McGraw-Hill, Professional Publishing, 2 Penn Plaza, New York, NY 10121-2298. Or contact your local bookstore.

High Performance Project Management is a trademark of The Lewis Institute, Inc. The Lewis Method is a registered trademark of The Lewis Institute, Inc. PMI, PMBOK, and PMP are registered trademarks of the Project Management Institute. MicrosoftProject is a registered trademark of Microsoft Corporation. Mind Map is a registered trademark of Tony Buzan. HBDI is a trademark of Herrmann International. The grid containing a thinking profile is also copyright by Herrmann International, and all such figures in this book are used by permission. MindManager is a trademark of MindJet.

Library of Congress Cataloging-in-Publication Data

Lewis, James P.
    Project planning, scheduling, and control : a hands-on guide to bringing projects in on time and on budget / by James P. Lewis.— 4th ed.
        p. cm.
    ISBN 0-07-146037-3 (hardcover : alk. paper)
    1. Project management.   2. Scheduling.   I. Title.

HD69.P75L493 2005
658.4'04—dc22   2005021825

This book is dedicated to the memory of
Lars, Neko, Fiona, and the score of other
feline "children" who have enriched my life
over the years. There are many ways in
which animals are smarter than people.

It is never too late to be
what you might have been.
—George Elliott

CONTENTS

SECTION THREE

PROJECT PLANNING

Chapter 7

Developing Project Strategy   183

CHAPTER 8

Implementation Planning   211

CHAPTER 9

Project Scheduling   261

PREFACE

When I attended my first project management seminar in 1975, there were only a very few programs available, and most were attended by engineers and construction managers. There weren't many more programs available in 1981, when I began teaching project management. Now interest is so strong that the Project Management Institute® has over 200,000 members, and is still growing at an exponential rate. It is safe to say that there has been a project management revolution. There are so many programs available that one hardly knows which to choose.

The same may be true of project management books. The first edition of this book was published in 1991, and at that time I never dreamed that it would have such an impact around the world. I have always written for the practitioner, rather than the classroom, but I have been pleased that the book has been adopted for use in a number of university courses on project management.

This fourth edition brings the book in line with current practice. There are not a lot of new practices in project management, but what does seem to be happening is that more people are following a structured approach to managing projects than was true 10 years ago.

I hope you will find the book useful in managing your own projects, and wish you the best in your career.

James P. Lewis
Vinton, Virginia
jlewis@lewisinstitute.com

ACKNOWLEDGMENTS

It is impossible to acknowledge all of the people who have contributed to this book over the years. Certainly many of the more than 30,000 people who have attended my project management seminars have contributed to my learning, which has found its way into the book. My heartfelt thanks goes to them.

There are some people who must be recognized by name. My wife, Lea Ann, has worked on each of my 12 books with enthusiasm, trying to bring them to life by illustrating the text, which might otherwise appear dull and uninviting. Lora Hansen has helped her turn her illustrations into computer graphics, as my wife does not use a computer.

Since I first began writing for McGraw-Hill, Judy Brown has typeset all of my books, and we have enjoyed a very good working relation. I appreciate her style and conscientious approach to her work.

I would also like to thank Pamela van Giessen, who first recognized the potential of this book in 1991. It is safe to say that publication of the first edition of *Project Planning, Scheduling, and Control* completely changed my life.

Thanks finally to my editors at McGraw-Hill. My first acquisition editor, Catherine Dassopoulous, decided to be a full-time mom last year, but she has avidly supported my projects over the years, and I thank her for that support. Stephen Isaacs, who took over for Catherine, has been equally excited about my projects, and I thank him for that as well. And Jeffrey Krames, who is not only my publisher but also a very fine writer, has given me great moral support over the years. My thanks to everyone at McGraw-Hill for bringing my work to life around the world.

PROJECT PLANNING, SCHEDULING, AND CONTROL

SECTION ONE

INTRODUCTION TO PROJECT MANAGEMENT

CHAPTER

An Introduction to Project Management

The news traveled from the palace to the Valley of the Kings with incredible speed—Nefertari, beloved wife of Ramses the Great, 19th Dynasty pharaoh of Upper and Lower Egypt, had just borne him another son. The messenger was out of breath as he entered the murky darkness of the burial chamber and greeted Ashahebsed, builder of the tombs for the family of the great king.

"The new child has just arrived," he announced breathlessly, "a son." Ashahebsed was well aware who he meant by "new child." The pregnancy of Nefertari, one of two royal wives of Ramses, was well known throughout the kingdom.

Ashahebsed shook his head. Another tomb would have to be added. How many was this now? At last count, the king had sired 30 sons and as many daughters. With two royal wives, two Hittite princesses acquired through diplomatic marriage, and four of his

**The "project" was
never-ending**

own daughters whom he had married, following Egyptian tradition, Ramses was more than prolific. At 60 years of age he was still fathering children at an alarming rate.

"By the great god Amun," Ashahebsed exclaimed, "at this rate, I'll never finish this project!"

"You're right," said the messenger. "I have been instructed to inform you that Isetnofret is pregnant again."

"The second royal wife of Ramses," thought Ashahebsed. "And so are the two Hittite princesses," he groaned.

"Don't forget Bant-Anat," the messenger offered.

Isetnofret's child, one of the four daughters the pharaoh had married.

"It is clear that I will be on this project until pharaoh dies," said Ashahebsed.

"It looks that way," agreed the messenger, as he turned to go out into the blinding Egyptian sun.

❧❀❧

Ashahebsed may very well have endured the most scope changes, over the most extended period, of any project manager in history. Ramses the Great had more than 100 sons and daughters over his 90 years. He was pharaoh for nearly 65 years, and no doubt the building of tombs for his progeny extended over much of that time. The best that can be said is that Ashahebsed had job security. The worst is that the project just kept on going and going and going . . .

WHAT IS A PROJECT?

The Project Management Institute (PMI®) is the professional association for project managers (more about them later). In the latest edition of the *Project Management Body of Knowledge,* or PMBOK® (2004), PMI defines a project as "a temporary endeavor undertaken to produce a unique product, service, or result." Temporary means that every project has a definite beginning and end.

> A project is a temporary endeavor undertaken to produce a unique product, service, or result (PMBOK, 2004, p. 5)

Unique means that this product, service, or result is different than others that may have preceded it.

Unfortunately, textbook definitions often don't reflect the real world. Ashahebsed's project definitely was not temporary; as the scope kept changing, the ultimate completion date slid out ever further until it disappeared over the horizon. And of course the budget had to change accordingly.

So this was certainly no textbook project. (In fact, if any of you know of a project that conforms to the textbook definition, please e-mail me about it, so I can write a case study!)

In reality, the only part of the definition that fits all projects is that all are jobs that produce something unique. Perhaps it would

There are
NO textbook
projects!

be better to say that they are *intended* to be temporary in nature, meaning a one-time job. A repetitive job is not a project. Neither is performing a single task. Nevertheless, a substantial number of jobs do qualify as projects, and there are many people managing them (or at least trying to).

Tom Peters (1998) has argued that as much as 50 percent of the work done in organizations can be thought of as projects. I believe that this number is far greater for many organizations. This means that, even though everyone is not called a project manager, they are *de facto* managing projects anyway. And, while they may not need the formality of critical path schedules and earned value analysis, they do need some skills in project planning and control.

Dr. J. M. Juran has also said that a project is a problem scheduled for solution. I like this definition because it makes us realize that a project is conducted to solve a problem for the organization. However, the word problem almost always conveys something negative. When someone says, "We have a problem," that is usually bad news. Environmental cleanup projects might be thought of as solving the "bad" kind of problem. But developing a new product or software program is also a problem—a positive problem. So "problem" is being used here in a very broad

A project is a
problem scheduled
for solution.
~ Dr. J. M. Juran

sense, and projects deal with both kinds of problems, positive and negative.

WHAT IS PROJECT MANAGEMENT?

The 2004 edition of the PMBOK defines project management as ". . . application of knowledge, skills, tools and techniques to project activities to meet project requirements. Project management is accomplished through the application and integration of the project management processes of initiating, planning, executing, monitoring and controlling, and closing" (op cit., p. 8.). These processes are further defined in the PMBOK, and it is the objective of this book to explain how all of these are accomplished in practice.

I think it is important to mention that these processes do not fully capture the essence of project management. Much of project management consists of dealing with political issues, trying to get team members to perform at the required level, and negotiating for scarce resources. These activities are not really captured by the PMBOK processes, and no single document can do justice to the true complexity of project management.

"Instant-Pudding" Project Management

In December 1999 I met with a project manager in Germany, and we discussed whether project management in Germany was the same as in the United States. I showed him my model of project management, which I call The Lewis Method®, and compared it to his process. We found that his method and mine were nearly identical.

"I have been trying to explain project management to senior management here, but I'm afraid with very little success," he said sadly.

"In one meeting, one of our vice presidents got very frustrated and said, 'I don't understand why we don't just buy Microsoft Project® and do it!'" He added, "Meaning, of course, why don't we do project management."

I almost laughed. "It's the same in the United States," I assured him. "Senior managers there also assume that project man-

agement is just scheduling, and that if they buy the tool for everyone, they will have instant project managers."

He looked a bit relieved.

"I think we should put the scheduling software in a box and rename it 'Instant Project Manager'," I said. "On the side of the box, the instructions would say just add water, stir, shake, bake, and you will have instant project managers—sort of an 'instant pudding' approach to project management."

He thought for a moment. "That's actually what we are doing now, isn't it? Practicing instant-pudding project management!"

"Yes," I agreed. "And I can tell you that it is an approach followed throughout much of the world."

Tools, People, and Systems

Project management is not just scheduling.

It is not just tools.

It is not a job position or job title.

It is not even the sum total of these. But my experience shows that few people understand this. They believe project management is scheduling, and that if a person can do some technical job (using the word technical in a very broad sense), then that individual can manage.

This is a pervasive problem. We forget that there are two aspects to all work, including projects—the *what* and the *how*. The "what" is the task to be performed. The "how" is the process by which it is performed. But process also applies to how the team functions overall—how they communicate, interact, solve problems, deal with conflict, make decisions, assign work, run meetings, and every other aspect of team performance. The tools they use—such as scheduling software, computers, project notebooks, and daily planners—help with both the what and the how. But the tools do not make an instant project manager of a person who has not been trained in the *how*. (See Figure 1.1.)

F I G U R E 1.1

Project Management Is Tools, People, and Systems

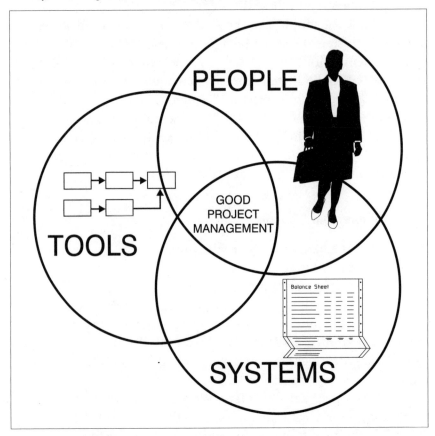

Organizations and project teams *are* people. I think we forget this. An organization has capital equipment, buildings, inventory, and other paraphernalia for the sole purpose of enabling human beings to do work that will result in desired organizational outcomes.

Yet managers often focus on everything but people. I have been told of many mangers who are brilliant with computers, but absolutely horrible at dealing with people. They are rude, condescending, and dictatorial. You wonder how such individuals survive in their jobs, but they do.

In any case, the message should be understood—organizations are people, and people engage in processes to get results. If the people do not function well, neither will the processes, and if the processes don't work, task outcomes will suffer. The sad thing is that we know more about how to get performance from capital equipment than from people.

As I already said, project management deals with tools, people, and systems. The tools are work breakdown structures, PERT scheduling, earned value analysis, risk analysis, and scheduling software (to name a few). And tools are the primary focus of most organizations that want to implement project management.

Tools are a necessary but not sufficient condition for success in managing projects. The processes or techniques are far more important, because without employing the correct processes for

Organizations are people, and people engage in processes to get results

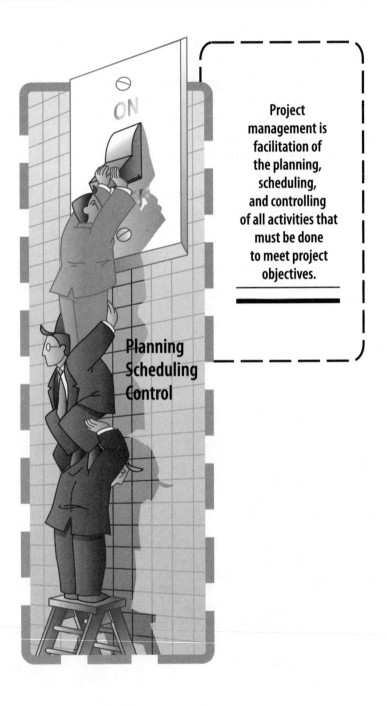

Project management is facilitation of the planning, scheduling, and controlling of all activities that must be done to meet project objectives.

managing, the tools will only help you document your failures with great precision.

A simple example is that you give a person an automobile so that he can get around, but you give him no training in how to drive the car. He must learn by trial and error. By the time he has become a competent driver (if he ever does), he has battered up the car pretty badly, and in the process done quite a bit of damage to others. This is what happens when you give people scheduling software with no training in how to use it properly.

On the other hand, training someone who has no car how to drive is a waste. Absent the car, the training is irrelevant.

In short, the PMI definition of project management is not bad, as long as you understand that you must include dealing with politics, exercising leadership, and, for good measure, a small dose of public relations expertise.

The Four Project Constraints

It has been common to talk about the triple constraints in project management—performance, time, and cost. Colloquially, they are often referred to as good, fast, and cheap, and as the saying goes, "Good, fast, or cheap—pick two." The point is that you can only dictate two of them, and the third will have to vary.

When I wrote the first edition of this book, I realized that there was a fourth constraint—scope. The magnitude or size of the job is also related to the other three, and I started pointing out that you could assign values to any three of them, but the fourth must be al-

> **Scope:** the magnitude or size of the project.

lowed to vary. In fact, scope changes probably cause more missed project deadlines and cost overruns than any other factor short of incorrectly defining project requirements to begin with.

I have learned during the past couple of years that many people are confused by the term *performance,* so I want to clarify it here. A project is intended to produce a result of some kind. Construction projects produce buildings for people to occupy, roads for them to travel on, or dams that provide water to communities. Product development projects provide products for people to use; software projects do the same.

There are two kinds of performance requirements, which together are called specifications. One is *functional requirements.* These describe what the deliverable is supposed to do. The other is technical requirements, which describe the features of the deliverable. They may specify dimensions, weight, color, speed, horsepower, thrust, or any of a million other specifications that can apply to a deliverable. As a former engineer, we used to ask if a change would affect the form, fit, or function of a product. You can see how this relates to what has just been said.

Defining project requirements is a major aspect of project definition, and doing so incorrectly or inadequately is, I believe, the single most common cause of project failures. I was once told a story by a fellow that illustrates this beautifully. He had a friend over at his house one day and they were doing some yard work. He said to his friend, "You see this small tree in front of my house? How about trimming the limbs off this tree to a height about like this?" He indicated what he meant by holding his hand a certain distance above the ground.

He then left his friend to trim the tree and went to the back of the house to do some work. When he returned to the front of the house, his friend had just finished the job. It was nicely done, except for one significant detail. His friend had cut all of the limbs off the top of the tree, down to the proper height, when what the fellow wanted was to have the limbs trimmed off the trunk of the tree from the *ground up* to the height he had indicated!

What happened here is all too common. "Trim the tree" meant something different to each of them. We call this is a communication problem. And because communication problems happen so frequently, we had better take care to achieve a *shared understanding* of what is supposed to be done in the project. We will talk about how this is done in Chapter 5.

Elsewhere I have said that project management is the application of knowledge, skills, tools, and techniques to project activities to meet project requirements. These requirements are defined by the PCTS targets and are the constraints on every project, no matter how large or small. Because you can never escape them, you must understand how they interact.

P = performance requirements: technical and functional

C = labor cost to do the job. (Note that capital equipment and material costs are accounted for separately from labor.)

T = time required for the project

S = scope or magnitude of the work

The relationship between them is given by the following expression:

$$C = f(P, T, S)$$

In other words, cost is a function of performance, time, and scope. Ideally this could be written as an exact mathematical expression. For example:

$$C = 2P + 3T + 4S$$

However, we are always estimating the values of these variables, so their exact relationship is never known.

One way to think of the relationship that exists between the PCTS constraints is to consider a triangle, as shown in Figure 1.2. P, C, and T are the lengths of the sides, while S is the area. If I know the lengths of the sides, I can compute the area. Or, if I know the area and two sides, I can compute the length of the third side.

F I G U R E 1.2

Triangles Showing PCTS Relationship

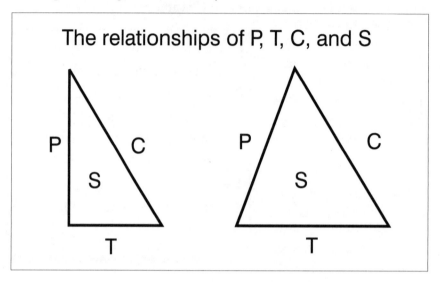

The relationships of P, T, C, and S

What is important about this illustration is that I cannot arbitrarily assign values to all three sides and the area. If three are specified, the fourth can be determined, but if you try to assign values to all four, they will only "fit" by accident.

In projects, however, it is common that the project sponsor or some other manager wants to dictate values for all four. This is, in fact, a common cause for project failures. As a project manager, it is

Principle: You can assign values to only three of the constraints. The fourth will be whatever the relationship dictates it will be.

my job to tell the sponsor what I need to do a project. So consider the most common case, in which values for P, T, and S are given. It is my job to tell the sponsor the cost to achieve those targets.

It is also true that when I do so, the sponsor may have heart failure. The response is often, "My goodness, how can it cost so much!!?," followed by protests that "We can't afford it!"

Then my response is, "Tell me what you can afford, and I'll tell you what I can do." This means that either scope will be reduced or perhaps time will be extended. In general, it is not acceptable to reduce performance.

Notice that this is a common tradeoff that we make at home. We have a list of things that need to be done. The roof is leaking and needs to be repaired before it ruins the house. The car is making a strange noise. My 13-year-old daughter needs braces on her teeth, which will cost a bundle. And on and on.

Trouble is, I can't afford it all.

So what am I going to do? I'm going to establish priorities for the items on the list. If the car quits, I won't be able to get to work to make the money to pay for everything, so perhaps it is number one on the list. The roof comes next. And goodness knows when I'll be able to afford braces for my daughter's teeth. Maybe she will grow up and marry someone who can afford them, but for now, they have to wait.

Interestingly, we are forced to prioritize at home, but in organizations we often try to do it all, thereby spreading our resources too thin, the result being that nothing gets done well or on time. (We will return to this issue in the section on control.) For now, the point is that you can't have it all, so choices have to be made, and my job is to help my boss or sponsor make those choices by providing the best information I can on what is needed to do the project.

The Time-Cost Tradeoff

In today's "hurry-up" world, the heat is on to finish projects in record time. This is due in part to the pressures of competition, especially in developing products, software, or new services. If you take too long to get it done, the competition will get there first,

In today's "hurry up" world, the pressures are on to finish projects in record time.

and the first to market with a new product often captures 60 to 70 percent of the market, leaving the rest of the pack to pick up the scraps.

Furthermore, there is pressure to reduce the cost to do the job. Again, this is partly because costs continue to rise over time, and also because if you can develop something faster and cheaper while leaving scope and performance constant, you can recover your investment sooner and protect yourself from the dynamics of the marketplace. (We will examine this in more detail in Chapter 14.)

Look now at the time-cost tradeoff curve shown in Figure 1.3. Notice that there is some duration for a project in which costs are at a minimum. That is, there is an optimum duration. The problem is, we seldom know just what that duration is, but we aren't too concerned about it.

What is important is to note that going past that point (extending the duration) causes project costs to rise, because you are being inefficient. You are taking too long to do the work.

Time-Cost Trade-Off Curve

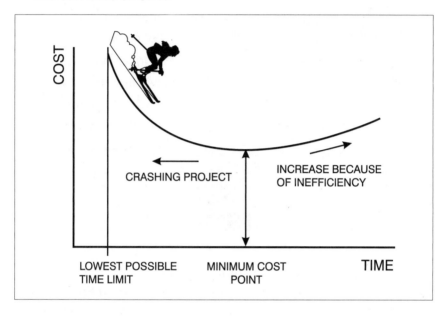

To the left of the minimum point, we are trying to reduce the time needed for the job. The common term for this is that we are trying to "crash" the project. That doesn't mean destroy it, but rather that we are trying to do it faster than the optimum time.

You can see that costs start to rise as you reduce time, and they rise very steeply. This is because we usually speed up a project by assigning more resources. In common language, we "throw bodies at it."

The difficulty is that, as we throw more bodies at a project, they begin to get in each other's way. The work can only be subdivided so far, and we hit what is called the point of diminishing returns. One way to think of this is that, if one person can do something in 10 hours, two people won't be able to do the same job in 5 hours. It may take 6. And four people may take 4 hours. So we don't get a linear gain in time.

As we throw
more bodies at
a project, they
begin to get
in each other's way.

In addition, there is a lower limit below which you cannot go, no matter how many people you put on the job. I call this the "forbidden zone." Naturally, there is always someone who thinks that if you just put enough people on a project, you can get it done in almost zero time, but that simply is not true.

Further, there is a principle called Brooks' Law, originally specified for software projects, that says, "Adding people to an already late project will just make it later." I believe this principle applies to all kinds of projects—not just software.

BROOKS' LAW

Adding people to an already late project may only make it later.
— Fred Brooks, 1975

Worse than that, you can actually destroy a project by adding people at the wrong time. This is shown in Figure 1.4. If you add someone new to the project, that person must be "brought

The Rework Spiral

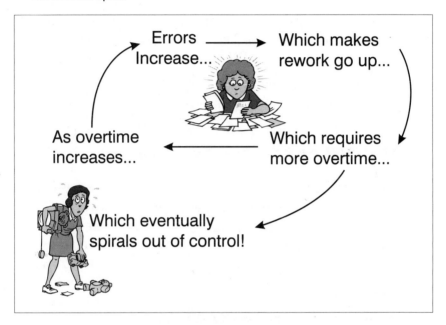

up to speed." That means that orientation and training are needed. Who is going to do the training?

You, most likely, but perhaps some other member of the team. No matter who, that person's productivity will drop. In order to keep from delaying the job, that person will have to work overtime. In doing so, she will get tired, thus losing more ground. She will probably also make more errors, which means she will have to correct them. This is called rework. As rework increases, she will have to work more overtime to keep up, thus getting more tired, which causes more errors, which increases rework, *ad nauseum*.

In other words, the project is likely to spiral downward, out of control. The message is, be very careful about adding people to help get the job done on time.

If You Always Do What You've Always Done

Now let's come back to the pressures that we feel to get the job done faster and cheaper at the same time. The time-cost tradeoff curve shows that, if you are below the minimum point on the curve, crashing the project costs more money. Yet we are being told to reduce costs *and* time simultaneously! Are we being set up?

Maybe.

> If you always do what you've always done, you'll always get what you've always got.

There is a saying in psychology, "If you always do what you've always done, you'll always get what you always got."

And there is a corollary. "Insanity is continuing to do what you've always done and hoping for a different result."

> Insanity is continuing to do what you've always done and hoping for a different result.

The message is that, if what you're doing isn't working, you have to change the way you're doing it. That is, you must change the *process*. In fact, that is what formal project management is all about.

Many of you have been managing projects for a long time in an informal way. I call that "seat-of-the-pants" project management, and I

> **Principle:** If what you are doing isn't working, you need to change the process by which it is done.

know, because I did it that way for about 10 years. Why? Because I didn't know any other way.

And I got the job done—usually to everyone's satisfaction.

The trouble is, we didn't know the work could be done any better.

Can formal project management (a change in process) really help you get the job done faster and cheaper at the same time?

I believe so.

Estimates are that about one-third of the cost to do many projects is rework. As someone has said, that is equivalent to having one of every three people on the job working full time to just redo what the other two people did wrong in the first place. That means, of course, that the cost is extremely high.

Why all the rework?

I think it is safe to say that it is the result of taking a ready-fire-aim approach to the project. The job is ill conceived, poorly defined, and inadequately planned. Everyone just wants to "get the job done."

It is said that haste makes waste. It is very true. But in our hurry-up-and-get-it-done world, there is little patience with "wasting time" on all that planning. So the result is rework, which is 100 percent waste.

I would suggest that, if you find a way to measure it, you will find that the rework in your projects ranges from 5 to 40 percent. As I have heard Tom Peters say on a tape (I forget which one), this is a good-news, bad-news story. The bad news is that it can be so high. The good news is that there is lots of room for improvement!

The nice thing about measuring rework is that you can show progress fairly soon. If you try to do baseline comparisons, you often find that baseline data for previous projects does not exist. With rework, you simply plot trend graphs. Such a graph is shown in Figure 1.5.

Quality

I have always considered this to be the forgotten aspect of project management. It has to do with the performance constraint. If the

F I G U R E 1.5

Trend Showing Rework Declining

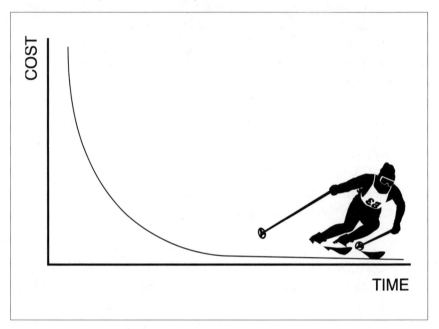

functional and technical requirements of the job are not met, you have done a poor-quality job. So, to some extent, performance is synonymous with quality.

If you put people under pressure to get the job done really fast, and won't allow them to reduce scope, then you can almost bet that they will sacrifice quality in the process. Furthermore, as a former quality manager at ITT, I learned that, if you improve quality, you get jobs done faster and cheaper, so in addition to improving processes, we must improve quality. In fact, the two go hand-in-hand.

In the past, quality has been defined in two primary ways. One was that quality was conformance to specifications. Another was that quality was meeting customer requirements. Of course,

**QUALITY:
The forgotten
aspect of
project
management.**

specifications should be written so that if you meet them, you meet customer requirements. Thus the second definition could be said to be the better of the two.

In the development of the six-sigma approach to quality at Motorola, a new definition of quality was also developed. This definition says that *quality is a state in which value entitlement is realized for the customer and provider in every aspect of the business relationship* (Harry & Schroeder, 2000, p. 6). This new definition recognizes the profit motive of every for-profit organization, whereas the old definitions focused only on the customer.

Harry and Schroeder say that most organizations are producing product and service quality levels at about three sigma. This refers to the number of errors that occur in a given number of opportunities. For 1,000,000 opportunities, a three-sigma level will yield 66,807 errors. At six sigma, there will only be 3 errors in 1,000,000 opportunities!

They also say that a three-sigma quality level means that of every sales dollar earned by the organization, approximately 25

Meeting customer requirements is very important.

to 30 percent (or 25 cents) is lost because of poor quality. This is called the cost of poor quality (COPQ). Most executives think that the COPQ is a few percent, and are horrified to learn that it is this high.

That cost comes from three factors: prevention, appraisal, and failure (PAF). Prevention is anything that we do to keep errors from happening in the first place. As an example of this, Alan Mulally, director of engineering at Boeing when the 777 airplane was being designed, explains how toy company Fisher-Price foolproofs the assembly of their model airplanes so that you can put them together with no hassle. "Fisher-Price makes a little notch in their wheels so that you can only put the right wheel on the right hub and you can only put the left wheel on the left hub" (Sabbagh, 1996). This approach has been used by the Japanese in manufacturing processes for years.

Appraisal cost results from the inspection of a finished part to be sure that no errors have been made. A basic given in quality is that you cannot inspect quality into a product—it must be designed in and built in to begin with. In fact, the work with

six-sigma programs has shown that "80 percent of quality problems are actually designed into the product without any conscious attempt to do so" (Harry & Schroeder, 1999, p. 36). When the problem is designed into the product, you can't inspect it out.

Failure cost is incurred once the product leaves the plant and reaches the customer. It includes warranty costs, repair costs, and so on. And almost impossible to track, but a part of failure cost nonetheless, is lost customers.

The important thing to note is that an increase in money spent on prevention leads to significant reductions in inspection and failure costs. This is shown in Figure 1.6. Most of our quality costs should go into prevention, so that we reap significant savings in the other two areas. If you want to see how significant these savings can be, I suggest you read Harry and Schroeder.

As for projects, if you improve your processes so that quality is improved, then you will also reduce time and cost of project work simultaneously. Again, this is because you eliminate rework, which adds no value to the project. Large gains can be made if more attention is paid to quality improvement in projects.

**Principle:
If you improve
quality, you reduce
total project costs.**

F I G U R E 1.6

Reduction in Total Cost of Quality When Prevention Is Increased

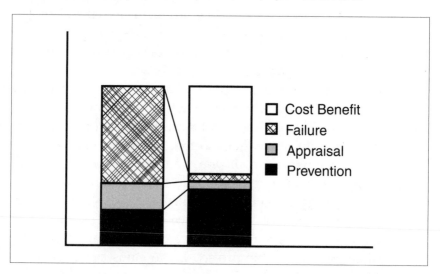

Have Your Cake and Eat It Too

In Figure 1.2, I showed the relationship between P, C, T, and S as a triangle and said that these are the quadruple constraints of a project. There is a problem with using a triangle as an analogy. Suppose I want to hold P, C, and T constant and increase the scope of the job. Based on the triangle analogy, this is impossible. If I increase scope, at least one of the three sides of the triangle must get longer.

However, if I think of the triangle as being drawn on the surface of a sphere, then this is no longer true. If I change the radius of the sphere, it will change the area bounded by P, C, and T.

In Figure 1.7 is a sphere with a spherical triangle drawn on it, and inside the spherical triangle I have also drawn a plane triangle. If I assume that the sides of both the spherical and plane triangle are the same lengths, then the spherical triangle has a greater area, which represents project scope, so the scope has been increased

F I G U R E 1.7

The PCTS Relationship Shown on a Spherical Surface

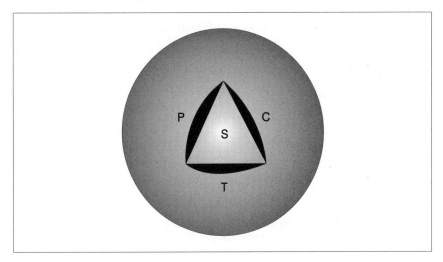

F I G U R E 1.8

The PCTS Relationship Shown as a Pyramid

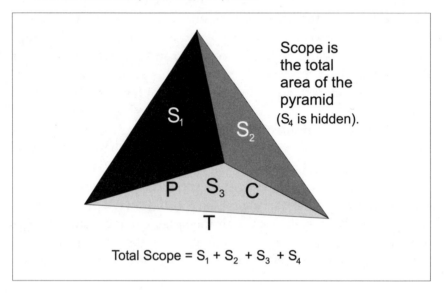

Scope is the total area of the pyramid (S_4 is hidden).

S_1 S_2

P S_3 C

T

Total Scope = $S_1 + S_2 + S_3 + S_4$

while holding the sides of the triangle to constant lengths.[1] What does the radius of the sphere represent? I suspect it is a measure of how well the process works.

There is still another way to think of the relationship between the variables. Suppose P, C, and T are the sides of the base of a pyramid. This is shown in Figure 1.8. Now the scope is the entire area of the pyramid. What would be the physical meaning of the vertical sides of the pyramid? Perhaps they are factors of P, C, and T. Furthermore, it may be that the height of the pyramid represents how well the process performs. If it is a poor process, the height of the pyramid diminishes until you simply have a conventional triangle (the base of the pyramid).

---

[1] For the mathematically inclined, the drawing is, of course, not correct, but I am trying to explain the concept in simple terms for the benefit of those readers who have no background in spherical geometry.

These figures help us understand that by changing the process by which we do project work, we can get more for our money. We can reduce rework, increase productivity, decrease time, and so on.

Earlier I mentioned that Alan Mulally wanted the 777 airplane to be designed like a Fisher-Price toy, so that it would go together easily. In addition, Boeing changed the process by which the airplane was designed. There were two aspects to this change, one technical and the other human.

The technical change was to utilize completely three-dimensional computer design. When you design parts in two dimensions, it is impossible to know ahead of time that, for instance, components inside the wing are going to run into each other. You have to build a model to find these problems. Correcting them is extremely expensive. By modeling the plane in three dimensions, these interferences can be detected on the computer screen and corrected before a prototype is built. It isn't perfect, and there may still be problems in the design, but this approach is a vast improvement over two-dimensional methods.

The human change was expressed by the slogan "Working Together." In most organizations you find various teams building silos around themselves. When conflicts arise, they fall into an us-them mode and snipe at each other. The Boeing approach was to tear down those silos and create a climate in which people understood that the success of the project meant that they were totally *interdependent* on each other (Dimancescu, 1992).

Teams were encouraged to discuss their problems freely. Mechanics and assembly workers were involved with the design teams to produce a product that would be easy to build and easy to use. The chief test pilot for Boeing worked closely with the designers to produce a plane that would be accepted by other pilots, because this design departed from the conventional approach of using cables to move the flaps and rudder of the plane to a fly-by-wire method of controlling these components electronically. Because this causes the plane to lack the "feel" that pilots are accustomed to, it was important to make the difference as unobjectionable as possible.

Most significantly, representatives from the first customer, United Airlines, were part of the team, to make sure the plane would meet their needs when it was finished. There was ongoing dialogue between all of these parties to ensure that all interests were represented in the design of this twenty-first century jet (Sabbagh, 1996).

The ultimate result was that United Airlines accepted the 777 airplane on the first test by their own pilots! This had never happened before. It is a world-class example of what good project management can achieve.

Facilitation

Previously I said project management is *facilitation* of planning, scheduling, and control. That word is very important. A project manager does not develop a project plan for a group. The general rule is that the people who must do the work should participate in developing the plan.

There are two reasons for this. One is that they know best how they will do their own work and how long it will take. The second is that they are likely to think of everything that must be done,

**Principle:
The people
who must
do the work
should develop
the plan.**

whereas if you plan the project by yourself, you may forget something. And, because they know that your plan is likely to be flawed, if you develop it by yourself and try to "lay it on them," they will most likely reject it. So, if you want to have a valid plan that is accepted by your team, get them involved in the planning process.

How about one-person projects? Well, I suggest that it is very helpful to have someone else review your plan, so they can spot those things that you may have overlooked. Forgetting something is one of the top 12 causes of project failure. If you can't get someone to review it for you, then the best alternative (if feasible) is to "sleep on it" for a few days. When you do go back to it, you will probably see things that you missed before.

Nature of Projects

Projects often draw on many different disciplines. Consider a simple home-building project. Carpenters, plumbers, electricians, landscapers, roofers, and painters are all involved. These different disciplines often don't talk the same language, see the work of the

**Principle:
The nature of
projects changes
at each phase
in their life cycle.**

other disciplines as interfering with their own work, and, in the final analysis, don't cooperate very well. Furthermore, the project manager often does not understand all disciplines. This is especially true in high-tech projects. That presents problems of evaluating progress and quality of work.

Projects also have various phases. All too often, the sequence is as shown in Figure 1.9. The project is kicked off with great enthusiasm, but soon things begin to turn sour. The next thing you know, the team is in chaos. After the boiling point is reached, they sit down to define the project requirements. Naturally, this should have been done first!

That is why I advocate the life-cycle model shown in Figure 1.10. My model is meant to be generic. It consists of five phases. Some models consist of only four phases: definition, initiation, execution, and closeout. Note that a project always begins as a concept, and a concept is usually a bit fuzzy. Our job as a team is to clarify the concept, to turn it into a *shared understanding* that the entire team will accept. Failure to do this causes many project failures.

In fact, I believe that projects almost always fail in the definition stage. They may hang around for a long time, going through the other phases, but if the initial definition is wrong they cannot succeed. We will return to this theme in Chapter 5.

HOW DO YOU DEFINE SUCCESS?

It seems reasonable to believe that, if you meet the P, C, T, and S targets for a project, it would be considered a success. Unfortunately, it doesn't always work that way. There are projects that meet all of the targets and are considered failures, and there are those that don't meet any of the targets and are considered successful.

To a person who likes to use numbers to judge outcomes, this is heresy. If you can't use the numbers to gauge success, what *are* you going to do?

The Typical Project Life Cycle

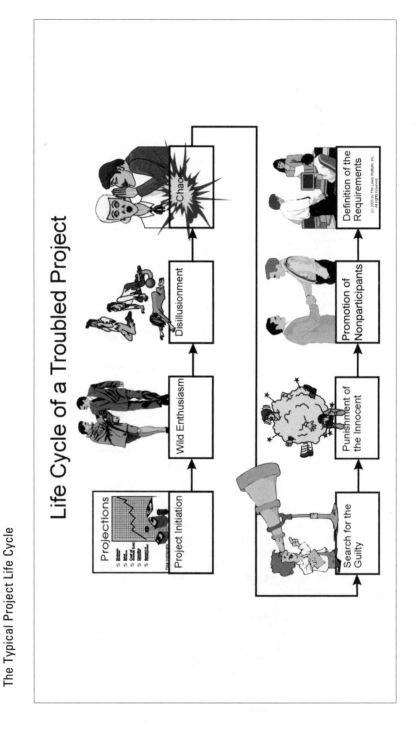

Life Cycle of a Troubled Project

F I G U R E 1.10

Life-Cycle Model for Projects

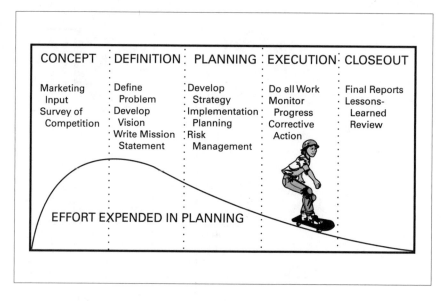

**How
do you
define
success?**

Good question.

The answer is that part of the definition process is to clarify requirements by having stakeholders state their expectations, understand what the results must be, and then determine what the deliverables must be to get those results and satisfy those expectations.

> The only truly successful project is the one that delivers what it is supposed to, gets results, and meets stakeholder expectations.

Consider a project in which a vendor has been chosen to provide certain equipment for a facility. One member of the staff preferred a different vendor. His expectation was that the team would follow his recommendation, but they chose someone else. Even if that vendor meets all P, C, T, S targets, he will judge the project negatively. So the project manager needs to win this person over. This is the politics of project management, and will be discussed later in the book.

Consider Figure 1.11. The only truly successful project is one for which you can answer "yes" at each point on the tree. A truly failed project is one for which you answer "no" at each point. (Other combinations are logically possible, but don't make any sense and are highly unlikely.)

THE PROJECT MANAGEMENT SYSTEM

There are seven components that make up a proper management system. These are shown in Figure 1.12. Note that I have arranged these to show how they interrelate.

Human Component

The human component is on the bottom, because dealing with people underpins the entire structure.

38

Expectations, Deliverables, and Results

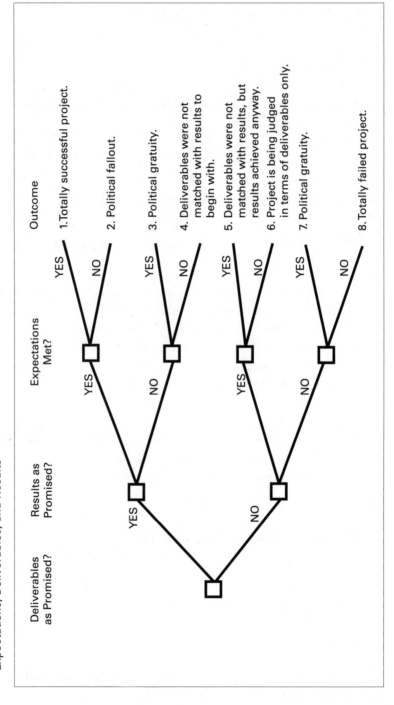

F I G U R E 1.12

The Project Management System

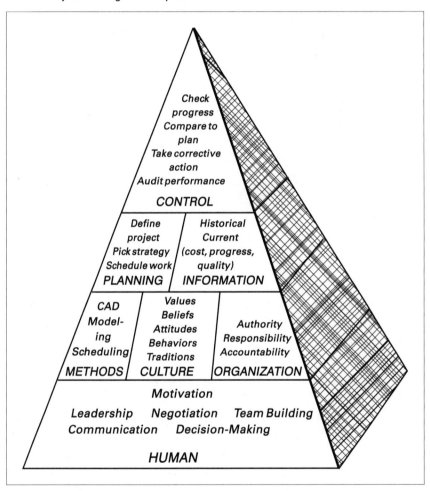

Projects are people! They are not critical path schedules or Gantt charts. Those are the tools we use to manage projects.

If a project manager cannot deal effectively with people, the project is likely to suffer. In fact, I have never seen a project fail because the manager or her team didn't know how to draw a critical

Principle:
Projects seldom
fail because
of tools. They
fail because
of people!

path schedule, but I have certainly seen many of them encounter serious difficulty because of "people problems."

A project manager has to be able to do all of the things listed in the box: deal with communication, conflict, motivation, leadership, decision making, politics, and so on. And the list is by no means complete.

I have had technical people look at the list and say, "Oh, man, I really hate that part! Projects would be okay if you could just get people to be logical!"

I say to them, "If you really mean that, I suggest you rethink your career. Don't be a project manager—or any other kind." I say this because dealing with people is what managing is all about. If you hate people problems, you probably won't handle them very well, and they will drive you crazy to boot. In my value system, life is too short to spend doing something you hate. Choose to be a technical person instead.

On the other hand, some people say, "I'm not very good at some of the interpersonal skills, but if I could learn them I would be willing." In that case, I suggest that they set for themselves a learning objective. All of the skills identified in the model can be learned, even leadership skills. Everyone may not be equally good at all of them, but everyone can definitely improve.

Culture

On the next level up, we have a component that is related to the human system, but is so special that it must be considered separately. This is culture. The word culture designates the sum total of the values, attitudes, traditions, and behaviors that exist in an organization. In fact, one way you know when people are talking about their culture is when they say, "We don't do it that way here."

Cultural differences come from geographic differences within a given country, from ethnic background, race, religion, and so on. Broadly speaking, there is nothing good or bad about these differences (not everyone would agree with this). However, the differences lead to conflicts, misunderstandings, and disagreements.

Because projects are becoming more global in nature, and teams are often more culturally diverse than in past years, it is important

that project managers learn about and value cultural differences and how to deal with them. A few examples will illustrate.

In Japanese society, it is considered impolite to say "no" directly. Furthermore, the word "hai," which we interpret to mean "yes," actually means "I am listening." So when a foreigner asks a Japanese person, "Do you agree?" and he says "Yes," it sounds as if an agreement has been reached. Later, when the Japanese individual seems to be violating the agreement, and this is mentioned, he may say, "Well, we agreed to *this*," and it will have a shade of meaning different than what the foreigner thought it had.

Americans like to be very informal and are quick to call each other by first names. When I was a boy, we never called anyone over 25 by their first name, but our culture has changed. So, when we go to countries like Germany on business, we are quick to call managers by their first names. Many Germans find this offensive. I recently met a German engineer who has been working for his manager for eight years and still does not call him by his first name.

On one of my first trips to Malaysia, I learned about Malaysian cultural taboos so I wouldn't offend anyone. A book called *Understanding the Asian Manager* (Bedi, 1992) offered some good tips.

I taught for a company in Kuala Lumpur, and following the program I had to fly to Singapore. They arranged for a company driver to take me to the airport. He was driving a van. As is customary in the United States, I started to get into the back seat. He looked back at me and said, "Sir, you're kind of fat. You would probably be more comfortable up here in the front seat."

It was all I could do to keep from laughing. I could picture this poor fellow coming to the United States and working as a limo driver. He makes this remark to a passenger, who complains, and he is fired. "What's wrong," he protests. "I was only trying to be helpful."

And he was.

What Bedi's book taught me is that being fat in Asian countries does not bear the stigma it does in our twiggy society. It is actually a sign of affluence, because over the years, unless a person was wealthy, he didn't eat a diet that was very fattening. Not knowing this, of course, it would seem insulting to an American to be referred to as fat.

One last example. A German man came to the states to work with a company in Seattle for a couple of weeks. One day he went to the men's room, as it was being cleaned, and used the facility. The woman cleaning it was incensed. She filed a sexual harassment grievance, alleging that he had deliberately come in and exposed his private anatomy to her.

Such a furor ensued that the president of the German company had to write a formal letter of apology, explaining that it is common in Europe for women to clean the men's restrooms without closing them. I have experienced this myself in Zurich and Frankfurt, as well as in Malaysia and Singapore.

All of these examples show the importance of being sensitive to cultural differences. The difficulty is that you don't know that you are violating someone else's culture until you do it, and they often don't tell you. And unfortunately, there aren't a lot of sources for training or education in such differences. You simply have to be sensitive to the cultures of other people, and if things don't seem to be going well, discuss openly what is wrong so the problem can be corrected. (For an in-depth treatment of cultural differences, see Hampden-Turner & Trompenaars, 2000.)

Methods

The methods component of the model indicates the tools used to manage projects. This includes scheduling methods, earned value analysis, work breakdown structures, and so on. I don't find this to be a significant problem for most people. Tools are easily learned. The biggest struggle seems to be with scheduling software, and the reason this is such a problem is because organizations provide the software to managers without training them in how to use it. Even the most basic scheduling program today has considerable power; and the more power it has, the harder it is to use superficially, much less master. Giving a person a saw and hammer does not make her a carpenter. She needs training and experience in the art of carpentry. The same goes for scheduling software.

Organization

This component deals with how a project is organized, as well as how the company is organized. Every organization must delineate the limits of an individual's authority, responsibility, and accountability. A common complaint from project managers is that they have a lot of responsibility but very little authority. I always tell people who say this that they may as well get used to it. As far as I can tell, it isn't likely to change.

However, there are two kinds of authority, and we need to note the differences. One is to be able to tell people to do something and expect them to do it. This is authority over people, which project managers won't usually have. So you have to get things done through influence—and this is true even for managers who do have authority over people. So concern about having no authority over people is an exaggerated issue, in my opinion.

The second kind of authority is to act unilaterally, without having to get one's actions approved by 12 people in advance. This is most evident where spending is concerned. It is still one of my pet peeves that organizations require that project managers get approvals for purchases over $25, when they are managing projects that have million-dollar budgets. This is ludicrous.

In my system of managing projects, as you will find as you read on, once a plan (which includes a budget) is developed and signed off, there should no need for further approvals so long as the project manager is spending in accordance with the pre-approved plan. Requiring such approvals simply makes more work, slows down the project, and sends a clear message to the manager that she is not trusted with company money. Then why give her such a large project?

Control

I want to take this one out of order. I will return to planning and information later. The entire reason for managing a project is to make sure you get the results desired by the organization. This is commonly called being in control, and it is what is expected of a project manager.

> **Con • trol:** the act of comparing where you are to where you are supposed to be, so corrective action can be taken when there is a deviation from the target.

Like many words in English, the word control has a couple of meanings. One is almost the same as the word power. Authoritarian managers attempt to control people through the use of power.

In management, the word control should have another meaning—that of guidance or an information systems definition. As you can see in the box, control is exercised by comparing where you are to where you are supposed to be, then taking steps to correct for deviations from targeted performance. This can only be done if the two components of the model labeled planning and information are functioning correctly.

Planning and Information

If you have no plan, by definition, you have no control, because it is your plan that tells where you are supposed to be in the first place. Further, if you don't know where you are, you can't have control. This knowledge comes from your information system.

Most organizations have difficulties with both of these. They don't do a very good job of planning. In many cases, it is

**Principle:
If you have no
plan, you
have no
control—by
definition!**

cultural. The company has grown from a one-person, garage-lo-cated business to be a prosperous concern with hundreds of em-ployees. As the business grows, managers begin to realize that the old, "loosey-goosey" way of managing is not working any more, and they try to impose some structure. This is often re-sisted. "We've never had to do it before, and we've been success-ful," people complain.

"Yes, but we can no longer continue to be successful this way," management tries to explain. In fact, there is considerable danger for an organization that is successful, because people tend to become complacent.

Most organizations do a good job of providing information systems to track inventory, payroll, orders, and other measures, but they don't have systems for tracking projects. Why? They didn't realize that they needed such a system. This means that most pro-ject managers have to track projects manually, which actually isn't too hard in most cases. Also, most scheduling software provides the capability to do earned value reporting, so generating your own progress reports is fairly simple.

Note that the information component also includes historical data. This is needed to estimate project time, cost, and resource requirements. If I ask you how long it takes to clean your house or mow your lawn, you can tell me the approximate time because you have done it so often. The same approach is used for project estimates when history is available. This means that a database must be set up to record task durations.

This works okay on well-defined tasks, but when you try to apply it to engineering, software, or scientific research, it turns out not to work as well. The reason is simple. You seldom do the same task twice, so it is harder to develop good history for knowledge work. Such records do have some value, though, and we will discuss estimating in a later chapter. Additionally, alternative methods of estimating knowledge work will be presented.

PROJECT MANAGEMENT AND ISO 9000

I am sometimes asked about the relationship between project management and ISO 9000. As I understand ISO, organizations are required to document their processes and procedures so that everyone does them the same way. You need to develop a project management methodology if you want to be ISO certified. Many of my clients have developed a methodology that requires their members to follow The Lewis Method™ of project management (as presented in this book).

PROJECT MANAGEMENT AND SIX SIGMA

People also ask about the six-sigma model, which deals with acceptable errors in processes or products. The idea is to reduce such errors or defects to extremely low levels.

If you draw a normal distribution curve that represents conformance of a process or product to its requirements, you find that going plus or minus three standard deviations on either side of the mean will contain 99.74 percent of the population. That is,

0.26 percent of the measures you take will fall outside these limits. If you consider only one side of the mean, then 0.13 percent of measures will be unacceptable (assuming that a product that performs better than expected is acceptable). This is shown in Figure 1.13.

If you draw the normal distribution curve to cover ± 6 standard deviations, then the percentage of nonconforming measures drops to 3.4 in a million. The six-sigma system requires that performance targets be set to this level.

Project management and six sigma, then, are different. Project management offers tools to help organizations achieve six-sigma performance targets.

Earlier I said that estimates place rework figures in projects at between 5 and 40 percent. That means that many projects are not even achieving three-sigma levels. If you go one standard devia-

F I G U R E 1.13

Conformance to Requirements

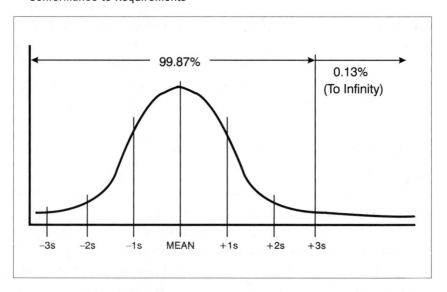

tion below the mean, you have 84 percent of the population conforming to requirements. That means, of course, that 16 percent of the population does not conform. Thus we are not achieving even three-sigma levels if we have rework that exceeds 0.13 percent.

THE LEWIS METHOD OF MANAGING PROJECTS

I attended my first seminar on project management around 1978. Since then, I have looked at project management systems of all kinds, and have developed my own model for managing projects. I call it The Lewis Method and have a trademark for the term. Other models exist. Probably the best known, the Kerzner Approach®, was developed by my colleague Harold Kerzner. If they are valid, all methods are similar. So you may find that you want to combine characteristics from several models to arrive at one that best fits your project requirements.

Does One Size Fit All?

The question you might ask is, "Does one approach work for all projects?" The answer is "Yes—and no." The "yes" part comes from the fact that project management is a disciplined way of thinking about how a job will be done. That disciplined way of thinking is shown by my flow chart, and it can be applied to any kind of project. It can be brain surgery, preparing a meal, developing hardware or software, or constructing a power dam. The overall approach is the same.

> **Principle:** The thought process can be applied to any project, regardless of type or size.

What differs is the tools used. I believe that there are some projects that are so small that to do a critical path schedule would be a waste of time. On the other hand, there are projects that could not possibly succeed without a good schedule. What you need to do is pick and choose what tools you use.

My Projects Are Too Small to Use This Stuff!

For some reason there are people who think that formal project management techniques are only valid on large projects. What I believe troubles them in many instances is that they are confusing documentation with the thought process. If I were preparing a meal, I would still go through the thought process outlined in my model, but I wouldn't create a lot of paperwork to do the job.

I am a strong advocate of the KISS (Keep It Simple Stupid) principle in managing projects—don't do any more than you must do to get the job done. (But don't do any less either!) I also like to call this the laziness principle, and I am lazy by nature. I don't want to spend more time or effort than needed to get the job done.

**Principle:
The thought
process is not
the same
thing as
documentation.**

So go through the thought process, then decide how much of it should be documented, and do that. Keep it simple!

An Overview of The Lewis Method

My method conforms to the five processes defined by the PMBOK: initiating, planning, execution, control, and closeout. The model has been applied by thousands of project managers and forms the basis for many organization methodologies. It is a practical, no-nonsense approach that, when followed, helps managers avoid many of the pitfalls that cause projects to fail. This even includes some of the more common behavioral issues that seem to plague projects.

The model is presented in Figure 1.14 as a flow chart. This chart can be carried around and used as a memory jogger, rather than carrying the book around. Notice that there is another component of the model shown in Figure 1.15. This chart is necessary because step six of the model consists of a number of substeps, so rather than make one very large chart, I have broken step six out into a separate diagram.

The model will be covered in depth in the various chapters. For now, I will provide just a summary of the main phases of the model.

Initiation

As the model shows, a project almost always begins as a concept. We need something. Or we have a problem. The project is designed to solve that problem or meet that need. Remember the definition of projects offered by Dr. Juran? A project is a problem scheduled for solution. So we are solving a problem with a large-scale effort when we do a project.

Where we get into trouble is in forgetting that the way you solve a problem depends on how it is defined. So the first stage in a project is to make sure you have correctly defined the problem being

FIGURE 1.14

The Lewis Method® of Project Management

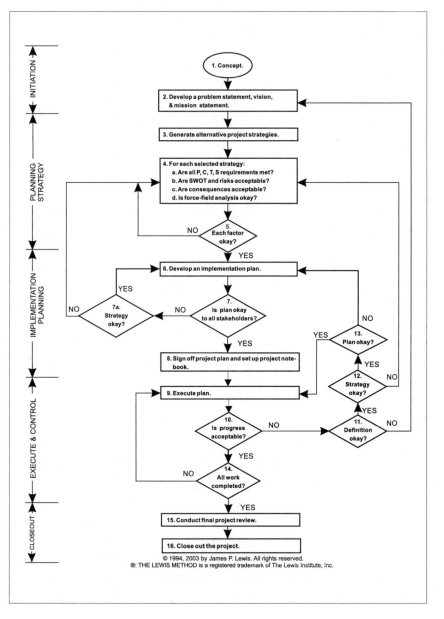

F I G U R E 1.15

Step 6 of The Lewis Method Expanded

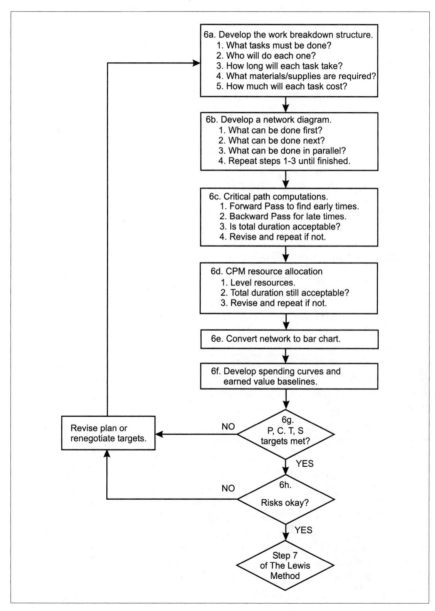

solved, that you have developed a vision for what the end result will be, and that you have stated your mission. As I said earlier, failing to properly do this results in headless-chicken projects.

This phase is covered in Chapter 5.

Planning: Strategy First

The word strategy means that you have an overall approach to running a project. This step is often brushed over lightly. There is always a strategy or "game plan" implied by how a project is run, but that strategy is not chosen by comparison to other approaches. It is simply a default approach. Choosing a proper project strategy can mean the difference between success and failure, and the procedure for doing so is covered in Chapter 7.

Planning for Implementation

This is what most people think of as planning. This is where you dot all of your i's and cross all your t's. You work out all of the details of how the project will be done—what must be done,

The word strategy means that you have an overall approach to running a project.

who will do it, how it will be done, how long the steps will take, and so on.

Execution and Control

In all too many cases, people jump directly from concept to execution. When they do this, they really have no control, since they have no plan that tells where they are supposed to be. This was discussed previously. Execution and control will be covered in Chapter 12.

Closeout

This stage is often aborted. At the Frontiers Conference on project management conducted by Boston University a few years ago, the keynote speaker asked an audience of some 400 people to raise their hands if they conducted regular end-of-project reviews for purposes of learning lessons. About 12 hands were raised. Then he asked a most compelling question.

"How many of you who put up your hands have a mandate that, before you do your next project, you must show your boss how you will avoid the mistakes you made on your last project?"

Two hands went up.

And that is common. My own surveys in my seminars indicate that this response rate is pretty standard. This topic will be covered in Chapter 14.

IN SUMMARY

There you have it—a concise overview of project management. The rest of this book is aimed at expanding this overview into a complete treatment of how to manage projects. However, I should say that the word complete is an exaggeration. The subject is too big to cover in one book. But what you will get in this book are the core methods, principles, and practices of project management.

2 CHAPTER

The Project Management Institute and the PMBOK

If you check the phone book you will find that there is an association for almost every profession, and project management is no exception. The Project Management Institute (PMI), is the association for those of us who consider managing projects to be more than just a temporary phase that we are going through on our way to maturity. PMI has experienced almost exponential growth for the past several years, as more people have become aware of the value of a structured approach to managing projects. In 2004, PMI passed the 100,000-member mark, and continues to grow at about 20 percent a year. You can get more information on PMI by checking their Web site: http://www.pmi.org.

PMI also attempts to promote project management as a profession, thereby raising the perceived status of project managers, and they have developed a certification process that confers on those who meet the requirements the designation of Project

Management Professional, or PMP®. As a broad example of requirements, a candidate must log a certain number of work hours to sit for the exam, which consists of 200 questions. At present the time limit for the exam is four hours. Applicants are also required to affirm that they will abide by a code of ethics in conducting their work. To find out more about the PMP certification process, check the PMI Web site.

The exam is based on the contents of the PMBOK. With the PMBOK, or *Project Management Body of Knowledge,* PMI attempts to define what a project manager should know in order to be a professional. At present, this knowledge falls into nine categories, described very briefly below. The PMBOK does not attempt to fully document all of these (it would take a tome weighing about a ton to do so!); many volumes from other sources have been written on each topic. The PMBOK was revised in 2004, and a new exam was released in September 2005. In addition, the passing grade is tentatively being raised.

PROCESSES VERSUS KNOWLEDGE AREAS

A process is some action, or a series of actions, that brings about a result. The PMBOK identifies two kinds of processes:

- Project processes are those such as planning and controlling that ensure that the *product* produced by the project matches what was intended at the beginning.

- Product processes are those actions taken to produce the product. These may include engineering design, construction, or other actions.

There are five project processes defined by the PMBOK:

- *Initiating:* doing whatever must be done to authorize a project.

- *Planning:* identifying all the work that must be done; developing policies, procedures, and other documentation that defines the project.

- *Executing:* applying labor and materials to develop the product (in this case product is a general term for whatever the project produces—whether item, service, or other result).

- *Controlling:* monitoring progress against the plan and taking whatever actions are necessary to keep the project on *track.*

- *Closing:* formal acceptance of the product and documentation of activities throughout the life of the project.

KNOWLEDGE AREAS

As mentioned above, there are currently nine knowledge areas. These will be described briefly in the following text.

Project Integration Management

Every facet of a project needs attention, and integration management is the effort made to ensure that everything comes together. This means that scope, cost, control systems, and so on have been defined and set up to function properly. Furthermore, the product being produced is inseparable from the project management itself, as managing the job is done to ensure that the product will be what was intended at completion.

Scope Management

Scope essentially defines what is to be done, and not done, in managing the project. In effect, it defines how large the job is. One cause of considerable difficulty for project managers is scope changes, as was shown in Chapter 1 with Ashahebsed trying to provide tombs for the expanding family of Ramses the Great. When work is contracted to someone else in a project, scope management takes on a particularly important role: ensuring that the contractor does everything called for by the contract.

Time Management

My personal feeling is that this is a most unfortunate choice of terms. To thousands of people, the term *time management* conveys managing one's personal time using a planner of some kind or a personal digital assistant (PDA). But the PMBOK defines it as developing the project schedule.

Because of the importance of project deadlines, scheduling receives a lot of attention, and scheduling software sells in large numbers.

Cost Management

As the term implies, controlling project costs is highly important. The difficulty with cost and schedule is that durations for tasks are estimated, and these estimates may not be very good—especially for poorly defined work. The net result is that there can be large variances from the estimates when actual work is performed. Organizations should recognize that all processes vary, that the variation can be reduced but never eliminated, and that there will be normal tolerances on all estimates that must be accepted.

Quality Management

As I pointed out in Chapter 1, it has long been customary to talk about the triple constraints in projects, but in doing so, the quality and scope components are combined. While they may be related, they are not identical, so we should discuss the quadruple constraints. In any event, quality is often the forgotten constraint. When you place people under pressure to finish a project in record time, quality sometimes suffers. Quality management is aimed at preventing this outcome.

Human Resources Management

Although it should be obvious to any thinking person, *projects are people,* and project managers should have a high level of *people skills* before they are allowed to manage projects. In addition, every project must have the right people assigned to do various tasks, and most of the time project managers don't get to choose their team members. Nevertheless, this knowledge area deals with all aspects of managing human resources, including staffing, evaluating, motivating, and so on.

Communications Management

The first thing to be clear about is that communications management does not deal with the processes of communicating, but with determining the various stakeholders to the project who need information, at what intervals, and in what formats. Information is vital to the health of a project, and this process is often overlooked in the planning stage of a project.

Risk Management

My colleague, and co-author of our book on preparing for the PMP exam (Lewis & Dudley, 2005), said to me once, "Project management is really all about managing risks." I think that is a pretty good observation. Because of the need to estimate task durations, resource requirements, and costs, a project faces many risks. And this doesn't even begin to take into account all of the things that can go wrong and shipwreck your project—weather, accidents,

contract disputes, illnesses, and so on. It can well be said that you must either manage risks or they will manage you.

Procurement Management

Most projects make use of materials and services that must be procured from outside sources. Note that the common term people use is purchasing, but not everything is purchased. Some things are licensed; others are leased. Clearly, regardless of how they are acquired, a project team can't meet deadlines if they don't have things when they need them.

Professional Development Units (PDUs)

One requirement to be a PMP is that you must obtain continuing education credits, called PDUs, both to take the certification exam and to maintain your certification over time. These credits can be obtained through participation in PMI chapter meetings, teaching project management, writing books, and so on. There are various organizations that are designated as Registered Education Providers (REP) with PMI. These organizations are required to meet certain standards to be registered, and courses they offer are pretty much automatically considered valid by PMI for obtaining PDUs. Check the PMI Web site for a list of these providers. My company, The Lewis Institute, Inc., is a REP.

SUMMARY

There you have it—a 36,000-foot view of PMI and the PMBOK. If you want to get down to ground level and see the actual trees, the Lewis and Dudley PMP Exam preparation book gives in-depth information on the entire subject (op cit.).

3

CHAPTER

The Role of the
Project Manager

As I wrote in Chapter 1, the PMI definition of project management does not completely capture the true nature of project management. I don't know if it is really possible to convey. One reason is that project management is a *performing art,* and it is difficult to convey in words what an actor, athlete, or artist does. However, we can describe the various roles of a project manager, and that will be the focus of this chapter. What should be clear is that you can't very well become something if you can't describe and define it, so this is a necessary exercise.

I have been involved in project management for over 40 years. First I was a project manager myself. Then, when I decided to start teaching seminars, I taught a program entitled "Leadership Skills for Project Managers." Altogether, about 30,000 individuals have attended my seminars on project management, and my goal has always been to turn out the best project managers I could develop.

The focus of most management training is on analysis and planning. As I have already said, management is a performing art, which is more right-brained in nature and can only be learned through practice. Perhaps it is my age (64), or maybe I've become jaded, but quite frankly, I am disappointed in the results I've achieved, and I am skeptical about the quality of managers in the United States in general. The focus of management training, whether it is the traditional MBA program or management seminars in general, has always been left-brain oriented (for more on brain dominance, see Chapter 5). The curriculum teaches tools—especially analytical tools for measuring financial progress—but analyzing data is not the same thing as managing.

> The focus of most management training is on analysis and planning. Management is a performing art, which is more right-brained in nature and can only be learned through practice.

Ray and Myers (1986) wrote about this when they published their book, *Creativity in Business*. They tried to inject some right-brain thinking into the MBA program at Stanford. Henry Mintzberg (1989) has also criticized the totally analytical focus. One of his suggestions is that people plan on the left side (of the brain) and manage on the right side.

IT'S ALL ABOUT PEOPLE!

The first thing you must recognize is that project management is about *people*. It isn't about technology. Yes, technology may be center stage, and you may have to be a techie to manage a given project, but generally speaking you don't need a high level of technical skill. In fact, I believe that being a technical expert can actually be detrimental to a project manager, because such individuals are inclined to get too involved in technology and neglect managing the project. Nevertheless, I have worked with a number of biotech companies and would never consider trying to manage a biotech project, simply because I understand virtually nothing about the work being done.

> Projects are people, and project management is about dealing with people, getting the best possible performance from them.

However, given that you know enough about the technology to understand individuals' jobs and problems, the main thing you need to be able to do is deal effectively with people—and not just those on your project team. You have to deal with all kinds of stakeholders—customers, suppliers, functional managers, finance people, public officials, and so on. One of the core activities of a project manager is dealing with politics. That's right, politics.

A lot of project managers with technical backgrounds hate the very word, and dealing with politics is to them a fate worse than

Project management has become a very popular career during the past decade.

death. Nevertheless, every act you perform in an organization has a political implication, and you may as well recognize and accept it. You certainly aren't going to change it. Like death and taxes, politics are with us for the long term.

As a project manager, you are constantly being bombarded with crises. A vendor shipped the wrong part and it is going to delay completion of xyz module. A team member from the mechanical engineering group is being a pain and you have to deal with him. A senior manager from another division is demanding that you accommodate his concerns about a market that has almost nothing to do with your product—but he thinks it does, and he outranks you about seven levels in the corporate hierarchy, so you have to deal with him. Then there is the squabble that has broken out between the industrial designers and the marketing department, which is about to escalate to nuclear proportions if you don't defuse it.

So, do you really want to be a project manager?

Not if you hate dealing with these kinds of issues. Life is too short. Go back to your technical job and use my book as a door-

Project management is about people. You have to deal with all kinds of stakeholders.

**Leadership is
the art of getting
others to want
to do something
you believe should
be done.**
~ Vance Packard

stop, so you see it fairly often and remind yourself that you don't
want to go that route.

Here's an anecdote to emphasize the importance of what I'm
saying. I have a close friend who has a number of project managers in his department. One of them had to be removed from the
position because he was constantly getting into conflicts with various stakeholders to his projects. My friend spent a lot of time doing damage control because the project manager simply did not
know how to deal with people. His technical skills were great, but
he couldn't get the job done without people skills.

What this really boils down to is that you need to be a project
leader, not just a project manager. Leadership is about getting people to follow you. My favorite definition is that leadership is the art
of getting others to want to do something you believe should be
done. The operative word in this definition is *want*. You can get
people to do what you want done through coercion or compensa-
tion. But getting them to want to do something—now, that's an art!

And, since project managers usually have a lot of responsibility and no authority, you need good leadership skills to get people

to do the work that must be done. Again, it's all about people. (For in-depth treatment of project leadership, see my book by that title [Lewis, 2002].)

So You Still Want to Be a Project Manager?

Okay, so you don't mind dealing with people problems. Fine. But do you *really* want to be a project manager—or any kind of manager, for that matter? Or are you following a script laid on you by society? In *Scripts People Live By*, Claude Steiner shows that we often follow a life script that was imposed on us by our parents, significant others, or society (Steiner, 1990).

In American society, success is defined as having status and money (and other countries seem to be rapidly catching up with us in this regard). The two generally go hand-in-hand. Managers have status, while engineers, clerks, accountants, and other positions do not. Thus, following our definition of success, these people are less successful than managers. So, if you want to be seen as

So you
want to be
a project
manager?

successful, you have to be a manager. At least, that's how it seems to many people (I was once one of them myself).

Another factor that makes people want to be managers is the desire to be in control, rather than being controlled. The need for independence is very strong in some of us, so we think we will gain that freedom if we just become managers. It turns out to be a myth at mid-management levels in most organizations, so the individual strives to reach the top—to be CEO, because then real independence will be achieved. That, too, is largely a myth, as any CEO will tell you. They have more bosses than anyone—the stockholders, board of directors, and every employee in the company.

Please don't misunderstand my message—there is nothing wrong with being a CEO or a project manager. I am simply pointing out that you should want to be one for the right reasons, not the wrong ones.

There are two kinds of project managers—dedicated and accidental. If you are a dedicated project manager, you own the project from cradle to grave. Not your grave, but the project's grave. It is your total responsibility from project initiation to project close out. If that is not your situation, then you aren't a dedicated project manager, with all the rights and accolades that accrue to that position.

Also, if you are a real project manager, you are proactive, not

> **Management is proactive, not reactive.**

reactive. I know, I know, you're sick of hearing about people who are proactive. You want to leave as soon as someone uses the term. But it's true whether you like it or not. A project manager absolutely must take the project and run with it. If you aren't doing so, you need to get with it.

Proactive means being assertive, as well as taking initiative. The difference between assertive and aggressive is important. To be assertive means to stand up for your own rights while simultaneously

The assertive person stands up for her own rights while respecting the rights of others. The aggressive person runs over other people.

respecting the rights of others. The aggressive person simply runs over others to get what he wants.

I was recently asked by someone in a seminar, "What do you do when a project is stalled?"

"Tell me what you mean by that," I said.

"Well, we refurbish buildings," he said. "One day you come in and realize that the gas needs to be turned off before some work can be done, and you have no idea how to go about getting it done. What do you do?"

I must confess that I had a hard time keeping a straight face. If you were a true project manager, wouldn't you be thinking ahead about this sort of thing? This person was not being proactive; he was totally reactive. I would say he was a project coordinator at best.

I don't mean to be condescending when I say this. He was an accidental project manager. He may not have wanted to be a project manager in the first place, but the job was thrust upon him, and he didn't fully understand the role. I believe this is true of many individuals who have become project managers in the same way as this person.

A Lesson about Authority

One reason that project managers sometimes fail to be proactive is that they don't have any authority granted by their position, and they think they have to get permission before they can take an action. In fact, organizations tend to establish this as a procedure. You can't purchase anything without having it approved, often by three levels of managers above yourself.

Naturally, we can't do anything about the red tape. However, we can ask ourselves, "Where could I exercise discretion in my job?" As an example, I once worked for an absentee boss. He traveled all the time, so he was never around when I needed a decision on something. I was fortunate enough to read somewhere that the best approach was to assume the authority when it wasn't given to

> You have as much authority as you are willing to assume.

me, so when I couldn't reach my boss I would decide what to do and later tell him what I had done. I am convinced that this behavior contributed to my rise in the organization from an entry-level position to chief engineer in about seven years. *The lesson was that you have as much authority as you are willing to assume.* If you wait for someone to give you authority it may never happen, because you haven't demonstrated that you can handle it.

Another aspect of this was taught to me by a colleague. His favorite saying was, "It's always easier to get forgiveness than permission." I think he's right, and in those environments that are so rigidly controlled that this is not true, I would ask myself whether it is the place I really want to be.

DO YOU REALLY WANT TO MANAGE?

In the 30-plus years of my career I have observed that there are a lot of people who want to be managers but don't want to actually *manage!* Part of the reason is that managers have status, some authority, and generally make more money than do nonmanagers.

Even in technical organizations that claim to have dual career paths, the managerial path usually goes higher than the technical path, both in terms of hierarchical

> A lot of people want to be managers, but many of them don't want to *manage.*

level and salary. In fact, I met a fellow once who had done a study for his MBA degree on organizations with dual career paths, and he had found that the number of companies actually having such paths was very small. In many cases, the technical path was a dumping ground for individuals who could not make it in management.

So, before you can really understand project management, you need to understand management in general. One common definition is that management is getting work done through other people. It is easy to see why this definition is inadequate. A guard over a prison work crew gets the prisoners to work, but would hardly be called a manager. And there are countless people who are called managers who really don't manage very well.

Peter Drucker, considered by many to be the father of modern management thinking, has written that management is making an unsolicited contribution to the organization (Drucker, 1973). That is, a manager does not wait until a situation exists that requires a reaction; rather, a manager is proactive. Furthermore, a manager is looking for ways to improve the functioning of the organization. He or she is forward thinking.

Mintzberg (1989) has argued that very few managers whom he has shadowed fit the theoretical mold of careful, reflective planners. I agree with him. But I would argue that this is because so many managers find themselves caught in the firefighting mode that they simply don't have time to do the careful, reflective

One common
definition is
that management
is getting work
done through
other people.

thinking and planning that they really should be doing. In addition, according to Mintzberg's experience, they are being interrupted at the rate of once every eight minutes, so they can't get
their everyday jobs done.

I think of managers as being very similar to pilots. The pilot's
job is to get an airplane to a distant destination. She begins with a
flight plan. She checks out the plane to ensure that it is functioning properly. Then she practices principles of navigation to guide
the plane to that final goal. She compares where she is to where
the flight plan says she should be, and makes course corrections as
necessary to get the plane back on target when it has drifted because of crosswinds. The same could be said of managing.

A manager has a goal in mind. He makes a plan for how he
will reach that goal. Then he sets in motion steps to reach the goal,
compares progress against the plan, and takes corrective action
when there are deviations from plan.

This is called control, and it is a primary function of management. Now note that, if you have no plan, you don't know

where you are supposed to be, so control is—by definition—impossible!

So a manager is like a pilot, guiding his or her organization to a predetermined destination. Of course, a pilot occasionally finds that the airport at the desired destination is fogged in, and must divert to an alternate until the fog lifts. Managers must sometimes do the same thing, and occasionally, they decide that the original destination should be changed because the environment in which they operate has changed, so that pursuing the original goal would be inappropriate.

> Control is exercised by comparing progress against planned performance, and taking steps to correct for any deviations from the proper course.

The Law of Requisite Variety

An organization is like an organic system. Such systems attempt to adapt to the changing conditions in the environment so that they can survive. A law in systems theory states that, in any system of humans or machines, the element in the system that has the greatest variability in its behavior will control the system.

We have seen that managing is essentially a process of controlling the behavior of an organization so that it can reach a desired goal. Thus, the law of requisite variety suggests that a manager must have more variability in her behavior than any other element in the system, or she won't be in control; some other element will be.

There are two possibilities for achieving such control. One is be to increase your flexibility to be greater than that of any element in the system. The other is to decrease the variability of the system elements so that you can match or exceed the variation in the system.

Any experienced manager knows how difficult it is to be flexible enough to respond to all the variations in the system. There are simply too many of them. We live in a turbulent environment, and chaos theory (Gleick, 1988) has shown that even minute variations in some system element can lead to extremely large excursions in overall system performance. The best expression of this is the premise that a

> **The Law of Requisite Variety**
>
> In any system of humans or machines, the element in the system that has the greatest variability in its behavior will control the system.

butterfly flapping its wings in San Francisco will, a few days later, affect the weather on the East Coast of the United States.

For this reason, some authors have argued that planning is futile, as the effects of chaos soon wipe out your efforts to control (Wheatley, 1992). I think this goes too far. A more balanced approach is recommended by Stacey (1996), who suggests that long-range planning should be tentative and

> You must increase your flexibility, or reduce variation in the behavior of the organization.

broad-brush in nature, but day-to-day planning can and should be more detailed.

The Negative Approach

Because increasing one's own flexibility is so difficult, I believe that most managers resort to the second approach, which is to try and limit the variation in the system. Unfortunately, they do this in a negative way rather than a positive one.

By this I mean that they try to limit variation with rules, regulations, and procedures that often stifle the variation the organization actually needs in order to survive in its environment. Another way to say this is that they create the ultimate bureaucracy, as bureaucracies are known for being highly rule governed.

> The negative approach (reducing system variation) tends to stifle the system and does not lead to real control.

The rules and regulations are essentially *thou shall nots*. Thou shall not go over budget. Thou shall not go around thy manager to his boss. Thou shall not spend more than $25 of company money without approval from the three lords above you.

Tom Peters (Peters, 1987) has argued that these policies (as they are usually called) don't guarantee that people behave in acceptable ways. All they do is give the organization grounds to exercise sanctions over anyone who violates the rule.

The Positive Approach

A better way of reducing variation in system behavior is through proper planning. If every member of the organization knows what he or she is supposed to be doing and how to do it, then variation in behavior is constrained by the plan, and the manager has control. And this is the only way. Unless every individual in the organization is in control of his or her own behavior, the manager won't have control.

> Control cannot be achieved through micromanaging.

This cannot be accomplished through micromanaging, either. In the end analysis, micromanaging means that you can only supervise one person, and I submit that one of you is redundant.

**The only way
you will ever
have control is
if every individual
in the organization
is in control
of his own
behavior!**

Rather, what is required is that conditions exist that allow every employee to be in control of his or her own behavior. How this is accomplished is covered in detail in Chapter 12.

A Word of Caution

It would be easy to conclude that, because few managers spend much time planning, this is appropriate for project managers. Every major study that I have seen on the correlates between the project manager's actions and project success have shown planning to be vital. It is important to recognize that good project managers *facilitate* good project planning; they don't do it themselves. As I have written in all of my books, the first rule of planning is that the people who must do the work should do the planning. There are two principle reasons why this is true:

1. They have no commitment to someone else's plan—not because of ego, but because it is generally not correct, either in estimates, sequencing, or inclusivity.

2. Collectively, the team will think of things that no one individual (namely, the project manager) would think of.

It is a fact that project managers are supposed to be in control, in the sense of getting results from the project team. And since control is defined as comparing where you are to where you are supposed to be, so you can take corrective action when a deviation occurs, it follows that if you have no plan, you have no control, since you have nothing to compare progress against. For that reason, planning is not an option—it is a requirement! Perhaps if more general managers spent time planning, fewer organizations would be operating in crisis mode.

> Just because few managers do much planning does not mean that project managers should abandon planning. If you have no plan, you have no control!

Managing versus Doing

Many managers have risen to their jobs after having first been technical experts in some field. In their new role as manager, they feel a bit like a fish out of water. They aren't very comfortable with it. I recently was told by a woman who has just been promoted, "I sometimes wonder if what I'm doing is what I *should* be doing." Her boss is in another location, so she seldom gets to talk with her, much less receive any guidance. I assured her that most of us experience the same anxiety. The only way out of it is to be extremely clear about what you want to accomplish with your department or project team. This means you have a clear mission and vision in mind.

Even then, however, it is easy to fall into the "doing trap." This happens when someone on your team has a technical problem that you could solve blindfolded. Or perhaps it is a bit of a challenge (that's the most dangerous kind.) Next thing you know,

Project
management
is about
managing risks.

you're spending a lot of time working on the technical issue and neglecting your management duties.

Or, you may have a tendency to micromanage. You don't fully trust your direct reports or team members to do the job as well as you would do it, so you resort to supervising them very closely. Either way, the managing suffers.

The Working Project Manager

Another trap, one that is imposed on project managers by the organization, is that they are expected to do some of the work that is being done by other members of the project team. They are called *working project managers*. The problem with this setup is that, when there is a conflict between getting work done and managing the team, the work always takes priority and the managing suffers. I would personally rather see a person be given several small projects to manage, with no work responsibility, than to have everyone trying to manage the project and do work at the same time. It just never works.

It is easy to
fall into the
"doing" trap!

MAKING YOUR CAREER DECISION

Graham and Englund (1997) have written that there will eventually be no more accidental project managers. Rather, project management will be recognized as a true profession, and we will have dedicated project managers with their own special career paths. They also observe that project management will be the proving ground and possibly the path taken to CEO status (as I mentioned earlier in this chapter).

The reasons are that project managers are exposed to almost every facet of the organization; they require exceptional political and interpersonal skills; and if they can manage projects successfully, they probably can manage the entire organization.

If, after reading this chapter, you are still undecided about whether you want to pursue project management as a career, you should read *World-Class Project Manager,* by Bob Wysocki and myself (Wysocki & Lewis, 2000). We offer a fuller treatment of project management as a career than is possible in this book, together with diagnostics and other aids to help you make your decision.

4
CHAPTER

How to Achieve High-Performance Project Management™

This chapter does not deal directly with how you, as an individual, should manage projects. My intent is that it serves as a guide that you can present to senior managers on how to make project management a core competence in your organization, so you can thrive in an environment that supports what you are learning from this book. In fact, we have a PowerPoint® presentation, which you can download from our Web site, www.lewisinstitute.com, on how your managers can achieve high performance project management. Look for the free downloads in the company store.

THE HIGH-PERFORMANCE PROJECT MANAGEMENT MODEL

No doubt you have heard about a quality improvement program called six sigma. The approach has been adopted by a number of companies, one of the most notable being General Electric. According to the six-sigma providers, most organizations operate at a three-sigma quality level. This means that for every one million tasks they will make about 36,000 errors. These errors will cost them about 20 to 40 cents of every sales dollar. This is the cost of poor quality! (For those who are interested in reading more about six sigma, see Michael George: *Lean Six Sigma*. McGraw-Hill, 2002).

> Most organizations and projects function at a three-sigma quality level, which means that for every million things they do, they make 36,000 errors. That means they waste 20 to 40 cents of every dollar spent!

When an organization can improve its performance to the six-sigma level, they then make only 3.4 errors for every million operations, and this reduces the cost of poor quality to about 3 cents on the dollar—a huge improvement that goes directly to the bottom line.

My High-Performance Project Management (HPPM) model defines project management maturity in five levels, with the first two being bare awareness and minimal performance. These two levels are equivalent to the three-sigma level mentioned above. When an organization reaches the third level, which we call the bronze level, they are probably around a four-sigma quality level. The fourth level, or silver level, is five-sigma, and the fifth level, or gold, is a six-sigma quality level for projects.

In addition to reducing errors, you only achieve HPPM when you consistently meet the PCTS targets for your projects. Remember that three of these can be dictated, and the fourth must be allowed to float. And since these targets are estimated, what we are really saying is that your ability to estimate has improved considerably.

Given the difficulty of estimating some kinds of work—such as creative design, programming, developing life sciences products, and so on—it is possible that some organizations can never consistently hit their targets, but this should be the objective. As Phil Crosby said about zero defects, you may never achieve the target, but it should be the target nonetheless (Crosby, 1980).

The Benefits of HPPM

Although most managers know that they need some form of project management in their organizations, I am not yet convinced that all of them distinguish between "seat-of-the-pants" project management and a structured approach that really gets high-performance results. One reason for this is that many senior managers were project managers before being promoted to higher level management jobs. However, they had no formal training in project management, so many of them used an unstructured approach to managing their projects. They did a good job—good enough, in fact, that they were promoted. And because of this success, they see no need for a structured approach.

Distinguish between seat-of-the-pants project management and a structured approach.

Consider though that even the most successful sports teams know that if they don't find new and improved ways of playing, they will not maintain their success. Continuous improvement has to be the standard approach for all organizations in today's highly competitive world. But just what can a formal, structured approach to project management do for an organization? Following is one such example.

The Four-Hour House

In 1983, the San Diego Building Association sponsored a competition to see just how fast a typical single-family home could be built. They chose as their design a single-story house built on a cement slab, with approximately 2,000 square feet of floor space. Such houses typically take from three to six months to build.

Highly detailed plans were developed—plans that defined activities down to 10-minute increments. A practice run was held, in which the two competing teams built identical houses for practice. The best time during the practice run was six hours. The plans were revised based on lessons learned from the practice session. The revised plan predicted that a house could be completed in about 3 hours and 39 minutes, so they called the competition the "four-hour house project."

It is important to bear in mind that these houses were not prefabricated. They were built from "raw" lumber, wallboard, and so on. The sites had been cleared and the placement for the cement slabs was marked, but the slabs were not poured ahead of time—they were poured when the starting gun for the "race" was fired. The competition ended when the first house was completed; that is, it was ready to move into—fully wired, carpets installed, sod grass in the lawn, shrubs in front, and all appliances (refrigerator, stove, etc.) installed. Each team consisted of 350 workers, all highly motivated to win the contest.

The winning team set a record that is recorded in the *Guinness Book of World Records*. They completed their house in an incredible 2 hours and 45 minutes! If you don't believe me, watch the documentary video, which can be ordered by calling the San Diego Building Association at (619) 450-1221.

A couple of very important points should be noted. First, as already mentioned, the practice houses required six hours to complete. Through a lessons-learned review, they were able to reduce this time by more than 50 percent in the competition. This illustrates the importance of lessons-learned reviews on projects! Secondly, good planning contributed significantly to the winning team's success. Without a truly well-developed plan, there would be no way to build a house in such a short time. But what about the cost? After all, there were 350 workers on each house.

One of my seminar students recently calculated that the house built in 2 hours and 45 minutes actually cost less (with 350 workers) than a house built with fewer workers over a longer time. Furthermore, if you consider that the house can be sold almost immediately, you have a cost-of-capital advantage. So, while less than 3 hours may not be the target we should have for all homes of this type, it does show that building times can be reduced significantly.

You may also realize that the planning took far longer than the execution time, and ordinarily this would not be so. This demonstrates the importance of a plan if you want to get a job done very quickly, and thus counters the claim that "we can get it done faster if we don't *waste* time working up a plan."

One last thought. I know some of you are thinking, "I wouldn't want to live in it." You are thinking that they must have cut corners, thereby sacrificing quality in order to build a house in such a short time. And you would be justified in thinking this. However, to prevent sacrificing quality for speed, building inspectors, wearing referee shirts, inspected the work as it was done, and

they insisted that each house meet code or they would not consider it a valid completion.

Another example of the benefits of good project management
comes from a former client who is now a friend. George Hollins
was Director of Design and Construction Services at the University of Iowa when I met him. He brought me in to teach his archi-
tects and engineers how to manage projects, then used my
methods as the foundation for his own methodology. During the
next five years, he estimates that the formal approach to managing
projects saved the university almost five million dollars in change
orders alone! Not a bad payback on his training investment, I'm
sure you will agree.

THE NEED FOR A NEW APPROACH

Since I began training people in 1980, I have conducted three-day
project management seminars for over 30,000 individuals. Many
of these programs were
conducted for compa-
nies that were trying to
improve project man-
agement in their organi-
zations. In one company
alone, I taught over 800

> No more than 33 percent of what is
> taught makes it back to the
> workplace.

people in sites scattered along the East Coast. In spite of this, I
learned that very few people actually applied what I taught them.
And I have found this to be true of many other clients as well.

This has been a big disappointment to me. I don't want to
just deliver training. I want to deliver training that *gets results!*
And this simply isn't happening.

As I pondered this over several years, I learned that it is a
typical situation. I once read a study that reported that no more
than 33 percent of what is taught ever makes it back to the job (I
no longer remember the source of this data). There are several pri-

mary reasons for this finding. One is that people are not supported for doing what they learned. Neither are they required to demonstrate what was taught. So soon after the program, they revert to their old ways and the learning never "takes."

One of the strongest examples of lack of support was related to me by a fellow who went home from one of my programs feeling very excited about his newfound knowledge. He immediately convened a planning session with his group to develop a project plan. His boss came by the conference room and called him outside.

"What are you doing in there?" his boss wanted to know

"Putting together a plan for our project," said the fellow with enthusiasm.

His boss glared at him. "We don't have time for that nonsense," he said. "Get them out of the conference room so they can get the job done."

This attitude toward planning is widespread. Managers are task-oriented. They want to see people doing work, not drawing work breakdown structures or critical path diagrams. Strangely, this fellow's manager continued sending him to a project management certificate series consisting of six three-day seminars. I have no idea why. He clearly does not understand the essence of project management.

Solving Problems

Since nearly 30 cents of every dollar spent on projects is wasted due to project mismanagement, this represents a problem to be solved by the organization. However, the way a problem is defined affects the solution possibilities, and the typical definition is that people running projects need to be trained. And this is true. However, it is only one component that contributes to poor project management, and if the other components are not addressed, the problem will be only partially solved. The components that

Nearly 30 percent of every dollar spent on projects is wasted.

must be addressed were introduced in Chapter 1 and are repeated here in Figure 4.1.

People

As shown in Figure 4.1, issues with people must be addressed to develop project management competence in an organization. If you want to understand how to develop the skills of people, you should observe athletic coaches, surgeons, and actors. Coaches have been learning how to improve the performance of athletes for centuries. Surgeons and actors, too, spend years on mastering their craft.

> Can you imagine a surgeon sitting through a lecture and going directly into the operating room to perform surgery on someone?

Can you imagine a surgeon sitting through a lecture and going directly into the operating room to perform surgery on someone? Of course not! Yet we do something similar when we send people to a seminar and expect them to per-

Tools, People, Systems Figure.

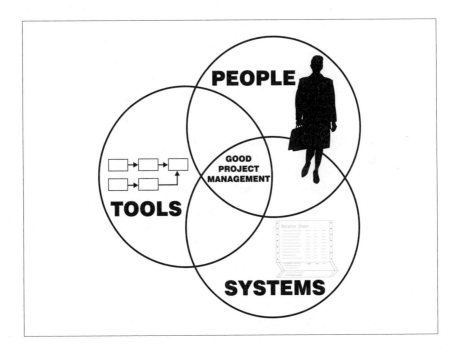

form immediately after they return to the job. Fortunately, poor project management skills seldom kill anyone.

Consider athletes. No coach would ever consider a single training session to be adequate to fully develop a player. Rather, players are coached over time. They practice, receive feedback, and practice some more—until they eventually get it right. But notice that this is a lifelong endeavor. No athlete who is any good ever thinks she is finished with learning or improving. Interestingly, it has been estimated that nearly 85 percent of skills are lost in a few months unless the person is coached over time. This means that we must adopt the sports model for coaching athletes in order to develop the skills of project managers over time.

Managers in organizations overlook the fact that managing is a *performing art*. It has less to do with knowledge than with behavior—applying skills in dealing with people—because projects are people, not technology. And you only learn these skills through practice, feedback, and more practice—until you get it right. The problem is, thousands of managers have never had any coaching. And there are thousands

> Managing is a *performing art*. This is not learned through lecture, but by rehearsing.

who are not very good at dealing with people. These managers generally don't understand that behavioral skills are important. After all, they get the job done. Their bosses are happy. The company makes money. And they continue to progress up the corporate ladder. So why all the fuss? All you really need to do (many of them believe) is just kick some behinds and this will get people moving.

To use the term from the cartoon strip, "Dilbert," these managers are *clueless!* They don't get it, and probably never will.

To summarize, we need to provide project managers with training in the tools and techniques of project management, together with skills in dealing with people. And this must be supported by ongoing feedback on how they are performing, together with coaching to improve that performance. Finally, the application of these tools, techniques, and skills must be supported; in fact, senior managers should demand that they be practiced properly. These skills should be assessed as part of the project manager's performance appraisal.

Tools

The next of the three components is tools. Here we find that managers think the only important tool is a scheduling software program. As I wrote in Chapter 1, this is "instant-pudding" project management—just give a person a copy of MicrosoftProject®, or some other such program, and he will be an instant project manager.

There are two problems with this scenario. First, giving me a saw won't make me a carpenter. I need some training in carpentry first. So people should be given a course in project management first, then taught the software. Secondly, scheduling software is so complex that it is unrealistic to expect a person to sit down and use it out of the box. They need at least two days of training in order to be able to use such software effectively. I have found over the years that most people are simply using the software to develop nice presentation graphics. They have imposed so many "must-start" and "must-finish" dates on tasks that the software can only regurgitate what it has been told—it is unable to do what it is intended to do, which is to tell the user on what dates tasks can be started and finished.

Systems

Peter Senge (1990) has shown that *systems generate behavior*, regardless of the people in the system, and that unless you change the system, you will continue to get the same behavior. A management simulation called the Beer Game shows one such example.

In this simulation, convenience stores sell a beer called Love beer. It's not a big seller—most of them only sell about four cases a month. Suddenly sales of Love beer take off, and the store managers learn that it is because the beer is mentioned in a popular song. So they increase their orders for

> Systems generate behavior! If the behavior is unacceptable, change the system, not the people.

the beer. But because this is going on throughout the region, the beer distributor is soon swamped with orders. The brewery can't fill them fast enough.

Systems generate
behavior,
regardless
of the people
in the system.

They have no choice but to increase capacity, so they initially ask people to work overtime. They also increase orders for grain and hops to make beer, and this puts a strain on the supply chain. But they all work hard to respond. Still, this is not enough to meet the demand, so the brewery begins hiring for a second shift.

Unfortunately, the market is fickle. The song loses popularity, the beer isn't a great beer, despite the temporary demand, and so people quit buying. Panic sets in. The stores begin canceling orders for beer, forcing the brewery to cancel orders for supplies and to lay off the newly hired second-shift employees, plus canceling all overtime. It is a snowball effect.

Now for the compelling fact. Senge says that they have run this simulation with a large number of groups consisting of members with all kinds of backgrounds—educational, ethnic, and so on—and the result is always the same. The conclusion: the system generates the behavior, regardless of the people involved.

This is a profound finding, and one that no manager can ignore with impunity. If the system generates the behavior, then just how accountable can people be within the system? Clearly there is a need for us to examine causality in situations where people don't seem to be performing acceptably.

Another example of the effect of systems on behavior was provided by Dr. Edwards Deming (1986), who demonstrated the same thing using a bowl of beads, some of which were white and some of which were red. The objective of the person in the demonstration was to insert into the bowl a paddle into which a large number of holes had been drilled, and extract only white beads. Red beads were regarded as defects. Of course, it is clear that it is impossible to consistently do this and pull out only white beads. However, what baffled many participants was that Dr. Deming said there were exactly 10 percent red beads in the bowl, and asked the audience what they expected the average defect level to be as the paddle was inserted and withdrawn and the beads were dumped back into the bowl—thus keeping the population constant.

Everyone guessed 10 percent. Deming asked why this number. They asserted that he had told them the population was 10 percent red beads. Deming then asked what that had to do with anything.

After considerable head scratching, someone usually suggested that maybe the process had something to do with the result. Deming then declared that it did, indeed, affect the outcome. He had three paddles. One would produce an average of 9.8 percent, another 10.0 percent, and the third would produce about 10.2 percent—in spite of the fact that the bead population was 10 percent red.

As he then told the audience, you have given workers a system that is going to inherently produce a certain defect level—no matter how they do their jobs—and you can admonish them to "do it right the first time" and it will make no difference. They cannot produce results better than the system is capable of producing!

Because most organizations have been functionally organized for so long, systems to support projects often do not exist.

They must be installed for good project management to be achieved. This includes the reward system, tracking, evaluation, budgeting, and so on. As an example, companies usually budget on a fiscal basis. Projects often span multiple years. It makes no sense to insist that a project manager spend exactly what he was supposed to on an annual basis, but this is what companies do.

Finally, we must examine the reward system in the organization. Most reward systems encourage individuals to maximize their performance, even though it may be at the expense of other people in the group. And functional groups are rewarded for excellent functional performance, rather than for supporting projects. Unless you change the reward systems to support good project performance, you won't get it.

Joint Optimization

One mistake that must be avoided in developing high project management performance is to optimize each of these three factors (tools, people, systems) independently of the others. You will note that the intersection of the three circles in Figure 4.1 is where good project management occurs. The reason for this is shown by considering how you might build the world's best car. You find the best transmission in the world, combine it with the best auto engine, brakes, body,

> Systems must be jointly optimized. Improving a single system can worsen, rather than improve, overall organization performance.

and so on. Chances are pretty good that you won't have a very good car because these various components have not been designed to work with each other. If the engine is too powerful for the transmission, for example, you will destroy the transmission as soon as you hit the accelerator. For this reason, you must develop your tools and systems to match the capabilities of your people.

STAGES OF DEVELOPMENT

No athlete becomes a star overnight, and no company develops project management competence immediately. Most project management maturity models have five levels of capability, and it takes most companies about one year per level to develop their capability. For the impatient, this is terrible news. Nevertheless, it is reality. Experience cannot be accelerated beyond certain limits. So long as this is recognized and expected, there are very few problems. But when it is not, we find companies abandoning project management because they do not get immediate benefits.

Too Many Projects

One of the major reasons that organizations have problems with projects is that they are trying to do too many projects given their resources. The result is that people are constantly jumping from one project to another in an attempt to keep everything going. In doing so, they must get re-oriented each time they shift tasks. This re-orientation is called *setup time* in manufacturing, and it adds no value to the work process itself. We have known for a long time that setup time should be reduced as much as possible, as it depresses productivity.

> Unless you have unlimited resources, you can't do everything at the same time. Prioritize projects and do them in priority order!

The only way this can be done is to allow a person to work on one thing until it is completed and then move to something else. Heresy, you say! Maybe so, but one company found that their productivity nearly doubled when they quit trying to multitask and prioritized their projects, so that each person had a priority-one project and a backup. So long as it was possible, the

One of the major
reasons that
organizations
have problems
with projects
is limited
resources.

person worked on the priority-one project and used the backup to fill dead time on the first project. Is it clear that if you double your productivity, you will get everything done in the same calendar time as when you were trying to do everything, but your productivity will be so much higher that your costs will go down dramatically? Multitasking creates the illusion that a lot is getting done. It is, but at low levels of productivity.

Consider one simple example. Many of you have probably found that you can't get anything done during the day. So you come in early or stay late. Why? Because during the day you are constantly being interrupted. Drop what you're doing and go to a meeting. Answer the random phone calls. Chat with your colleagues who need your help. And report on what you're doing to your boss. Interview candidates for jobs. And on and on goes the list. It is all important "stuff" that must be done, but it takes time that you can't spend doing your work. And it's called multitasking!

The Negative Environment

You can't have high performance in an environment that has a negative climate. This includes a climate of blame and punishment for things that go wrong. Don't get me wrong. It is appropriate to punish people who break rules or act irresponsibly. But when the climate is such that failure to meet project targets is seen as a sign of weakness on the part of people, and they are chastised for it, you have an environment that does not support high performance.

Remember, all project targets are estimates—which is a kinder word than guesses, but they are guesses just the same, and can be expected to be missed fairly often until you have enough history to know how long things really take. And even when you have history, the time it takes to do any given activity will vary because of factors outside a person's control. Variance is a fact of life and must be accepted.

Turf battles are also detrimental to high performance. A team spirit—one of cooperation—must exist, and this must be promoted

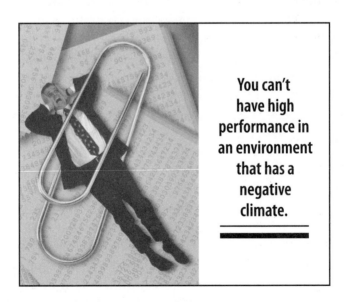

You can't have high performance in an environment that has a negative climate.

by senior management. I have known many senior managers who did exactly the opposite. They promoted competition between people in the workplace, believing that this brings out the best in them. This is a carryover from sports. In sports, competition does tend to bring out the best in people. Unfortunately, it also brings out the worst in them, as we have witnessed from the violence toward fans and other players that sometimes erupts when winning becomes all that matters. And the same happens in organizations.

I knew about a textile mill in South Carolina that decided to use competition to improve production. They had a three-shift operation, so they told their people that the shift with the highest production for the week would receive an award. All members of that team would get a dinner at a very nice local restaurant. This did initially spark enthusiasm and increase production.

Soon, however, teams became discontented to simply work hard to win. They began to consider how they might actually create a disadvantage to the other teams—to slow them down. The most obvious thing was to adjust the settings on their machines so that they would not run right. They did this at the end of the shift, so that the people who followed them would have to waste time resetting the adjustments on all the machines. This gave the preceding team an advantage and enabled them to win.

Of course, it only took a short time for everyone to catch on to what was being done, so each team now left their machines misadjusted at the end of their shift. When management learned what was going on, they established a new rule—a team was only eligible for the award if the team that followed reported that all machines ran properly when they came on board!

This is by no means an isolated incident. Alfie Kohn (1999), in a book entitled, *Punished by Rewards,* wrote that almost all reward systems tend to blow up over time. Employees always try to maximize their rewards, and they will do so at the expense of cooperation and even actual performance. The only legitimate reward system is one in which people are rewarded by true

A team spirit—one of cooperation—must exist.

achievement and pride in the work they do. All carrot-and-stick systems create problems.

This is not a popular notion. Kohn was strongly criticized for his assertions. People want to believe that they can hold carrots in front of people and get them turned on. After more than 50 years of research that demonstrates that money is not

> The only legitimate reward system is one in which people are rewarded by true achievement and pride in the work they do.

an actual motivator, but rather a symbol for those things that really motivate people, there are a lot of people who refuse to accept the results. They cling stubbornly to the belief that you only have to pay people well to motivate them.

To return to the central premise of this section, a negative environment will not produce good project results. And, while project managers are limited in how much influence they exert over the work environment, they should be aware of those factors that

**A negative
environment will
not produce
good project results.**

contribute to environmental climate and do their best to make
the project environment as positive as they can. In general, the
most important thing they can do is try to match team members
to work that they find enjoyable and challenging. And they
should strenuously try to create a climate of mutual respect and
cooperation.

As a general guideline, I would recommend practicing the
principles developed by the president and CEO of Boeing Commercial Airplanes, Alan Mulally. These were documented in my
book, *Working Together* (Lewis, 2002), and I will not repeat them
here (as that would require inserting a full book into this chapter!). When applied properly, they mitigate against many of the
concerns that I have expressed above.

Finally, developing high-performance project management
does not happen overnight, any more than a championship team
can be developed overnight. It takes time and hard work.

The benefits are worth the investment.

5

CHAPTER

Whole Brain Project Management

You can't solve a problem with the same thinking that caused it.

—Albert Einstein

No doubt most of you have heard about left-brain/right-brain orientations in thinking. Left-brain thinkers are more analytical, logical, and sequential than are right-brain thinkers, who are more parallel thinking, intuitive, and global thinkers.

Does this matter to project managers? If so, how do you make use of it?

To answer this question, I'll share an experience with you. I once hired an engineer who worked for a very prestigious company. He was supposed to design communications equipment. I asked him a number of questions during the interview about communications technology, which he answered flawlessly. Unfortunately, he didn't know how to translate the theory into design practice. In a word, his design work was inadequate.

At the time I had no training in psychology, so I had no idea what was wrong. However, I knew that his former position had been a manufacturing engineering job in which he helped solve problems with products that were already in manufacturing. I offered to transfer him to an equivalent job on the basis that if he had done satisfactory work in such a job previously, then he should work well for us.

He saw this transfer as a demotion and refused it. Then he worked for another project manager for a time before returning to my project. The other manager had similar problems with him.

His performance deficit finally came to a head. We gave him the option of finding another job, taking the transfer, or terminating him. He chose to find another job.

What I didn't know then, but do now, is that the design job requires different thinking than the manufacturing support job. The design engineer must be able to think in terms of synthesis, whereas the manufacturing engineer must think more analytically. Synthesis is a right-brain mode, and analysis is a left-brain mode. So I actually hired the wrong person for the job based on his thinking preferences (and ability). Now, exactly what does this mean?

THINKING STYLES

Ned Herrmann was a training manager at General Electric's Crotonville Management Training Center. Ned was originally educated as a physicist, but was very interested in the social sciences, especially art. He was a gifted painter.

He heard about research that indicated that the two hemispheres of the brain seem to control different kinds of thinking, and wondered how those differences might affect learning, management, creativity, and other aspects of human performance. Because the field was in its infancy, Ned had to do a lot of research himself, and he found that the left/right dichotomy did not suffice to explain thinking differences, and he postulated another axis

HBDI Profile of Thinking Styles

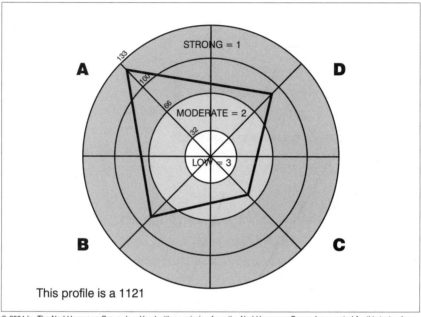

This profile is a 1121

based on cerebral/limbic thinking (Herrmann, 1995, 1996). When this dimension is added, you have four pure styles that combine to yield a wide range of different thinking styles. Ned developed an instrument that measures these preferences, called the Herrmann Brain Dominance Instrument (HBDI™)[1], and the respondent receives a profile like the one shown in Figure 5.1.

In this profile are four concentric circles or bands, divided into about 33 points per band, so raw scores range from 0 to 133. However, to give a person a raw score implies a measurement precision that simply does not exist, so Ned chose to give a ranking instead. The outer two bands have a rank of 1, meaning the

---

[1]   HBDI™ is a trademark of the Ned Herrmann Group, Inc.

person has a very strong preference for thinking in the specific mode. The next band has a rank of 2, which is weaker but still significant. Finally, the inner band yields a rank of 3, which is a very low preference. In fact, a score in this band indicates that the individual may actually reject this mode of thinking most of the time. There is no such thing as a 0 rank, as everyone uses all four modes to some degree. Note also that the instrument measures *preferences,* not skills or abilities.

> The HBDI measures one's preference for thinking in certain ways, not one's ability.

However, there is a correlation between preference and skill. If you have a strong preference for engaging in a certain mode of thinking, you will tend to do so frequently and thus get pretty good at it. So, over time, preference probably does lead to skill.

Herrmann believed that the preference for the various thinking modes was based on brain physiology, which involves both chemistry and genetics, but whether this is true is still open to question. In the January 2005 issue of *Scientific American's* special publication on the mind, research by a German team was reported in which they used the MRI, rather than just the standard EKG, to observe brain activity, and found that specific areas of the brain do not cleanly correlate with certain kinds of thinking. Rather, various stimuli activated multiple parts of the brain at once. Thus, the idea of left-right hemispheres and limbic versus cerebral as determinants of certain thinking may not be accurate, but it is not important for our purposes. The fact is that four distinct modes of thinking have been identified and the HBDI does a good job of measuring them.

At this time the Herrmann International database contains over a half-million profiles of people who have taken the HBDI. most find that the measures represent them fairly well. Seldom does anyone say, "That's just not me!"

Profiles

As you might expect, an individual can have a preference for thinking in only one of the four modes. The HBDI profile for such a person, called *single-dominant*, looks a bit like a kite, so we sometimes refer to a profile as a kite. Only about 5 percent of the population is single-dominant. A sample profile is shown in Figure 5.2.

When an individual likes to think in two modes, the profile is called *double-dominant*, and there are two forms that can be taken by the kite. In one the two preferred quadrants are side-by-side. In the other they are diagonally opposite each other. The two possibilities are shown in Figure 5.3. Naturally, the adjacent preferences can be

F I G U R E   5.2

A Single-Dominant HBDI Profile

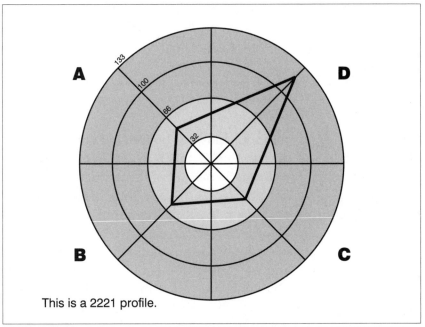

This is a 2221 profile.

F I G U R E 5.3

Double-Dominant HBDI Profiles

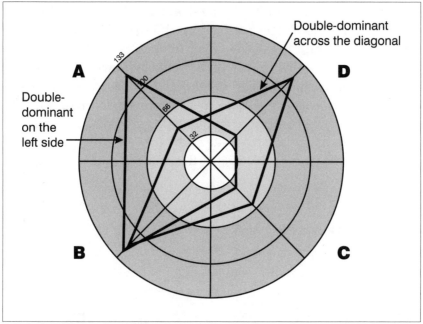

both left, both right, both top, and both bottom quadrants, and the diagonally opposite can be A to C and B to D. Double-dominant preferences account for about 56 percent of the population.

The *triple-dominant* profile can be any three adjacent quadrants, and approximately 36 percent of the population falls into this category. A triple-dominant profile is shown in Figure 5.4.

Finally, a mere 3 percent of the population prefers to think in all four quadrants, and of course this profile is called *quadruple-dominant*. Such individuals are called multidominant translators, and Ned believed that they should make excellent CEOs, because they can interact effectively with people from each of the

F I G U R E 5.4

The Triple-Dominant HBDI Profile

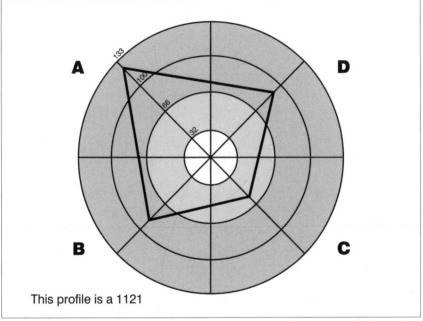

This profile is a 1121

quadrants. This may be hard to demonstrate, since the numbers are so small, and of those people who are quadruple dominant, only a certain percentage will ever become CEOs, so we may never know if they are good candidates. Furthermore, one's thinking preferences do not guarantee that a person will be able to deal effectively with others, so thinking is only part of the picture. A quadruple-dominant profile is shown in Figure 5.5.

What are the differences between the four modes, and how do these differences affect various work functions in a project? Since the model is a grid containing four quadrants, each of which represents a different thought mode, we will begin in the upper left, or A

F I G U R E 5.5

A Quadruple-Dominant HBDI Profile

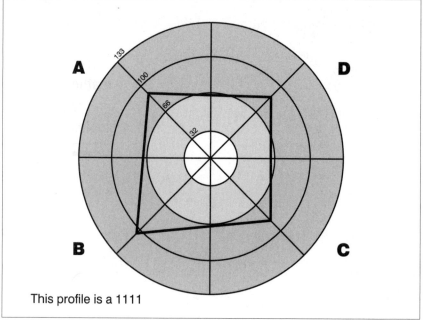

This profile is a 1111

quadrant, and explain each mode by progressing in a counterclock-
wise direction through the quadrants. Note that the progression is
A-B-C-D and that in the profile received by respondents, each
quadrant is colored, in the sequence blue-green-red-yellow.

THE A QUADRANT

The thinking associated with the A quadrant can be described as
logical, analytical, technical, mathematical, and problem solving
(see Figure 5.6). Such thinking can be thought of as dealing with
facts and figures. It seems reasonable that people who like dealing
with facts and figures would be attracted to jobs or professions

Quadrant A can be
described as
logical, analytical,
technical,
mathematical,
and
problem solving.

F I G U R E 5.6

The Herrmann Whole Brain Model—Thinking in Each Quadrant

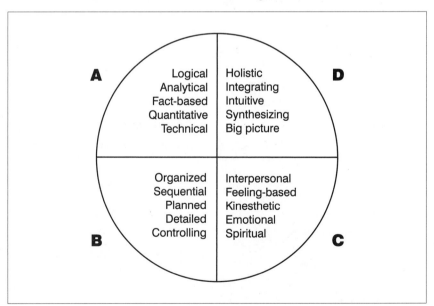

that require such thinking, and this is true. Examples of such careers include technical, legal and financial areas (including accounting and tax law), engineering, information technology, science, mathematics, and the analytical aspects of management.

A project manager with a single-dominant profile in quadrant A could be expected to be very logical, interested in technical issues affecting the project, inclined to analyze status reports carefully, and keen on problem solving. Such a project manager may be seen as cold, uncaring, and interested only in the problems presented by the project. However, since only 5 percent of the population is single-dominant, such project managers should be correspondingly rare.

THE B QUADRANT

The B quadrant is similar to the A quadrant, but with significant differences. Words that describe the B quadrant thinkers are organizational, administrative, conservative, controlled, and planning.

Quadrant B is organizational, administrative, conservative, controlled, and planning.

This is the preferred thinking of many managers, administrators, planners, bookkeepers, foremen, and manufacturers. Individuals who have single-dominant profiles in the B quadrant could be expected to be concerned with the detailed plans of a project, and with keeping everything organized and controlled. Note that individuals with financial interests who are dominant in quadrant A will probably be financial managers, whereas those with dominant B quadrant profiles may be drawn to cost accounting.

If you want someone to pay close attention to details, you want someone who displays a strong preference for this quadrant. If they have a single-dominant profile, however, they may see the trees and be unaware of the forest.

THE C QUADRANT

People with single-dominant profiles in the A or B quadrants probably see individuals with strong C quadrant preferences as being very "touchy-feely." Words that describe this quadrant are

Quadrant C are often nurses, social workers, musicians, teachers, counselors, or ministers.

interpersonal, emotional, musical, spiritual, and talkative. Individuals with single-dominant C profiles are very "feeling" and people-oriented. They are often nurses, social workers, musicians, teachers, counselors, or ministers.

A project manager with a single-dominant C profile would naturally be concerned with the interpersonal aspects of the project, perhaps to the detriment of getting the work done. Such an individual would be drawn to the coordination of project activities with people both inside and outside the team, and would be a relationship builder. This would be a good bias to have for highly political projects, as long as other members of the team are attending to the work itself.

In fact, you will remember that we have said several times that projects are people, and dealing with people is one aspect of project management that some individuals find distasteful. So you could expect that this aspect of the job will bother the person who has very low C-quadrant scores on the HBDI. My counsel is that you can develop the skill if you have the desire, but given very low scores in the C-quadrant naturally means this is not your "cup of tea." So you will have to work very hard at this aspect of the job if you want to manage projects.

There is an interesting finding about how we behave in terms of our least-preferred thinking styles. I have a very strong D-quadrant preference, with B-quadrant being my least preferred. This means that I love developing concepts and dislike doing detail work. However, if I must do detail work in order to get one of my ideas to see the light of day, then I am very motivated to do so. This means that you can be motivated to deal with the "touchy-feely" stuff if it means achieving success in terms of your other thinking preferences.

THE D QUADRANT

Words that describe this quadrant are artistic, holistic, imaginative, synthesizers, and conceptualizers. Individuals who have single-dominant D quadrant profiles are often drawn to careers that involve entrepreneurial effort, facilitation, advising, or consulting, being sales leaders and artists. These are the "idea" people in a team, and they enjoy synthesizing ideas from several sources to create something new from that combination.

This is the natural domain of people who are perceived to be creative. At the beginning of this chapter we discussed the need for creative thinking in projects. So you may conclude that if you are primarily a left-brain thinker having strong preferences for A- or B-quadrant thinking, and low preference for thinking in the D quadrant, then you are out of luck. Not so. It turns out that it is easier for left-brain thinkers to learn to do conceptual or "creative" thinking than it is for conceptual thinkers to learn analytical or detail thinking.

Project managers who have single-dominant D-quadrant profiles could be expected to be "big-picture" in their thinking—they run the risk of seeing the forest without realizing that it consists of distinct trees. They are generally good at thinking strategically, so in planning a project the D-quadrant thinker will develop a gameplan but will need help from B-quadrant thinkers to make it workable.

Quadrant D are often entrepreneurs, in facilitation, advising, consulting, sales leaders, and artists.

Double-Dominant Profiles and Project Management Styles

Since only 5 percent of our population has single-dominant profiles, it would seem more reasonable to examine multidominant profiles. The simplest analysis would be for double-dominant profiles because they comprise 56 percent of the population, and this will give us insight into a host of project managers. A diagram showing the characteristics of each of the adjacent-quadrant double-dominant profiles is shown in Figure 5.7.

F I G U R E 5.7

Management Styles of Single and Double-Dominant Managers Using the Herrmann Model

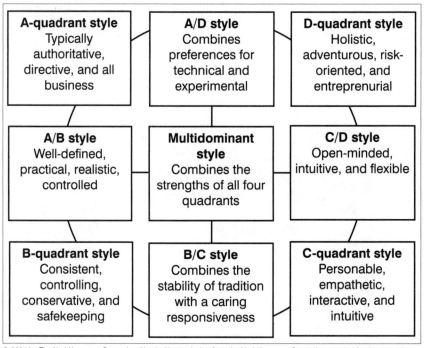

© 2004 by The Ned Herrmann Group, Inc. Used with permission from the Ned Herrmann Group, Inc. granted for this text only.

WORK MOTIVATION AND THE HBDI

One aspect of thinking preferences that you should consider is that you probably have a least-preferred thinking style (or several). Mine is the B-quadrant, which requires great attention to detail. I would find a project requiring such thinking to be drudgery.

When I was an engineer, I disliked the detailed work involved in reviewing drawings or making sure a bill of materials was exactly right. It was vital work, but I hated it. So knowing your most-preferred and least-preferred thinking styles should help you determine when a particular kind of project is a good match for you, or what you should do when there is a mismatch.

> People are motivated to engage in various patterns of activity, and these are derived from preferred thinking modes.

As a matter of fact, a person's motivation is derived from his preferred quadrants. If the preference is single-dominant, you will have a single motivation pattern. If your profile is double-dominant you will have two patterns, and so on. These patterns of activity motivate a person. As an example, a person with a strong preference for thinking in the D quadrant may be very innovative. A person whose preference is the A quadrant may be a good trouble-shooter, which requires analytical thinking.

Thus, a person's profile is a pretty good indication of the kind of activities that motivate her. If you understand the characteristics of the job, you will know whether it is likely to motivate the person or not.

Is There a Best Profile?

Ned Herrmann was always careful to say that individuals with almost any profile *can* do most jobs. The HBDI measures one's

The HBDI measures one's preference for thinking, not one's ability.

preference for thinking, not one's *ability*. As I pointed out earlier, there is a relationship, but presumably a person with any profile can develop the ability to think in all four modes and become skilled enough to be able to perform in any job.

Also, as I mentioned earlier, Ned did postulate that there may be an ideal profile for a CEO (chief executive officer), that being a square—a quadruple-dominant profile. The reason is easy to understand. A CEO must deal with people who think in all four quadrants, and if she prefers to think in all four, then she can translate between them for all parties involved.

I met one such individual, and sure enough he was a turnaround CEO who specialized in saving hospitals from financial disaster. Unlike some individuals who specialize in turnarounds, this man tried to employ measures that saved as many jobs as possible. The turnaround CEO with very low C-quadrant thinking is often concerned only with the bottom line, and the quickest way to improve financial performance is to eliminate jobs regardless of the cost in human suffering. Naturally they will justify such action by saying that sacrificing a few jobs is better for everyone in the long run.

The Herrmann group pulled a composite profile for all of the project managers that they had in their database, and that overall profile was square. They had 1,250 profiles for project managers, with the population being almost perfectly split 50-50 between men and women. These profiles are shown in Figures 5.8 and 5.9. For the overall population, there is a small "tilt" toward the A quadrant for men and a small tilt toward the C quadrant for women, and this was also true of the profiles for project managers.

F I G U R E 5.8

HBDI Composite Profile for Female Project Managers

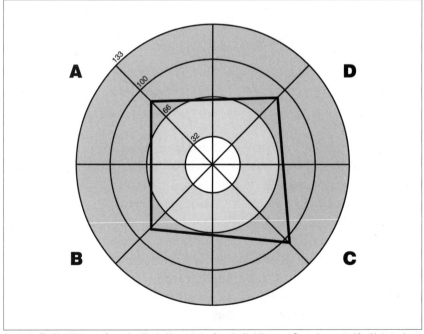

HBDI Composite Profile for Male Project Managers

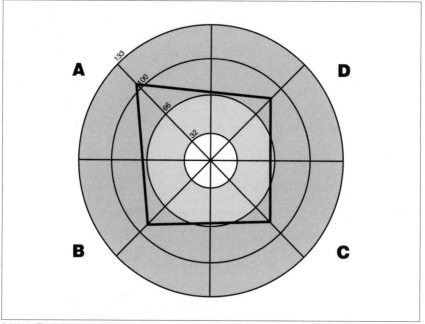

This suggests that project managers come in all shapes and sizes. There has to be a fairly even distribution of profiles to get a composite square, so the distribution for project managers is not very different than for the population in general.

As has been stated above, an individual's thinking preference will affect his style of managing projects. One concern would be with project managers who have very little preference for C-quadrant thinking, the reason being that age-old problem of project managers: they have a lot of responsibility and very little authority, so that the only way they can get anything done is through influence, negotiation, begging, and selling. Project managers with very low preference for the C quadrant are inclined to say, "I hate dealing with people problems," and to them I suggest that they rethink whether they truly want to manage projects. This would be the one deficit that should enter into a person's decision about whether to be a project manager. If you hate dealing with people, then why subject yourself to the daily agony that you are sure to experience as a project manager?

> Your profile will affect your style of managing projects, and this could affect your success in certain environments, but any profile can be effective in project management.

Is there a *best* profile? Maybe.

In a recent seminar that I taught, entitled "Whole Brain Project Management," I discussed the attributes of project managers having various profiles, and concluded that of the double-dominant profiles, the one that is probably most effective is the C-D profile—that is, the person who is primarily right-brained. Because project managers

> I believe the project manager with a primarily right-brain preference has an advantage over other profiles in most situations.

must use influence to get things done, they need strong C-quadrant thinking. Furthermore, project managers have a major responsibility to help a team develop a shared understanding for the vision of the project outcome, and this requires a strong D-quadrant focus.

I also believe that a project manager is primarily a leader and facilitator. For that reason, she need not be highly analytical, nor be a very strong planner/organizer, as long as she recognizes the need for such thinking and gets the team to do it. In fact, I believe

Is there
a "best"
profile?
(NO)

that project managers who are strong in the A and B quadrants may be inclined to get too bogged down in technology or detail, and to possibly do too much of the planning rather than having the team do it, and this is not always good.

As a matter of fact, I have now met quite a few quadruple-dominant individuals, and although they may be good translators between the quadrants, they seem to me to have trouble making decisions. The simple reason is that they try too hard to cover all of the quadrants, to consider all of the issues in each one, and in doing so become paralyzed. I'm not certain that this is true, and would love to hear from any of my readers who can add insight into this question. Write me at jlewis@lewisinstitute.com.

Forming Teams Using the HBDI

One application of the HBDI that is now well documented is its use in assembling teams. A team should collectively represent a "whole brain," meaning that if you overlay the profiles of all members of the team, they will form a composite profile that shows preferences in all four quadrants. Otherwise, if they have a strong aversion to one of the quadrants, you could expect that issues requiring thinking in that area may not be handled very well. However, a word of caution is in order. Ned found that whole-brain, gender-balanced teams produce better solutions and work than homogeneous or single-gender teams. However, you can also expect much more debate to take place because people approach each situation from their own perspective, and team members with multiple perspectives have a hard time reaching agreement.

As I've noted, many teams do not collectively represent a whole brain. For example, technical groups often have a profile like that shown in Figure 5.10. They are strong in the A, B, and D quadrants and weak in C—the one having to do with interpersonal matters.

This means that they may very well attend to technical issues, are good at details, and generate good ideas, but they neglect the "touchy-feely" attributes that may undermine their team's performance. What should they do?

The important thing is that they be aware of the profile and know how to compensate for the low preference in quadrant C.

> When a team lacks a "whole-brain," members must learn to "walk into" the least-preferred quadrant and cover issues relevant to that quadrant.

Remember, it is not that they *can't* think in this quadrant but that they simply don't have a strong preference to do so. If they can understand that failing to deal with quadrant C issues is going to cause them problems in dealing with what they really care about (namely technical matters), then they are more likely to spend time working on such issues.

F I G U R E 5.10

HBDI Average Profile for a Technical Team

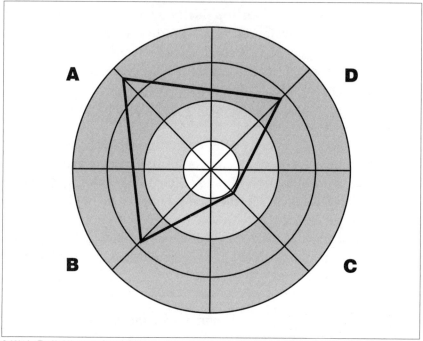

Figure 5.11 offers another example. This time we have a very creative group of people; they love ideas, are interpersonal, and like doing analytical work—but they dislike detail. We can expect that they will generate good ideas but have trouble executing them, at least so far as the details are concerned. It is said that "The devil is in the details," and the devil may just get this group!

Again, however, if they are aware of the low quadrant-B score for the team, they can compensate by working hard to ensure that details are not overlooked.

F I G U R E 5.11

HBDI Average Profile for a Creative Team

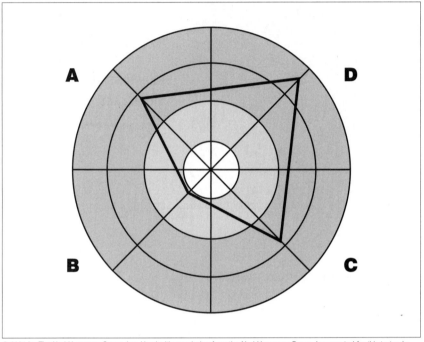

TEAM DYNAMICS

A project team is meeting to discuss an important project issue—a missed milestone. Everyone is a little apprehensive. They aren't sure how senior management is going to react to their failure to complete project work on schedule.

Wanda says, "I don't see how we could have done any better. We did everything humanly possible to complete the work on time. I feel really bummed out over the whole thing!"

Team dynamics affect problem solving significantly.

"In looking at the numbers," Chuck says, "I believe we were set up to begin with. We were allocated to the project at a 95 percent rate, which is too high."

"I didn't like the concept we started with in the first place," chimes in Karen. "It was too flaky."

Don had been studying the schedule. "We should have moved these two tasks in parallel," he offers. "Then we could have finished on time."

This sets Wanda off. "You're always changing the plan, Don," she insists. "Can't you see we did everything we could to meet the deadline?"

"But the schedule is the most important part of the project plan," Don says defensively. "If we don't use the schedule properly, we can't hope to complete the work on time. It's a question of being better organized."

"It doesn't matter how well organized we are if the concept is no good to begin with," Karen interjects.

At this point, the project manager, Beth, interrupts. "Okay, let's calm down for a moment," she says. "And let's look at what's going on."

They all lean back in their chairs and wait for Beth to continue.

"Wanda, you're concerned about the effort you've put into the job, and you're feeling a little guilty that it didn't pay off," Beth says. "In terms of your HBDI profile, you're thinking in the C quadrant."

Wanda nods in agreement.

"And Karen, you're in the D quadrant, thinking conceptually, as usual," Beth says.

Karen smiles and nods. Beth has her pegged.

Beth continues around the table. "Naturally, Don is concerned about the schedule. He's a predominantly B-quadrant thinker, and Chuck is analyzing the numbers—his normal A-quadrant thinking."

Everyone laughs.

"The bad news is that each of us sees the situation from a different perspective," Beth continues. "And the good news is that each of us sees the situation from a different perspective."

She pauses to let the impact of her comment sink in.

"That's true," Karen says. "If we all saw it the same way we would probably fall into 'groupthink' and really get into trouble."

"Exactly!" Beth says. "We need every perspective to be an effective team, but our different styles make us think the other person doesn't understand what we're talking about, and we get into conflict."

They all murmur their agreement.

"Now let's see if we can use our varying points of view to get a handle on this project," Beth suggests. "How about if we come back to Karen's contention that the concept is flawed. She's right. If it is, then the detailed plan can't be any good."

From this point on, the meeting proceeds to a solution.

**Principle:
Misunderstanding
sometimes occurs
because of
differences in
thinking
preferences.**

By understanding the fact that each member of the team sees the project in different ways, based on their individual thinking styles, Beth is able to draw on those preferences to the benefit of the project. Were she unaware of thinking preferences, she would probably see the team as dysfunctional and be tempted to disband it altogether, or perhaps ask a group facilitator to help her keep them in line.

Of course, this scenario has been framed somewhat unrealistically. I have treated each individual team member as though he or she had a single-dominant thinking style. Most of us think in more than one quadrant, but it is true that there may be a quadrant that does dominate our thinking. When we communicate with others who are in different quadrants than our own, we have difficulties.

The opposite is also true. A couple of years ago I met a fellow with whom I seemed to have almost instant rapport. We saw eye-to-eye on so many things it was almost scary. At that time I was aware of the HBDI, but had not yet been certified as a practitioner, so it didn't occur to me that this could be the source of our easy communication and understanding. I did know the Myers-Briggs, and found that we had similar temperaments. In any case, we became good friends.

After I became certified I sent a survey to my friend, and to our amazement his profile and mine are congruent to within a few points in every quadrant! No wonder we think so much alike. Naturally, we don't agree on everything, but the similarities are striking.

The danger for us, of course, is that we may too quickly agree on an issue without exercising the critical thinking that might change our opinions. As Beth told her team, we need opposing points of view to achieve a balanced perspective on issues.

Managing Conflict

If a team is to have creative capacity, it must be able to generate many ideas so that one good one will emerge. These ideas must be screened and the best one selected. During the screening process various ideas are critiqued, and it is at this point that conflict sometimes turns nasty.

There is a sense in which, if you criticize my idea, you are finding fault with me. So I respond by getting angry. Next thing you know, we are locked in an interpersonal conflict. These are often labeled as *personality conflicts*. They are in a sense. But they have a fundamental cause—we see things differently, and identify with our points of view and the ideas we have.

A project leader has to get people to generate ideas, and manage the critiquing of these conflicting ideas so that they don't develop into interpersonal conflicts. As this will sometimes happen, the project manager then has resolve that interpersonal conflict, and if people understand the concept of thinking preferences this will be somewhat easier than it would be otherwise.

"You Think Funny"

THE BALANCED SCORECARD

Kaplan and Norton (1996) developed the concept of using a balanced scorecard to measure the effectiveness of an organization. This concept can also be used to measure project performance. The idea is that most measures focus exclusively on financial aspects of the business and fail to consider other important factors, such as long-term strategies, developing human resources, knowledge management, and so on.

When you think about this, it is clear that the Herrmann model can be used to measure project performance. Each quadrant represents a domain of concern for project and/or organization performance. The A quadrant deals with the familiar financial measures and other numerical data. The B quadrant focuses on policies, procedures, and controls. The C quadrant provides a focus on people—training and development of employees, maintaining good relations with customers, clients, and key suppliers. The D quadrant concerns long-range planning—positioning the organization or project for the future and dealing with concepts, strategies, and the "big picture."

> Develop a whole-brain, balanced scorecard for a project so you can measure success from the perspective of each quadrant.

In planning a project it is important to decide what outcomes should be achieved in each quadrant, and what evidence will be used to show that these outcomes have been achieved. In other words, you should ask:

- What is the desired outcome?
- How will we know it has been achieved?

Once you know the desired outcomes and how you will know they have been achieved, you can develop plans to get you there. This approach will help you avoid focusing only on financials.

As an example, a project may meet all PCTS targets and still be judged negatively by a major stakeholder. This may be because he was not treated as he expected to be treated (C-quadrant). By paying attention to C-quadrant factors from the very beginning, such missteps can be avoided.

Figure 5.12 shows a general example of the factors that might be considered in a balanced scorecard for a project.

IN SUMMARY

There are many applications of the whole-brain model in managing projects, because projects involve all kinds of work. We have

F I G U R E 5.12

A Balanced Scorecard for a Project, Based on the Herrmann Model

A	**D**
Measurable performance outcomes Financial outcomes, ROI E-products, technical results Research data and analysis	Concept or model development Strategies and strategic thinking Ideation, creativity and innovation Global, culture issues
Administrative plans and policies Process improvement Operational efficiencies Quality improvement	Team process and effectiveness Customer or stakeholder relationships Training & development achievements Communication effectiveness
B	**C**

only scratched the surface in this chapter. I would encourage you to read Ned's book, *The Whole Brain Business Book* (1996), for a more complete exposition on the many applications. And check out the Herrmann International Web site, www.hbdi.com. It offers a number of resources that you may find useful.

PROJECT DEFINITION

6

Headless-Chicken Projects and How to Prevent Them

When I was a boy we lived in the country for a few years, and my parents kept some chickens around. In those days, if you wanted fried chicken for lunch on Sunday, you didn't go to a grocery store and buy a processed chicken. Instead, you caught one in the backyard and whacked its head off—that was your lunch (after cooking it, of course).

When you cut off a chicken's head, the body runs around spewing blood for a few seconds, then falls over, quivers a bit, and the chicken is "officially" dead. It is actually dead when you cut off its head, but it takes some time for the message to reach the rest of the body.

Projects are like that.

We whack off the project's "head" during initiation, and it runs around for a while spewing blood, finally falls over, quivers a bit, and becomes still.

**Principle:
Projects often
fail at the
beginning,
not the end.**

Someone says, "I think that project is dead."

It is. It was dead from the very beginning, but like the chicken, it takes a while for the message to reach the body.

I call these "headless-chicken" projects.

No doubt you have seen one yourself. They're all around us, projects that are doomed before they get started because we whack off their heads at the beginning.

THE COLD, HARD FACTS

Every year the Standish Group (www.standishgroup.com) surveys software development projects in the United States. How many succeeded, failed, or were changed dramatically? Results from a survey they did in 1994 are shown in Figure 6.1. This data is on their Web site, so you can review it for yourself.

As you can see, 83 percent of all projects suffer serious problems, with nearly a third of them being bad enough to be canceled. That means that of the $250 billion spent on software development in 1994, about $80 billion was wasted.

F I G U R E   6.1

Standish Group Survey Results

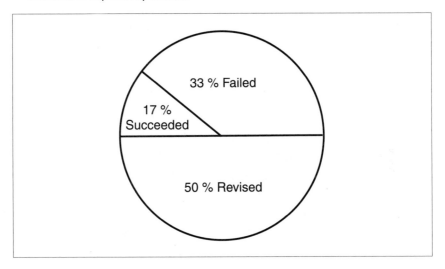

Since this data was collected over 10 years ago, I know you believe that the situation must be greatly improved now. After all, Microsoft has sold between one and two million copies of MicrosoftProject®, and thousands of people have teen trained in project management. I know of six companies with collective revenues of well over $100 million a year in project management training. So with all that progress, the success rate must be higher.

> Projects are perfectly planned to fail from the beginning.

Not so. Billions are still being thrown at software projects; what seems to have changed is that companies cancel losing projects sooner than they did in 1994.

This is a sad situation, to be sure, and corresponds to what I reported in Chapter 4, namely, that training does not transfer back to the job. This means that hundreds of millions of dollars a year are being wasted on training that does not result in better job performance! Scary thought—if I got paid for results, I would have starved long ago, or had to find a new profession.

I have already discussed the reasons why training doesn't transfer (in Chapter 4). So let's focus on the reasons for headless-chicken projects.

THE CAUSES

What causes headless-chicken projects?

First, consider how projects are launched. In many cases, the project sponsor conceives the need for the project. A project manager is recruited to do the job. She is told about the sponsor's concept, which both find very exciting. Of course, the sponsor has only a half-baked idea and is certain that the project manager can turn it into a fully baked cake that everyone will admire. The project manager is equally certain that she can do this.

She assembles a team, and with breathless enthusiasm tells them all about the project. She also congratulates them on being

**Consider how
projects
are kicked off.**

**Many people
are socialized
to remain silent,
even when
they don't
understand.**

selected for membership in this team, for they are truly the chosen ones; because the project sponsor is a high-ranking manager in the company, they are sure to have high visibility. She is certain that success will be handsomely rewarded.

Members of the team sit in rapt attention, nodding their agreement with the project manager's words of anticipation. She is overjoyed that they have so readily "bought in" to the general concept of the job, and she sends them forth to do the work, fully confident that they are bound for glory.

They leave the room, walking side-by-side down the hall, going back to their desks. Unknown to the project manager, one of the chosen team members, Matthew, asks Karen, "Did you understand what Heather was talking about?"

"I don't have a clue," Karen says, shaking her head.

"Boy, I was hoping you understood her," Matthew says. "Because I didn't get it at all. Maybe Susan got it," he says, as he notices Susan walking ahead of them.

"Hey, Susan, can we ask you a question?" Matthew asks.

"Sure." Susan pauses to wait for them.

"We were wondering if you understood what Heather wants us to do," Karen tells her. "Neither Matthew nor I have a clue."

Susan shakes her head, an obvious expression of dismay on her face. "I don't either," she admits. "But I was sure I was the only one in the group who was confused, so that's why I didn't say anything."

"I thought the same thing," Matthew confesses. "I guess none of us really understood, but were afraid to say so."

The Abilene Paradox

This is an example of what Jerry Harvey calls the Abilene Paradox (Harvey, 1988). Harvey made up a story about a family that lives in Texas. One hot Sunday morning, they are sitting around bored to death because they have nothing to do.

Someone asks, "What do you want to do today?"

Another member of the family suggests, "How about if we go to Abilene and have lunch at the cafeteria?"

Next thing you know, they all pile into an old car with no air conditioning. It's 110 degrees in the shade, but driving 75 miles an hour with the windows down creates enough of a breeze to make the 90-mile drive bearable.

They have lunch. Not a very good lunch. A cafeteria lunch.

Following the mediocre meal, they go out onto the streets of Abilene, only to find that there is nothing to do.

Now they are bored in Abilene.

There's nothing to do at this point but go home, so they make the 90-mile blast-furnace trek back home.

They park the car, and as they walk back to the house, someone says, "Boy, that was a waste of time!"

"I thought you wanted to go," another person protests.

"No, I just went because the rest of you wanted to go," replies the first person.

They look at each other sheepishly and take a poll.

It turns out nobody *really* wanted to go to Abilene—not even the person who first suggested it. She was only thinking out loud.

They have all made a 180-mile round trip to Abilene for a mediocre meal, when nobody really wanted to go at all! A paradox, to say the least.

Harvey makes a highly significant point about this. He says it appears to be a failure to manage agreement.

It is not. It is a failure to manage *disagreement!*

The reason? They never knew there *was* any disagreement, because no one said anything. They have fallen into the trap called "silence means consent." This is the nature of the Abilene Paradox.

Notice that the same thing happened to our project team. Because no one said anything, the project manager assumed that they were all in agreement and all understood the mission.

They didn't. But they were afraid to say so.

Why?

The false consensus effect is a failure to manage disagreement, because no one is willing to express disagreement.

Probably because they did not individually want to appear stupid to other members of the group. After all, *they could tell* from the smiling faces of their peers in the team that *they* all understood. "Surely," each of them was thinking, "I must be the only team member who doesn't understand."

Overcoming the Abilene Paradox

Notice that the way a project team falls into the Abilene Paradox trap is that the message is delivered in a way that allows the team members to remain passive. Furthermore, they are not yet a true team. They have been brought together to be *told* about the project, and in most cases the project manager does nothing to make them feel that they are a team. She is so excited about the project that she wants to dive right in and get them started. She is completely *task focused*.

This is a pervasive problem. We forget that there are two aspects to all projects—the what and the how. The what is called the task to be performed. How it is to be performed is called process. But process also applies to how the team functions in total—how they communicate, interact, solve problems, deal with conflict, make decisions, make work assignments, run meetings, and every other aspect of team performance.

And the lesson that many managers have not learned is that *process will always affect task performance!* We have understood this in manufacturing for many years. We have applied statistical process control (SPC) to manufacturing to detect

> Process will always affect task performance.

process problems. We have worked to improve processes, to eliminate non-value-added steps, to reduce scrap and rework, and we have even begun to recognize that nonmanufacturing processes should be improved. But we haven't gone far enough. We need to

pay attention to project processes as much as we pay attention to task outcomes. If the process is broken or defective, it can't get a positive task outcome.

For that reason, we must employ a process that will avoid the Abilene paradox. The best approach that I know of is to get the team members actively involved in defining the project, which includes examining the problem to be solved, then developing a mission statement that tells where the team is going and a vision for the end result they wish to achieve. I have found that the steps in Figure 6.2 meet this requirement.

In this procedure the team members are told the mission, but are then asked to put it into their own words. Each member writes out what he or she believes the mission to be. They then try to consolidate their individual statements into one that they can all support. This statement is then polished and published. From that point on, every time a question about the team's performance comes up, you ask how to answer the question, take the step,

F I G U R E 6.2

The Steps in Developing a Mission Statement

make a decision, or solve a problem in such a way that you support attainment of the team's mission.

Notice that this procedure makes team members active participants in drafting the statement. Furthermore, once the statement is written, it is used to keep the team on track and to guide them on how to address various issues as they arise. This makes the mission statement an operational, living document.

This is in sharp contrast to what usually is done. In many cases, the mission statement is drafted and then forgotten, leaving everyone wondering what all the fuss was about. In fact, more often than not, the mission is handed to the team and no one ever questions whether it is valid—until the project fails to solve the problem it is supposed to solve.

Furthermore, I have found that almost every team will have at least one member who is initially going the wrong way, compared to where the team is going. This is shown in Figure 6.3. Ideally, when they write out their individual statements and compare them, they will all be going in the same direction—the one represented by the big arrow. This means that they are aligned with the direction to be taken by the project. However, you usually find that someone has a different idea about what the team is supposed to be doing, and unless this discrepancy is resolved, the team will fail.

There are only three things that can be done to resolve the disconnect. The first response is to convince the person to go in the

> Suffer fools gladly. They may be right.
>
> — Holbrook Jackson

same direction as the others. This may be done through discussions in which any of the individual's misunderstandings are corrected. Or he may need to be convinced of the proper direction.

The second response is to change the direction of the entire team. It may well be that the "errant" person has thought of the mission in a way that everyone else missed. In this case, the team

F I G U R E 6.3

Misalignment of One Team Member with the Others

agrees to go in the direction advocated by the individual. This can happen when a paradigm shift occurs. You may recall that the Swiss invented the digital watch. However, they weren't impressed with it—it was just a toy in the eyes of "real" watchmakers. So they didn't even patent it. When Seiko and Texas Instruments learned about it, they began producing digital watches, and over the next several years the Swiss lost thousands of watchmakers.

Now imagine a team getting ready to design a new watch. One lone member thinks they should design a digital watch. The others think he is crazy—a nonteam player, who should be thrown off the project. But this is the one person who has it right, and unless they realize this and go in his direction, they will produce another product that is not wanted by the market.

In the event that neither of these responses is possible, the only remaining step is to remove the person from the team. You simply cannot have a successful project when a core team member disagrees with the mission as it is seen by the other members. This may be the most difficult step

> The first objective for a project manager is to achieve *a shared understanding* of the team's mission.

you will be called on to take, since you often do not get to choose core team members, but it really is necessary. And you can't kid yourself by thinking it isn't important. Ensuring that you have a shared understanding of the mission, vision, and problem is the most important action you can take as a project manager. Otherwise you are certain to have a headless-chicken project.

But beyond the process offered to avoid the Abilene Paradox, just how do you integrate the problem, mission, and vision statements for a project?

MISSION AND VISION

I have found that there is considerable confusion between the terms *mission* and *vision*. The reason seems to be that we use the terms almost interchangeably. So before we go much further, we should clarify the difference.

Let's begin with something simple. Suppose you have decided to change jobs and are moving to another city, far enough away that you don't plan to commute from where you presently live. So you will have to find a new home, apartment, or condominium. You turn in your resignation, and soon everyone knows that you are leaving. One of your friends passes you in the hallway and says, "Charlie, I hear you're leaving." You acknowledge that this is true.

"You look a bit distracted," says your friend.

"Yes, I have to find a new place to live," you say.

Your friend has apparently been to a project management seminar, because she says, "What is your mission?"

"To find a place to live," you say.

"And how about your vision," she persists.

"To have a place to live," you reply, somewhat confused.

"Well, those sound the same," she says. She pulls you over to a nearby desk and begins to draw on a sheet of paper. "Suppose

F I G U R E 6.4

The Empty Chevron

we think of it this way. Your problem is that you don't have a place to live in your new town, right?"

You agree. She then sketches the diagram shown in Figure 6.4.

"Let's put your problem statement here," she continues. "And let's state it as a negative. I'll explain why in a moment." She fills in the problem statement as *I have no place to live.*

That done, she asks, "Now, do you have an idea in mind for what kind of place you're looking for?"

"Yes, I plan to buy a house," you say.

F I G U R E 6.5

Chevron with Problem Statement Entered

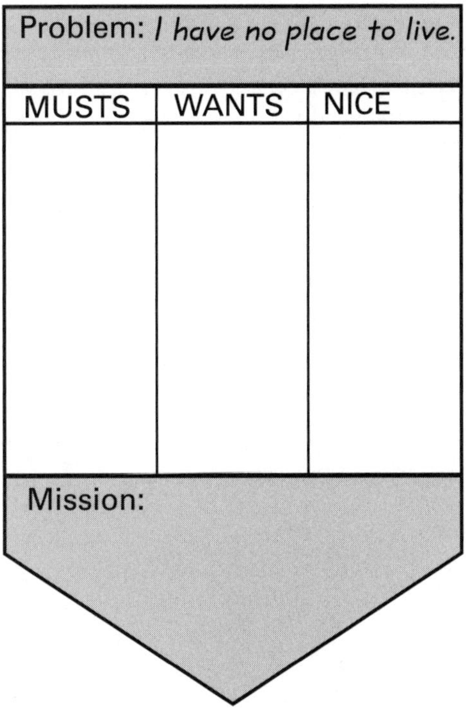

"Okay. Let's fill in the chevron. What are the characteristics of the house that are nonnegotiable? In other words, your must-have features?"

You name several features, and she fills in the must-have section of the chevron (Figure 6.6).

"Now, how about some things you want but you would be willing to give up if you had to?" she continues.

F I G U R E 6.6

Chevron with Must-Have Features Entered

Problem: *I have no place to live.*		
MUSTS	WANTS	NICE
2,500 square feet three bedrooms two-car garage basement 1 acre lot		

Mission:

You name a few such features and she enters them into the wants section. Then she asks about things that would simply be nice to have, and enters these into that part of the diagram. The final result is shown here in Figure 6.7

She says, "These features constitute your vision for the kind of home you want to buy. And your mission is to find such a place, thereby achieving your vision." She pauses for you to think,

F I G U R E   6.7

Chevron with "Wants" and "Nice-to-Have" Features Added

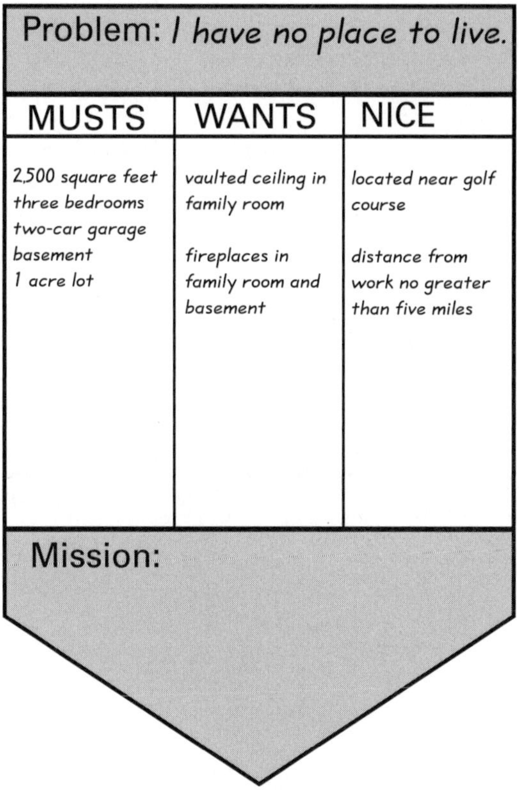

Problem: *I have no place to live.*		
MUSTS	WANTS	NICE
2,500 square feet three bedrooms two-car garage basement 1 acre lot	vaulted ceiling in family room fireplaces in family room and basement	located near golf course distance from work no greater than five miles

Mission:

then adds, "If you do these two things, then your problem is solved, agreed?"

You do agree. And the final result is as shown in Figure 6.8.

Chevron with Everything Filled in

Problem: *I have no place to live.*

MUSTS	WANTS	NICE
2,500 square feet three bedrooms two-car garage basement 1 acre lot	vaulted ceiling in family room fireplaces in family room and basement	located near golf course distance from work no greater than five miles

Mission: To find a place to live that has all of the must-have features and as many of the others as possible.

This is a simple way to understand the difference between the problem, mission, and vision for a project. It isn't always so easy to fill in all of the parts, but if you can do this with your sponsor and your team the battle is half won.

I do have one suggestion. Once you have filled in the nice-to-have features for your project, you should burn that list. Unfortunately, these things become tempting distractions to a project team, and they will often spend too much time on them and neglect the musts and wants. Do be careful.

> Mission: the goal or objective that the team must achieve. The mission is *always* to achieve the vision for the final project outcome.

What is a nice feature for one stakeholder may be a must feature for another. So you may have to spend some time getting consensus on your final list. Let's summarize what we have learned.

You must have a statement that tells everyone where they are going, and if you don't like the word mission, then call it goal, objective, or target. I'm going to stay with the mission because it is the correct term. And the mission is always to achieve the vision for the project outcome.

And the vision, quite simply, is a definition of the characteristics of that final outcome. It may be truly visual for tangible things like houses or hardware. But it may be simply a concept for something like software. In fact, the vision for software has more to do with how it functions

> Where there is no vision, the people perish.
> — Proverbs 29:18

than it does with actual visual effects. For example, a photo editing software program would allow you to crop a photo just by dragging a rectangle around the part of the overall photo you

If everyone doesn't agree on a vision, each person will try to achieve the outcome she imagines.

want to retain and clicking your mouse button; the unwanted part disappears. Can you "visualize" this functionality? If you have used PhotoShop® or other editing programs with this feature, you know what I'm talking about. But if you have not I would expect that my description still allows you to "see" it in your mind, and that is what we are talking about.

So a vision depicts the final result of the team's efforts. It's that simple. If you know what the final result will be, you will know when you're finished with the job. Otherwise, you may not be certain that the job is done.

Writing problem, mission, and vision statements is not a popular exercise. People often see it as a waste of time. When you have one member in a team who thinks you should be going in one direction and others who have their own ideas of the right direction, you can't expect to have a cohesive result. People will take you where they think you are going, not where you want to go.

Now that we have seen the difference between problem, mission, and vision, let's take a closer look at problems and how they are defined, because this is where many headless-chicken projects are created.

PROBLEMS, PROBLEMS

Dr. Juran defined a project as a problem scheduled for solution. That is, we are solving a problem on a large scale when we do a project. Building a bridge solves the problem of not being able to easily get across a river or gorge. Developing an automobile solves the problem of not being able to transport people easily from one place to another.

Developing an insurance package provides protection against financial ruin for people. Financial ruin would be a major problem—a problem that is solved by the insurance package.

> The uncreative mind can spot wrong answers, but it takes a creative mind to spot wrong questions.
>
> — Anthony Jay

In the same way, every project solves a problem for the organization, but we often make the mistake of assuming that we understand the problem when in fact we do not. As an example, let us suppose that you have a headache. You assume the cause is stress, so you take some capsules for pain, and the headache goes away. The next day it returns, so you again take some pain pills. It retreats.

This is repeated for an extended period until you finally become concerned and go to the doctor. After some exhaustive tests, the doc-

> The way a problem is defined determines how we attempt to solve it.

tor reports that you have a brain tumor that can only be removed by surgery.

You have been treating the *symptom*—not the cause—of the problem. The symptom is the headache itself. The cause is the tumor.

This is typical of so many attempts to solve problems. The way we define the problem always determines how we try to solve it. If the definition is incorrect, the solution won't work.

This is the major cause of headless-chicken projects.

We don't spend enough time working out the actual definition, and so we may very well develop the *right solution to the wrong problem,* leaving the organization with the original problem the project was intended to solve.

If we are to ensure that our projects don't solve the wrong problem, clearly we must spend more time on the definition stage. Furthermore, we need to have a clear understanding of what is meant by a problem, because the word is used so loosely that it means many things. We say that the headache is a problem, when it is actually a symptom of the underlying cause. We claim that the problem is slow sales, when this again is but a symptom of some larger cause. So there is a tendency to equate symptoms with problems, guess at the cause, and go off on a happy hunt for the witch that we think caused the symptom.

Every project is conducted to solve a problem for someone. Usually the sponsor has an idea in mind of what things will be like when the problem is solved. This is his or her vision for the final project outcome. The mission of the project team is to achieve that vision, which will presumably solve the problem.

However, you seldom receive a statement of problem when you are assigned a project to manage. Rather, you are given a description of the outcome you are supposed to achieve. Perhaps it is to develop software or a product. Maybe it is to build an office building. It may be a fundraising campaign. Whatever the nature of the job, you will be told that you are expected to make it happen—whatever "it" is.

In many cases this is fine. If you do what you have been told to do, it will solve whatever problem your sponsor has. However, if the sponsor has misdefined the problem to be solved, then you may do what you are told to do and the organization will still have the original problem. For that reason, when you are assigned

We need to have a clear understanding of what is meant by a problem.

a project, you should examine the problem to be solved and determine whether doing the project as assigned will actually achieve the desired result. If not, then you need to discuss this with the project sponsor, being careful to express your concerns diplomatically, of course. If the sponsor insists that you do the job assigned, even though you are convinced it won't solve the intended problem, then you may have to acquiesce, but in that case I suggest you have an up-to-date resume handy.

A problem is defined as a gap between where you are and where you want to be, confronted with obstacles that make closing the gap difficult. It is actually the obstacles that make the gap a problem. As an example, if you are at the end of a long hallway and want to go to the other end, that in itself is a simple goal. If, however, someone puts a large alligator in the hall, and you know the alligator will bite off your leg if you try to pass, then you truly have a problem. The essence of all problems is dealing with alligators! You must remove them, get around them, or momentarily neutralize them if you want to reach the other end of the hall.

There is another alternative. It may be that you want to reach a room just off the end of the hallway, and instead of going down the hallway that contains the alligator you detour to another path to get to the desired destination. You have avoided the alligator altogether. This is the essence of creative thinking—finding another route to the solution that can be easily navigated.

Open- and Closed-Ended Problems

There are two categories of problems—those that have single solutions and those that have multiple solutions. Those with single solutions are called *closed-ended pro*blems. Those with multiple solutions are called *open-ended problems.*

> Closed-ended problems have single solutions.
> Open-ended problems have multiple solutions.

Solving each category requires a different approach. Closed-ended problems are best solved using a left-brain analytical approach, whereas open-ended problems are solved by applying a right-brain synthesis approach. In terms of the Herrmann brain dominance model, we would expect quadrant-A thinking to be required for solving closed-ended problems and quadrant-D thinking to be required for solving open-ended ones. Remember, of course, that preference for thinking in a certain quadrant does not indicate *ability*. We all have a whole brain. However, if your preference is very strong for the A quadrant and very weak for the D quadrant, you will probably be drawn to analytical problems, and conversely.

Interestingly, American education is largely focused on solving closed-ended problems. Very little attention is given to solving open-ended ones, yet it is clear that there are far more open-ended problems in the world than closed-ended ones. The result is that we leave school with a mindset that all problems are closed-ended, and we have limited skills for solving open-ended problems. Of course, projects demand that we deal with both kinds of problems.

As an example, an environmental cleanup project is closed-ended. So is one to overhaul a piece of equipment, repair a car, or discover the cause of a disease. On the other hand, a project to develop new software or hardware is open-ended, as are projects to build a house, improve a process, sell a product, or develop a project-based organization.

> Solving closed-ended problems requires an analytical, left-brained approach, while solving open-ended ones requires a right-brained approach.

One way to think of these is that closed-ended problems are oriented to the past, while open-ended ones are oriented to the future.

Repairing a car is an attempt to return it to a condition that existed previously. Math problems are closed-ended; the solution exists already. We are simply trying to discover it.

Building a house, however, is open-ended. The house does not yet exist. There are several ways to build it. You

> Closed-ended problems are oriented to the past, while open-ended ones are oriented to the future.

may say that one approach is better than another, but that does not discount the fact that there is more than one way to go about it. The same is true for developing a new product; it does not yet exist, and there are a number of approaches to designing it.

DEFINING CLOSED-ENDED PROBLEMS

For closed-ended problems, the best approach to defining the problem is to use what is commonly called the scientific method, which consists of the following steps:

- Ask questions
- Develop a plan of inquiry
- Formulate hypotheses
- Gather data to test those hypotheses
- Draw conclusions from hypothesis testing
- Test the conclusions

Constructing a Good Problem Statement

Also, at this point, it is essential to develop a solid problem statement. The steps for doing this are:

1. The problem statement should reflect shared values and a clear purpose.
2. The problem statement should not mention either causes or remedies.
3. The problem statement should define problems and processes of manageable size.
4. The problem statement should, if possible, mention measurable characteristics.
5. The problem statement should be refined (if appropriate) as knowledge is gained.

Defining Closed-Ended Problems with Problem Analysis

As was previously stated, closed-ended problems have single solutions. Something that used to work is now broken. The remedy is to determine what has broken and repair it—a single solution. To solve closed-ended problems we use a general approach called

The diagram in Figure 6.9 shows the steps in the problem analysis process.

Problem Analysis Steps

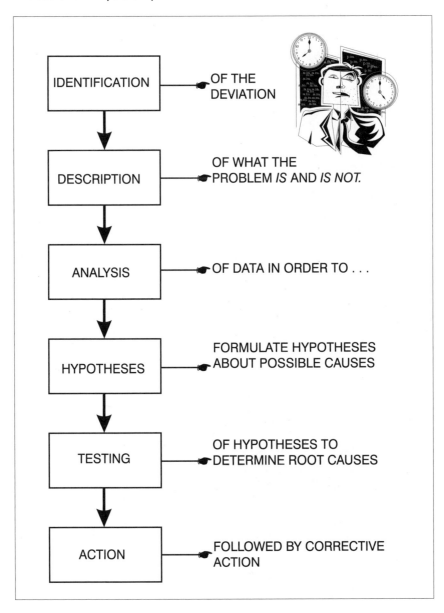

Identification

The first step in the problem analysis process is identification. "How do I know I have a problem?" In general, you know that you have a problem because a system that previously performed properly suddenly ceases to do so. *Symptoms* of this misperformance will tell you something is amiss. In the case of mechanical systems, strange noises may be coming from within the machine. Or the level of performance changes—an automobile quits running, for example, or a tire on your bicycle goes flat.

In biological systems (people, plants, animals), illness occurs. You have a severe headache. That is the symptom that something is wrong with your body. It is not performing as it usually does.

As previously stated, a problem is a gap between a desired state and a present state, confronted by obstacles that prevent easy closure of the gap. As just described, when a process is involved, that gap is a *deviation* from standard performance. In monitoring progress in a project, there is an index called a critical ratio, which should have a value of 0.8 to 1.1. When the critical ratio falls outside these limits, it's a signal that a potential problem exists with the task in question. This is where problem analysis begins in that

"How do I
know I have
a problem?"

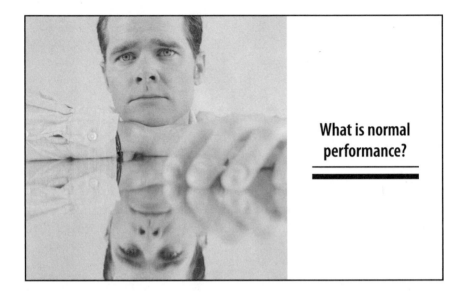

**What is normal
performance?**

situation. (Critical ratio, which is part of earned value analysis, is covered in depth in Chapter 12.)

What Is the Normal Performance?

When dealing with deviations, we have to know the performance *norm*. How is the system supposed to behave? The human body is supposed to perform pain-free. Your automobile is supposed to accelerate from 0 to 60 mph in a certain time. It should get so many miles per gallon on the highway. Of course, this will vary somewhat depending on road conditions and the driver's style. All systems exhibit variation around normal performance. Some systems will have very small levels of variation, and some will have large variation.

In the same way, some project work will have much more variability than other project work. For that reason, critical ratio limits for some tasks might be set tighter than for others. Once the normal variability is known we can determine if the deviation is significant, and whether it is positive (performance better than the norm) or negative (performance worse than the norm).

To summarize: a problem is recognized because of the *effects* produced being different than the normal outcomes expected from the system or process. Those effects might be a change in scrap level, higher or lower production, or a drop in customer purchases.

Determining the Cause

In order to correct for the deviation, we need to find its *cause*. For a desirable deviation, we must know the cause so we can replicate it. For an undesirable deviation, the cause must be remedied. To determine the cause of the deviation we employ a process called *description* of the problem.

Description Using Is/Is-Not Analysis and Stratification

Stratification and is/is-not analysis are ways to localize a problem by exposing underlying patterns. This analysis is done before collecting data (so the team will know what kind of differences to look for), and also follows it (so the team can determine which factors actually represent the root cause).

To stratify data, examine the process to see what characteristics could lead to biases in the data. For example, could different shifts account for differences in results? Are mistakes made by new employees very different than those made by experienced individuals? Does output from one machine have fewer defects than that from another?

Begin by making a list of the characteristics that could cause differences in results (use brainstorming here). Make data collection forms that incorporate those factors, and collect the data. Look for patterns related to time or sequence. Then check for systematic differences between days of the week, shifts, operators, and so on.

The is/is-not matrix in Figure 6.10 is a structured form of stratification, based on the ideas of Charles Kepner and Benjamin Tregoe (Kepner & Tregoe, 1965).

The Is/Is-Not Matrix

	Is Where, when, to what extent, or regarding whom does this situation occur?	**Is Not** Where does this situation NOT occur, though it reasonably might have?	**Therefore** What might explain the pattern of occurrence and nonoccurrence?
Where The physical or geographical location of the event or situation. Where it occurs or is noticed.			
When The hour/time of day/ day of week, month/ time of year of the event or situation. Its relationship (before, during, after) to other events.			
What Kind or How Much The type or category of event or situation. The extent, degree, dimensions, or duration of occurrence.			
Who What relationships do various individuals or groups have to the situation/event? To whom, by whom, near whom, etc., does this occur? (Do not use these questions to place blame.)			

Instructions: Identify the problem to be analyzed. Use this matrix to organize your knowledge and information. The answers will assist you in pinpointing the occurrence of the problem and in verifying conclusions or suspicions.

Analysis

Once stratified data have been collected, the differences can be analyzed so that hypotheses can be formulated as to causes of the problem. The following questions are designed to help identify differences:

> What is different, distinctive, or unique between *what* the problem is and what it is not?
>
> What is different, distinctive, or unique between *where* the problem is and where it is not?
>
> What is different, distinctive, or unique between *when* the problem is seen and when it is not?

The focus of these questions is to help us determine what has changed about the process. If nothing had changed, there would be no problem. Our search should be limited to focusing on the following question: What has changed about each of these differences?

Noting the date of each change may also help us relate the start of the problem to some specific change that was made to the process. Perhaps a different person was doing the job when the change in performance occurred. Maybe there was an electrical storm. Perhaps a new shipment of raw materials came in.

Hypotheses

A hypothesis is simply a conjecture or guess about the possible cause of a problem. We form hypotheses based on our data collection and analysis. Then we test them to determine if we have guessed correctly. At this point, *all* reasonable hypotheses should be listed. Nothing should be excluded because it seems improbable or because it was suggested by someone who is not deemed credible as an expert on the subject.

One of my favorite stories about solving problems came from a Japanese semiconductor plant. The plant was experiencing low-yield problems in making a new chip. The engineers were working frantically to determine the cause of the problem, but were making no progress. One morning an 18-year-old woman who had only recently taken a job at the plant was on her way to work. She rode a bicycle, and as she approached the plant a train passed by. She had to wait until the crossing was clear to proceed.

As she stood watching the train, she noticed that the ground was shaking. She had heard about the yield problem and wondered if the vibration from the train might be a factor. She posed this question to her supervisor, who passed it on to the engineering group. A member of the group decided to test the hypothesis. He rented a ditching machine, dug a large trench between the building and the railroad track, filled it with water to absorb some of the vibration, and the yield problem was solved! (Subsequently they shock-mounted their equipment—the ditch was a temporary fix.)

An important point about this story is that in many cultures this young woman would have been totally discounted because she was not an expert in engineering. In Japan, however, contributions from anyone tend to be welcomed.

Cause-Effect Diagrams

One of the most commonly used tools for formulating hypotheses is the Ishikawa or cause-effect diagram, also called the fishbone diagram because it resembles the skeleton of a fish. An example is shown in Figure 6.11. It can be used separately or in conjunction with is/is-not analysis to help formulate hypotheses. As shown in the diagram, four general categories of causes are standard. Here we use *manpower, machines, methods,* and *materials* (there are other possibilities, but these four are fairly common). For each category, we ask whether some change has occurred that might explain the problem. Has a person who is not properly trained been assigned to the job? Was someone sick on the day the problem began? Are they not following standard operating procedures? Is a machine out of adjustment? Is an improper method being used to do something? Are materials defective or incorrect?

F I G U R E 6.11

An Ishikawa Diagram

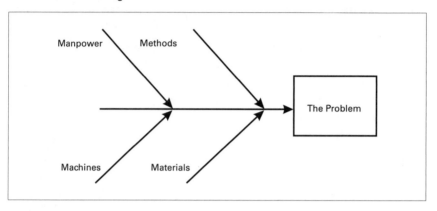

Using brainstorming by a group to generate ideas, all possible causes are listed on the branches. Again, it must be emphasized that censoring ideas is not allowed.

Test Hypotheses

Once ideas have been generated they must be tested. To test hypotheses, we first ask if the suspected cause can explain both sides of the description. That is, the cause must explain both the is and the is-not effects. If it cannot explain both, it is unlikely to be a real cause.

To save time, the group will usually try to determine which of many causes is the most likely one. This may be done simply through intuition. Headaches are most frequently caused by stress; thus, a doctor might ask a patient if she has been under a lot of recent stress. If this is not the case, then other possible causes would be examined, possibly by having the person undergo a number of tests, such as brain scans, blood tests, and so on.

The testing method is as follows:

- Test each possible cause through the description, especially the sharp contrast areas.

- Note all "only-if" assumptions.

The most likely cause will be the one that best explains the description, or the one with the fewest assumptions. To be certain, you must now verify the hypothesis quickly and cheaply.

One test is whether you can make the effects come and go by manipulating the factor that is supposedly causing the deviation. If you can, you have probably found the true root cause. If a doctor believed you were having headaches because of an allergy, tests would be run to determine if the allergy existed. If it did you would be advised to avoid that allergen. If the headaches ceased, then the allergen was the most likely cause. Note that we could test this by deliberately exposing you to the allergen, but most people are happy to have the headaches go away and are unwilling to submit to this second part of the test. In testing hypotheses in general, however, this is a valid method of confirming if a cause is "the" one we are looking for.

Action

While we are testing hypotheses, or trying to determine the root cause, there are three possible actions that we might take:

Interim action	You buy time while the root cause of the problem is sought. This action is only a "patch" for correcting symptoms. You may, for example, take painkillers while doctors try to determine the cause of your headaches.
Adaptive action	You decide to live with the problem or adapt to it. There are people who learn that they are allergic to certain foods, and should give them up, but they love them so much that they decide to live with the symptoms instead.

Corrective action   This is the only action that will truly solve
                       the problem. It is aimed at the actual cause
                       of the problem, rather than simply alleviat-
                       ing symptoms.

Design of Experiments

There are times when single causes do not account for problems.
As an example, a biotech product may have many ingredients,
each of which must have a concentration that falls within a certain
range or the final product won't perform correctly. I know of one
such case in which the suspected cause of product
misperformance was believed to be an enzyme, but it turned out
to be the concentration of a buffer that was incorrect. This was determined by running an experiment in which various factors
could be changed simultaneously and the outcome observed. This
approach allows testing of both first-order and second-order (interaction) effects. Second-order effects are particularly difficult to
identify unless such an approach is used. For example, it may be
that both the temperature and the concentration of a buffer must
be off for the defect in performance to occur.

It is outside the scope of this book to explain design of experiments. The interested reader should consult a good book on the
subject, such as Walpole, 1974.

Defining Open-Ended Problems

There are generally more open-ended problems than
closed-ended ones. This is especially true of projects. The problem
being solved by a project is likely to require different methods
than those presented previously for solving closed-ended problems. Even the approach used to define the problem is different.
For closed-ended problems, the scientific approach to analyzing
data can be used. A closed-ended problem has a *cause*. There is no

cause of an open-ended problem, so we need different methods for defining it. The techniques that follow are intended to help you develop good definitions for open-ended problems.

Remember also that open-ended problems do not have single solutions. When there is a cause of a problem, the solution is to remove the cause. For open-ended problems, no such action is possible. We often refer to these as creative problems, and they are characterized by the question, "How do I make something happen?" As examples:

- How do we design a product to perform in a certain way?
- How can I pay for my child's college education?
- How to we send someone to the moon and bring him back safely?
- How do we penetrate a certain market?

I should mention here that Dr. Edward de Bono is considered by many people to be one of the leading experts on creative problem solving, and his book, *Serious Creativity* (1992), covers the subject in more detail than this chapter can possibly do. I heartily recommend that the interested reader consult Dr. de Bono's works.

The procedure outlined in Table 6.1 is designed to help you develop a good definition for an open-ended problem. However, it is only one approach, and others are presented following the table. Note that you are not trying to solve the problem with this approach, even though there are questions that begin, "If I could solve the problem . . ." You are simply trying to understand what the problem is. Actually, you are really trying to understand the nature of your desired outcome. That is, when the problem is solved, where will you be, or what condition will exist? (You can download a form containing these questions from my Web site: www.lewisinstitute.com.)

I have had people do this exercise many times and they often find that, through this process, the problem they thought they

T A B L E 6.1

An Exercise to Develop a Good Problem Definition

1. Describe an open-ended problem that is important to you and for which you need answers that could lead to action. Take as long as you wish for this.

2. Again, taking your time, complete the following statements about the problem you have chosen. If you cannot think of anything to write for a particular statement, move on to the next one.

   a. There is usually more than one way of looking at problems. You could also define this one as . . .

   b. . . . but the main point of the problem is . . .

   c. What I would really like to do is . . .

   d. If I could break all laws of reality (physical, social, etc.) I would try to solve it by . . .

   e. The problem, put another way, could be likened to . . .

   f. Another, even stranger, way of looking at it might be . . .

3. Now return to your original definition (step 1). Write down whether any of the redefinitions have helped you see the problem in a different way.

were solving was, in fact, not correct. For example, a person might begin by stating the problem as needing to buy a new car and wondering how to afford it. On closer examination, she finds that what she really wants is reliable transportation to work every day; a car is only one way of accomplishing this goal.

The Goal Orientation Technique

Unless you are clear about your goal, you are certainly not likely to achieve it. Most importantly, there is little value in achieving the wrong goal—as would be true if a person bought a car only to realize that the real goal was getting to work, and that this could have been achieved with less expense.

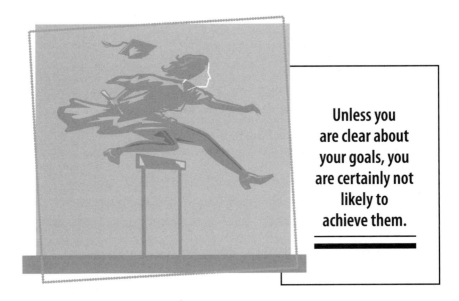

> **Unless you are clear about your goals, you are certainly not likely to achieve them.**

Goal orientation is an attitude, first of all. Secondly, it is a technique to encourage that attitude. Open-ended problems are situations where the boundaries are unclear, but in which there may be fairly well-defined needs and obstacles to progress.

The goal-oriented person tries to recognize the desired end-state ("what I want") and obstacles ("what's stopping me from getting the result I want?").

To illustrate the goal-orientation technique, consider the problem outlined in Table 6.2.

The Successive Abstractions Technique

Suppose a company that makes lawnmowers is looking for new business ideas. Their first definition of their problem is to "develop a new lawnmower." A higher level of abstraction would be to define the problem as "develop new grass-cutting machines." An even higher level of abstraction yields "get rid of unwanted grass."

T A B L E 6.2

Use of the Goal-Orientation Technique

Original problem statement

Adult illiteracy has reached alarming proportions. Ford Motor Company recently said they are having to train almost 25% of their workforce in basic reading, writing, and arithmetic, at considerable cost.

Redefinitions:

1. (How to) efficiently and effectively teach adults to read.
2. (How to) keep kids from getting through school without being able to read.
3. (How to) get parents to take an interest in their kids so they will learn to read in school.
4. (How to) eliminate the influences which cause kids to take no interest in school.

T A B L E 6.3

Successive Abstractions

Highest level	Get rid of unwanted grass
Intermediate level	Develop new grass-cutting machines
Lower level	Develop new lawnmower

Another definition of the problem, of course, might be to "develop grass that only grows to a height of only 'x' inches above the ground" (see Table 6.3).

Analogy and Metaphor Procedures

One really interesting way of describing problems is through the use of analogy or metaphor. Such definitions help increase the chances of finding creative solutions to problems and are especially useful in group techniques, such as brainstorming. In fact, they are

One interesting way of describing problems is through the use of analogy or metaphor.

actually preferable to literal statements, since they tend to be extremely effective in stimulating creative thinking. For example:

"How to improve the efficiency of a factory" is a down-to-earth statement.

"How to make a factory run as smoothly as a well-oiled machine" is an analogical redefinition.

"How to reduce organizational friction or viscosity" is a metaphoric definition.

Wishful Thinking

Many left-brained, rational people do not appreciate the value of wishful thinking. However, wishful thinking can provide a rich source of new ideas. Dr. Edward de Bono, in his work on creative thinking, talks about an "intermediate impossible"—a concept that can be used as a stepping stone between conventional thinking and realistic new insights. Wishful thinking is a great device for producing such intermediate impossibles.

Rickards cites the example of a food technologist working on new methods of preparing artificial protein. As a fantasy, she considers the problem to be "how to build an artificial cow." Although the metaphor is wishful, it suggests that she might look closely at biological systems and perhaps look for a way of converting cellulose into protein, which is what takes place in nature.

Remember the statement from Table 6.1: "What I would *really* like to do is . . ." Or try this approach: "If I could break all constraints, I would . . ."

Nonlogical Stimuli

One good way of generating ideas is through forced comparisons. This method can be used for developing ideas for solving a problem, or as an aid to redefinition. Table 6.4 is an example of the procedure, used in conjunction with a dictionary.

Design Tree

Another phrase for design tree is "mind map®," which is a trademark of Tony Buzan. The design tree has been used by many people to illustrate associations of ideas. For example, you can use the design tree to outline a book. You begin by writing a single word—representing the issue you want to deal with—then draw a circle around it. Next list all the ideas that come to you, connect them to the first word with lines, and continue by examining each new word in turn for the ideas it might trigger. I used the word *transportation* to illustrate the approach (see Figure 6.12).

Expectations, Deliverables, and Results

It would be nice if all we had to worry about was meeting PCTS targets in a project, but this is not the case. We also have to deal with the expectations of stakeholders, as I explained in Chapter 1. Clarifying stakeholder expectations is as much a part of project

T A B L E   6.4

An Exercise in Nonlogical Stimuli

For this exercise, you will need paper, pencil, and a dictionary

1. Write down as many uses as you can think of for a piece of chalk.

2. When you can think of no more ideas, let your eyes wander to some object in your range of vision, which has no immediate connection to a piece of chalk.

3. Try to develop new ideas stimulated by the object.

4. Now repeat stages (2) and (3) with a second randomly selected object.

5. Open the dictionary and jot down the first three nouns or verbs that you see.

6. Try to develop new ideas stimulated by these words in turn.

7. Examine your ideas produced with and without stimuli for differences in variety (flexibility) and total numbers (fluency).

F I G U R E   6.12

Design Tree for Transportation

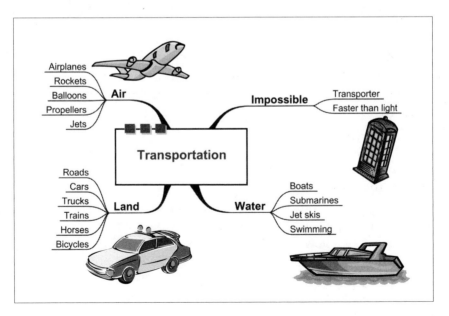

definition as anything else, and meeting those expectations is necessary for the project to be judged a success.

In addition you must ask, what results is this project intended to get and what must we deliver to achieve those results? The answers to these questions should help you in developing a crisp, shared mission and vision for your project.

Be aware that, if a stakeholder changes midway through the project, you will have to go through the process of clarifying the new stakeholder's expectations. You can't just assume that if you meet the expectations of the former stakeholder everything will be okay. The new person will see the job differently than his or her predecessor, and you will have to negotiate those things that can be accommodated and those that cannot. The new stakeholder may have totally unrealistic expectations about deliverables and results, and you must bring them in line with reality.

You may think of this as one of the political aspects of the project management job, and it is. Ignore it to your own risk!

THE FALLACY OF PROJECT MANAGEMENT ASSUMPTIONS

Everything I have written about managing projects would be ideal—if it could be made to work the way I have suggested. However, there is a huge fallacy in the assumptions we make about managing projects, and that is that the world will stand still while we execute our carefully constructed project plan. This simply isn't true, and we know it.

As I discussed above, stakeholders change, and with them come new expectations, which require that we adapt our project to meet those expectations or be judged negatively when the project ends. Furthermore, as projects evolve, we learn things we didn't know at the beginning. If we are developing software or hardware, we have new ideas about how the final product should function. For that reason, many products are *adaptive* in nature and cannot be planned *deterministically*.

**Principle:
The big fallacy in
our assumptions
is that the world
will stand still
while we execute
our project plan.**

I believe this is a major reason why software development projects have such high percentages of missed targets. Remember the Standish Group study that shows that only 17 percent of software projects meet the original PCTS targets? It's no wonder. The targets are constantly moving.

I speak from experience. I have just about finished designing an on-line training program for my Web site as of this writing. I started about a year ago by defining what I wanted it to do. As I neared project completion and started testing the program on a temporary dummy site, I began to realize that I could make the program far more effective by making some changes. I also thought of functions that never occurred to me a year ago. So the job has taken nearly twice as many programming hours as originally estimated, but I have a significantly better product as a result.

Could I have used the product in the form originally defined? Yes, but it would not have had the utility of the present version.

You must exercise caution, of course. If you continually make changes to a product in response to new ideas, you will never

**Principle:
Some projects
are adaptive in
nature and cannot
be planned
deterministically.**

release it. This is the trap into which perfectionists fall. They can never finish a design because they can always make it better.

You must decide if a change is needed to make the final result as functional as it must be in the final application. If the change is not made, can it be sold? Will it be accepted by the customer? If the change is made, will it delay product introduction to the marketplace so much that competitors will seize the market share and cost you all of your profits? These are not easy questions to answer, and should never be made unilaterally by technologists. Many technologists have very little grasp of market dynamics and will opt for technical improvements even if the product never sells.

The message here is that project planning must be done with the understanding that there must be flexibility enough to respond to legitimate environmental forces, without going so far as to become aimless. On construction projects and other fairly well-defined jobs, this is not such a big issue. Software, hardware, and scientific work (such as drug development), however, are more likely to require an adaptive, rather than deterministic, management approach.

PROJECT PLANNING

7

CHAPTER

Developing Project Strategy

In this chapter, we will discuss developing a strategy for a project. This involves steps 3–5 of my method, and these steps are repeated in Figure 7.1 for your convenience.

As I have written previously, there is a strong tendency for people to skip from step 1 in my model down to step 9. They want to just get on with it and get the job done. In the process, they fail to properly define the problem being solved and establish a proper mission and vision for the job. Consequently, the project fails.

Another mistake is to want to jump from step 2 down to step 6. People who do this understand that they must deal with step two, but they fail to consider project strategy. They simply want to construct a working plan—usually a schedule that is developed with some kind of software.

F I G U R E 7.1

Steps 3 to 5 of The Lewis Method

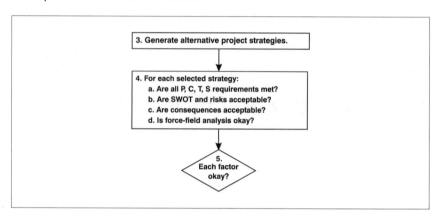

WHAT IS STRATEGY?

Strategy is an overall approach to a project. It is sometimes called a *game plan*. The difference between strategy and tactics is that tactics get you down to the "nitty-gritty" details of exactly how you are going to do the work. For example, if I have decided that the best way to build a house is to use prefabricated components, then I must work out how I am going to actually make the components. Do I assemble an entire wall and send it to the job site, or do I make it in small sections that can be joined together at the site?

Logistics involves how I am going to get the prefab parts out to the site, how I will supply workers with tools and other equipment, how I will feed them, and so on. Tactics and logistics will be worked out in step 6 of the flow chart during detailed implementation planning.

The Importance of Strategy

A manager once told me that he could not keep engineers, because the big manufacturers in his area could pay more, and no sooner would he get a young engineer trained than the big company would steal that person. He decided to adopt a new strategy. Instead of recruiting engineers, he would hire technical school graduates and teach them to be engineers. Since the big companies generally preferred engineers with four-year degrees, he very seldom lost a tech-school graduate to them. Certainly his tech-school engineers may not have been quite

> I became a good pitcher when I stopped trying to make them miss the ball and started trying to make them hit it.
> — Sandy Koufax

as qualified as those with full degrees, but they were capable enough for his needs, and the cost of constantly replacing engineers dropped dramatically.

In a similar vein, the United States has had a shortage of programmers for several years, and many companies have found that

> Without competitors there would be no need for strategy.
> ~ Kenichi Ohmae

they can get programming done in India at considerably less cost than if they had local programmers do the work. The programmers in India speak good English, are well educated, and work for considerably less than American programmers, since their cost of living is much lower than in the United States. This strategy has been used for a number of years to get projects done on time and at less expense than would otherwise be possible.

When the chunnel was built to connect France with England, the strategy was to start digging from both sides. Using laser-surveying methods, the crews met in the middle with only negligible error in position. This strategy allowed the project to be completed in about half the time it would have taken to dig from one side to another, as you can only dig so many feet per day. By going in both directions, the digging speed was essentially doubled.

My first engineering job was with a very small company that designed and built land mobile communications equipment. We had only 150 employees, and of course our engineering staff was very small. There was no way that we could compete directly with the big players in the game, as they had far more resources than we did.

So one of our engineers conceived the idea of doing modular design of radios. Instead of having to design every new radio "from scratch," we would design some circuits that could be used in all models. Good examples are audio amplifiers and intermediate frequency (IF) strips. By employing this method we were able to develop a family of products in relatively short time. We were leveraging our limited resources.

Air Industries has employed a similar strategy in its Airbus line of aircraft. In most cases, pilots are trained to fly a single kind of airplane. So a crew that can fly one plane can't fly one of the same design but having a slightly different configuration. Airbus has several planes with different seating capacities that can all be flown by the same crews. The cockpit layouts are the same and the planes handle so similarly that the crews don't have to be re-

It is better
to give away the
wool than
the sheep.
~ Italian Proverb

trained to switch from one to the other. In addition, the airline does not have to stock so many different spare parts because the planes all use the same ones. This represents a significant savings in inventory costs, pilot training, and so on.

Boeing designed the 757 and 767 airplanes so that the same pilots can fly them as well. As is true for Airbus, this saves money for the airlines.

Project Strategy and Technical Strategy

It turns out that there are often two aspects to project strategy. As an example, suppose you have to feed a group, and you are considering how to do it. You could (1) cook the meal yourself, (2) take everyone to a restaurant, (3) have a potluck dinner, in which everyone brings something, or (4) have a caterer deliver the food. You examine the alternatives and decide that you will cook the meal yourself. This is your project strategy. But how will you cook the food?

You could (1) cook it conventionally on your stove, (2) micro-wave it, or (3) have a backyard barbecue. These three approaches would be called technical strategy. Your preference is to have a backyard barbecue, but you discover that your grill is kaput. You don't want to cook on the stove or microwave, so you decide to have the meal catered. In other words, your choice of technical strategy may determine your project strategy (see Figure 7.2).

In a technological company, for example, you are considering developing a product by employing a new technology. However, no one in the company knows anything about the technology, so you may have to contract out that part of the work (a project strat-egy) or develop the capability.

A general guideline in selecting a technical strategy is that you don't want to employ cutting-edge technology when you

F I G U R E 7.2

The Difference between Project and Technical Strategy

have a very tight project deadline. Of course, this rule is violated frequently in high-tech industries, but deadlines are also missed occasionally, and sometimes products are released that later have field problems. This can do serious damage to a company's reputation.

Related to this rule is that you should separate discovery from development in a project. That is, you don't want to be trying to make some technology work when you are supposed to be developing a product. The best approach is to do a feasibility study, then, based on the outcome, launch a development project. If you are trying to prove feasibility and develop a product at the same time, and you can't make the technology work, that project will be judged a failure. However, no matter what result you get with a feasibility study—yes it works or no it doesn't—that should be judged a successful project, as you have conclusively answered a question.

GENERATING AND CHOOSING THE CORRECT STRATEGY

As you can see from my model, in step 3 you generate a list of alternative project and technical strategies that may apply to your project. In step 4 you select the combination that you judge to be best. Generating the list may be as simple as looking at existing strategies and listing them; or, you may invent a new strategy. Note that this step requires strategic or conceptual thinking. You can expect that individuals with a strong preference for quadrant-D thinking will be needed at this step (see Figure 7.3).

Inventing a Strategy

As an example of this, Charles Kepner and Benjamin Tregoe developed an approach to problem solving that was very rigorous. They convinced managers at General Motors to adopt it. In fact, GM wanted most of their employees to be trained in the new

F I G U R E 7.3

Quadrant-D Thinking Is Needed at This Step

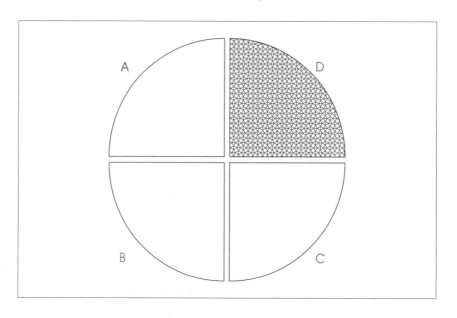

**Principle:
If no existing
strategy is acceptable,
you may have
to invent one.**

If you have to invent a strategy, you should use creative problem-solving methods.

method. Kepner and Tregoe knew that they could not possibly train all of those people themselves, so they were almost destroyed by success. So they conceived a new approach. They would train individuals within GM to deliver the training. They conducted a series of train-the-trainer workshops and made GM self-sufficient in doing their own internal training. All Kepner and Tregoe had to do from that point on was sell the classroom materials to GM, and that was how they made their income. This was an invented strategy at the time. It has become common since then.

If you have to invent a strategy, you should use creative problem-solving methods. The most common one is brainstorming, in which members of a group generate as many ideas as they can, without evaluation, then select one. There are many other approaches for developing good ideas. One good source of techniques is the book by Michael Michalko, *Thinkertoys* (Michalko, 1995). A number of idea-generating methods were presented in Chapter 6, so you may want to go back and review those.

Selecting Strategy

Sometimes it is a simple matter to choose a strategy. However, if a number of issues are involved, the choice may not be so easy to make. A step-by-step procedure is presented at the end of this chapter that will guide you through the process, but you should understand why the steps are followed before applying them in a rote way.

When you were generating ideas for project strategy, you were in quadrant D of the Herrmann model. To select the best combination of project and technical strategy, quadrant-A thinking is needed. Critical analysis is required to sort through the facts and details of the various choices, so if you have no one on your team who is really good at such thinking, you should bring in someone temporarily who is.

Ranking the Alternatives

To select the best combination of strategies, you should rank both lists (project and technical strategies). The easiest way to do this is to use the priority matrix as shown in Figure 7.4. There are several ways to go about this. One is to make each choice binary. Suppose, for example, that I have four strategies. If I had some way to quantitatively rank them, it would be easy to make a choice, but there may be a number of factors involved that affect the "measure" that each one would yield, and it gets too complicated to work out. So I simply ask myself if one strategy is better than another. If the answer is "yes," I put a one in the cell, and if it is "no," I put a zero. If I proceed across row one and ask this question for strategy one compared to each of the others, I get the result shown in Figure 7.4. This technique is called *paired comparisons*.

Next, I ask if strategy two is better than each of the others. However, you will note that when I ask if strategy two is better

F I G U R E 7.4

Priority Matrix for Four Strategies with Row 1 Filled In

STRATEGY	1	2	3	4	TOTAL	RANK
1	X	1	0	1		
2		X				
3			X			
4				X		

than one, I have already asked that question in row one, but in reverse. So whatever I put in row one under strategy two must now be the inverse in row two, column one. This is shown in Figure 7.5.

F I G U R E 7.5

Priority Matrix with Row 2, Column 1 Filled In

STRATEGY	1	2	3	4	TOTAL	RANK
1	X	1	0	1		
2	0	X	1	1		
3	1		X			
4	0			X		

In fact, it turns out that as you continue with the matrix, you will find that every entry in column one is going to be the inverse of what is in row one, so you can save time by simply filling in the rows of the matrix above the diagonal and then filling in the columns with the inverse of their rows. The final result is shown in Figure 7.6.

F I G U R E 7.6

Priority Matrix with All Entries Filled In

STRATEGY	1	2	3	4	TOTAL	RANK
1	X	1	0	1		
2	0	X	1	1		
3	1	0	X	0		
4	0	0	1	X		

Next you total each row, and the row with the highest total will be your first choice, that with the next-highest total will be choice two, and so on. If you find that two rows add to the same total, just look in the matrix to see which of the two choices outranks the other, since that decision has already been made. The final result for this matrix is shown in Figure 7.7.

F I G U R E 7.7

Priority Matrix with Totals and ranks Filled In

STRATEGY	1	2	3	4	TOTAL	RANK
1	X	1	0	1	2	1
2	0	X	1	1	2	2
3	1	0	X	0	1	4
4	0	0	1	X	1	3

This ranking should ideally be done by a team. When this is the case, you can still deal with the strategies in a binary fashion, but now you ask your team members how many think strategy one is better than strategy two, and you count the votes. Suppose, for example that you have six team members, counting yourself, and you ask for a comparison of strategy one versus two. When you enter the votes, you put the votes for strategy one on row one and the votes for strategy two in row two. This is shown in Figure 7.8.

F I G U R E 7.8

Matrix with Votes Tallied for Strategy 1 versus Strategy 2

STRATEGY	1	2	3	4	TOTAL	RANK
1	X	8	6	1		
2	2	X				
3	4		X			
4	9			X		

Continue in this manner until you have completed all voting, then total the votes in each row. This gives the result shown in Figure 7.9. This is a more finely tuned approach than using ones and zeros as you did previously.

F I G U R E 7.9

Matrix Completely Filled In and Totaled

STRATEGY	1	2	3	4	TOTAL	RANK
1	X	8	6	1	15	2
2	2	X	5	1	8	4
3	4	5	X	2	11	3
4	9	9	8	X	26	1

The Analytical Hierarchy

The priority matrix can be enhanced by evaluating various attributes of each choice. As you can see in step 4 of The Lewis Method, the first question is whether a given strategy can meet our PCTS targets. It may be that one choice will meet the CTS targets, but is not as good as another choice in meeting the performance objective. But are PCTS all of equal importance to the project?

It could be that performance is most important and time is second. Graham and Englund (1999) have written that *mind share* is what you want to achieve with a product in order to capture *market share*. For example, when someone mentions laser jet printers, Hewlett Packard wants everyone to think of their units as the best available. So performance may be the foremost requirement to be met. Then may come time, scope, and cost. If weights are assigned to these, you would then have a more complicated situation to analyze.

Now you would have to ask the question, is strategy one better than strategy two in terms of performance? In terms of cost? Time? Scope? And you would tally the votes for all four criteria for each paired comparison. To arrive at a numerical weight for each choice involves matrix algebra, which I long ago forgot and is best done with a software program called Expert Choice®. The program allows comparisons between quantitative and qualitative facets of a choice, making it an extremely powerful way of arriving at a correct decision. To find out more about the software, check out their Web site at www.expertchoice.com.

Conducting SWOT and Risk Analysis

In choosing the best project strategy, it is a good idea to do a SWOT and risk analysis. The acronym SWOT stands for *strengths, weaknesses, opportunities,* and *threats.* It is an analysis originally used in marketing analysis. Before entering a new market, it is useful to ask the following questions:

What are our strengths? How can we take advantage of them?

What weaknesses do we have? How do we minimize the effect of them?

What opportunities does this market offer us? How can we capitalize on them?

What threats exist that may impact our success? How can we deal effectively with these?

The best way to do a SWOT analysis is to simply fill in the form shown in Figure 7.10. I do suggest that you identify *all* the strengths you can think of, then answer the question of how to take advantage of them, rather than identifying a given strength followed immediately by how to deal with it in particular. This procedure goes faster as a rule. The same goes for the other three concerns.

Threats versus Risks

Notice that question two in step 4 asks if SWOT and risks are okay. The difference between risks and threats is that a risk is something that can simply happen—an accident, act of nature, or missed deadline—whereas a threat is something that may be posed by another entity. It may be a competitor who beats you to market, for example.

For practical purposes it is okay to combine threats and risks, because either way you look at it they both jeopardize the project if they happen.

Furthermore, it is not enough to simply identify risks and threats. The question is, what are you going to do about them? The essential point is that threats and risks should be managed so that they do not cause the project to fail.

There are two points in planning a project where risks should be analyzed and managed. The first is to address risks to

F I G U R E 7.10

A SWOT Analysis Form

SWOT Analysis Form

Project:

Prepared by:

Date:

Strategy, goal, or objective being considered:

List strengths of your team.	How can you best take advantage of these?	List weaknesses of your team.	How can you minimize the impact of these?
What opportunities does this project/strategy/goal present?	How can you best take advantage of them?	List those threats that might keep you from succeeding.	How can you deal with each identified threat?

the strategy itself. For example, to employ cutting-edge technology in a product development project is more risky than using proven technology. Unless the benefits to be gained far exceed the cost of failure, the cutting-edge approach would be undesirable. Even if the cutting-edge strategy is chosen, it is a good idea to have a contingency plan in place in case the strategy proves to be unworkable.

You also need to manage risks during implementation planning. Many things can go wrong in the execution of a project plan, and if these are identified ahead of time, plans can be developed to deal with them. You can sometimes eliminate a risk altogether with a small change in your approach to the project. As my colleague, Harvey Levine, says, it is better to avoid risks than to have to deal with them.

Risk management is covered in detail in Chapter 8. For now, suffice it to say that there are three responses to risk:

1. Mitigation—you do something to correct for the damage done by the event.

2. Avoidance—you attempt to avoid the risk in the first place.

3. Transfer—you transfer the risk to someone else. Insurance is an example of risk transfer. Contracting work to another party is also risk transfer.

Unintended Consequences

An unintended consequence is something that happens because of the action you have taken to solve one problem. For example, you decide to contract work to an outside vendor, and the consequence is that you lose control of that part of the project. Or you push everyone to complete a project by a certain date, and they unintentionally sacrifice quality (performance) in the process.

Unintended consequences are all around us. It has been said that most of today's environmental problems are the consequence of solutions to yesterday's problems. I also believe that many organizational problems are consequences of actions and decisions made previously to solve problems. For that reason, it is important to ask yourself if your chosen project strategy is going to lead to serious consequences that may actually be worse than the problem you were trying to solve when you selected it.

As an example, several years ago, I decided to change my way of printing seminar workbooks. In the past, I typed the text on my computer and left space for illustrations. My wife then pasted the art into the placeholders. These masters were then copied and used to reproduce the workbooks in quantity. The problem was that the final workbook, a second-generation copy, had lost some quality. It was also difficult to revise the copy. A significant change could cause page numbers to change, requiring new paste up. This was time-consuming.

To remedy this, I decided to utilize desktop publishing for the workbooks. In doing so, I found that some of the art wouldn't scan without degrading. Also, the computer would occasionally crash for some reason, costing time to redo files. To make a long story short, although there were times when I questioned the wisdom of my decision, I'm convinced that it is the right strategy for the long run.

Force-Field Analysis

Organizations and projects are, by nature, political. The basic nature of politics is that people try to gain and keep power. They choose sides on various issues and then try to have their side "win." This can affect a project when a certain strategy is not acceptable to certain individuals or groups.

As an example, a facilities engineer once told me about an experience he had refurbishing an office. He arranged to do the job over the plant shutdown that occurred for about a week around Christmas. He convinced some people from the plant to help move furniture, lay carpet, and paint walls, and paid them triple time because they were working during a holiday period. They completely overhauled the office, and it was ready for occupancy when the plant resumed its normal operation.

To his chagrin, when he walked into the office on the first day, the union steward was talking with the engineer's boss. He was outraged. "We would normally have taken several months to do that job," he snarled. "Now management knows it can be done in less time."

I asked him the boss' response.

"You should have known better," his boss told him.

This is a good example of a strategy that would have been rejected if it had been suggested to the union steward before the fact.

Force-field analysis is a process by which you consider all of the forces in the environment that may cause your strategy to succeed or fail because of acceptance or rejection by the parties involved. Essentially this entails paying attention to the politics of the project, and this is sometimes overlooked by project managers.

The process is to identify parties that may accept or reject a strategy, assess the strength of their support or resistance, and determine then if your strategy can succeed. The basic idea is that the sum of the supporting forces must exceed the strength of the sum of the resisting forces, or you can't make your strategy work. Such an analysis is shown in Figure 7.11.

The difficulty with this approach lies in trying to quantify the forces. I consider the attempt to do so a very iffy proposition. On top of that, we assume that all resistance is the same when we sum the resisting forces to get a total, and this may not be valid. You may be adding apples and oranges. I suggest that you forget about trying to quantify the forces and concentrate instead on managing resistance. After all, the positive forces are going to help you. You may, of course, try to bolster them or add to them.

F I G U R E   7.11

Force-Field Analysis

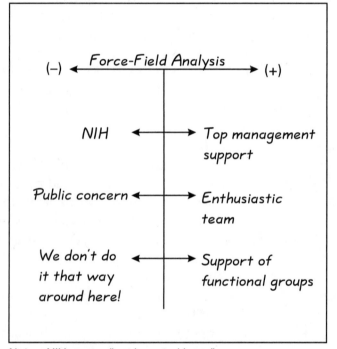

Notes: NIH means "not invented here."
Also, the forces across from each other are not opposites of
each other. They are just drawn this way for appearance.

There are four approaches to dealing with resistance:

1. Ignore it.
2. Overcome it.
3. Go around it.
4. Neutralize it.

Ignore

There are times when you should ignore resistance. If you pay attention to it, you may simply make it grow. This is valid when the resistance is low level, or the resistant person is in no position to do you any harm. The danger is that you may underestimate the level of resistance. In any case, if you later find that you should not have ignored someone's resistance, you can adopt one of the next three approaches.

Overcome

This is one of the most common approaches to resistance. You try to counter the person's resistance by arguing against it. Suppose, for example, that a person objects to a strategy for reasons of safety. You try to convince him that his concerns are unwarranted. He counters your argument with expressions of strong fear that someone will be injured and bring a lawsuit against the company. You go back and forth, offering argument and counterargument, until you are convinced that he is a stubborn opponent who will

Threats are done to us by outside entities.

never "see the light." Of course, he thinks the same thing about you. What has happened is that the strength of your opposing arguments has simply grown, and neither of you has been able to convince the other of the correctness of your position.

The nature of this conflict is a move-countermove exchange, which is called a *game without end*. This means that there is almost no way that the game can end because there are no rules within the system for changing its own behavior. (For more on this, see Watzlawick, et. al., 1974.)

When you see that you are getting into a game-without-end interaction, I suggest that you try another approach. Otherwise you may simply strengthen your opponent. In addition, even if you were able to convince him of your position, he has invested so much energy in his own point of view that to change now would make him lose face, which he may be very reluctant to do.

Go Around

To go around someone means that you go to that person's boss and ask that the boss have a "heart-to-heart" talk with your opponent. It might work, but you might very well regret your action over the long run. It is generally not considered a very wise choice. The only exception would be when some serious safety issue is involved and you have made no headway with other tactics. Otherwise this should be a last resort.

Neutralize

The word suggests that you are going to blast your opponent off the face of the earth—and you may well wish you could do so, but that is not the meaning of "neutralize" in this case. Here it means that you try to find a way to dispel the person's resistance.

The simplest approach is to ask the individual, "What would I have to do to convince you that this is a good strategy?"

The person has two possible responses. One is to tell you to forget about trying to convince her. She is never going to accept this strategy.

When I get this very negative response, I ask, "Really? There's absolutely nothing I can do to convince you?"

If the person is willing to meet you even part way, you will usually get the second response, which is, "Oh, I suppose if you could do (whatever it is) I would be convinced." The nice thing about this is that you no longer try to find out how to convince the individual, because she has told you.

I suggest that, even if you are able to do what the person suggests, you ask if there is anything else you need to do. The reason is that you may do what was originally requested, only to have the person say, "Well, I still have this concern . . ." By taking care of all her concerns at one time, you avoid the sense of playing games later on.

People, Problems, and Projects

I find that very few people take force-field analysis seriously. I'm not sure why. Perhaps they don't feel that they have the skills to deal with resistance. Maybe they think it will go away once the person sees the logic of the strategy. Or it could be that they are simply underestimating its importance.

This is a serious error of judgment. Recently I met with a company that sells heavy equipment and has developed software that allows users to get maximum advantage from the equipment. The user, recognizing this almost immediately, is eager to purchase the software.

The difficulty is with their own salesforce. For years they have sold heavy equipment. They don't know or care anything about software. They are resisting the new system.

This is a good example of a paradigm shift. The old paradigm is that the company sells equipment. The new one is that

A direct approach to resistance may back a person into a corner.

they sell a system in which the software makes the equipment more useful.

The initial response to all paradigm shifts is rejection. For example, when Henry Ford invented the automobile, people thought it was very impractical. After all, they argued, where was anyone going to get gasoline for it? Indeed, the infrastructure needed to support the auto did not exist at that time.

How many people ignored the impact of the personal computer, believing that it could never replace a mainframe unit?

Overcoming resistance to a paradigm shift is very difficult. Usually, evidence of the validity of the new paradigm grows to the point that people can no longer reject it, and then there is a landslide of acceptance. This is shown in Figure 7.12.

Some organizations have to accept that there will be a few employees who will not accept the new paradigm. These people become casualties of the changing direction of the business. This is unfortunate, but given the potential strength of resistance to change it may be unavoidable. However, it is always worth trying

Acceptance of a Paradigm Shift

the strategy that I have outlined above—ask the person what you must do to convince her of the soundness of the new paradigm. If you are unable to get a positive response, you can resort to some other action.

The important point is that projects often get into far more trouble because of these "people" issues than they do because the schedule was incorrect or someone didn't plan properly. As I said at the beginning of the book, successful projects can only be achieved when tools, people, and systems are jointly optimized. Unfortunately, the people side of the equation is more often overlooked than the other two.

PUTTING IT ALL TOGETHER

Following is a step-by-step procedure for developing and selecting project strategy.

Steps 3 to 5 of
The Lewis Method

Project strategy describes, overall, how the job will be done. It
is sometimes called a game plan. You should consider both project strategies and technical strategies when appropriate.
Since these may interact, the choice of a technical strategy
may affect your project strategy, and vice versa.

1. Brainstorm a list of alternative project and technical strate-
    gies. Remember, in brainstorming there is no evaluation or
    criticism until after all ideas have been listed.

2. Once the project strategies have been listed, rank them us-
    ing the priority matrix presented in Chapter 6. Do the same
    for technical strategies.

3. Is the number one technical strategy compatible with the
    number one project strategy? If not, decide which pair of
    the two will be compatible before continuing.

4. For the chosen strategies, can you meet your performance,
    cost, time, and scope targets? If "yes," continue to step 5.
    If "no," then select another strategy to evaluate, until the
    answer is "yes."

5. Fill in a SWOT form, in which you combine threats and
    risks. Don't bother to fill in the right panel of the threat por-
    tion of the form at this time. Note that you are doing this for
    strategy only, not for implementation steps.

6. Next fill in a risk analysis form in which you calculate RPNs (Risk Priority Numbers) for all threats and risks. (You will have to read Chapter 8 to do this.)

7. For all risks that have severities of 8 to 10 points, you *must* find a contingency to deal with the risk. Remember, you can avoid, mitigate, or transfer risk.

8. For all risks that have high products (regardless of severity), you should identify ways that these RPNs can be reduced, either by reducing probability or severity, or improving detection.

9. Are any risks serious enough that the strategy may not work? If so, you may have to select the next strategy in your priority matrix.

10. Are any identified weaknesses serious enough that they may jeopardize the strategy? Can they be overcome? If not, then you may need to select the next strategy in your matrix.

11. Now consider consequences. Will the chosen strategy lead to unacceptable consequences? If so, you may have to reject the strategy.

12. Finally, conduct a force-field analysis in which you identify the positive forces in the environment that will help your strategy succeed and the negative forces that may do the opposite. These forces can be political, social, or paradigm issues. Then ask yourself:

    a. Can I ignore any resisting forces? If yes, check them off your list. If not, then ask:

    b. Can the remaining forces be overcome? If not, then ask:

    c. Can I go around them without creating enemies for life? If not, then ask:

    d. Can I neutralize them by asking the following question: "What must I do to convince you that this strategy is okay?"

8
CHAPTER

Implementation Planning

We are now ready to discuss detailed implementation planning, steps 6-8 of The Lewis Method. These steps are shown in Figure 8.1.

In a previous chapter I wrote that people are inclined to jump from step 1 of my model down to step 9. When I am able to convince them not to skip the definition phase, they then want to jump from step 2 to step 6. They tend to think of planning as detailed planning, omitting strategy from their thinking altogether.

In fact, I still find many individuals thinking about detailed planning while they are trying to define the project. The inclination to do detailed planning seems to be virtually genetic! In terms of the HBDI, this is the place for quadrant-B thinking. You want people to work out exactly how to execute the strategy chosen in steps 4 and 5. In case you have forgotten where the B quadrant is, the model is shown in Figure 8.2, with the B quadrant highlighted.

F I G U R E   8.1

Steps 6 to 8 of The Lewis Method

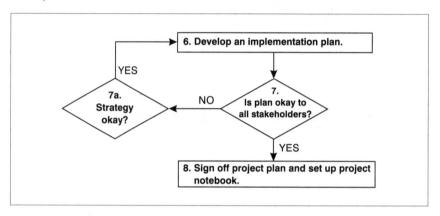

Please note that, even though much B-quadrant thinking is required in this step, it does not mean that you don't need the other quadrants. It is just that planning is particularly a B-quadrant activity. Nevertheless, you may need creative thinking (the D quadrant), and you especially should consider the C quadrant,

You must now determine all the steps that will get you there.

Quadrant B Highlighted

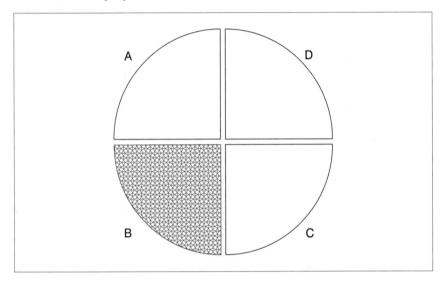

which deals with interpersonal issues, in putting together a plan. Whole-brain thinking would be very helpful at this stage of the project.

You are now ready to work out the details of how a job will be done. For example, if you were building the Chunnel, knowing that you will go in both directions and meet in the middle, you must now determine all of the steps that will get you there. Since there are many contractors performing various parts of the project, you must decide *who* does what, *when* it will be done, *how much* will each step cost, *what* will be needed, and so on. In fact, this illustrates the definition of planning. It is answering all of the who, what, when, and how questions, much as a reporter asks when writing an article.

This is not to say that planning is easy. In fact, I believe it is some of the hardest work we ever do. One reason is that estimating is involved. How long will a step take? Who knows? As one of my engineers told me once when I asked how long some work would take, "You can't schedule creativity."

I agreed with him at the time, but as I told him, "We have to pretend we can, because they won't fund the project unless we tell them how long it will take."

Since then I have changed my mind. You can schedule creativity (within reason, of course). In fact, the most motivating factor in creative thinking is a deadline. Ad agencies live with this all the time. So do the writers of daily "soaps." And so do engineers and programmers.

> Prediction is very difficult, especially about the future.
>
> — Neils Bohr

Dr. Edward de Bono, one of the world's leading gurus on creative thinking, has written that, when he teaches creative thinking to children, if he gives them a deadline, they produce great results. Otherwise, if they have no time limit, they just mess around.

I know a creativity consultant who took an engineering group to the mountains for a weekend to develop a design for a

The ultimate inspiration is the deadline.
~ Nolan Bushnell

new device. They started on Friday afternoon, and by Sunday afternoon they had developed a device that was patented. Using a structured approach to creativity enabled them to do this.

MISTAKES IN PLANNING

Before we go any further, it may be helpful to discuss the more common mistakes that people make in planning, so that you can avoid them. There are five fairly common ones.

Unilateral Planning

This mistake is made when the project manager plans a project for the group and turns it over to them to execute. The major reason this occurs is because no one individual can possibly think of everything in a project. Even a one-person project can benefit from the thinking of other individuals.

> **Mistake 1:** Not involving in the planning process the people who must do the work.

Furthermore, you must estimate task durations yourself when you plan the project by yourself, and your estimates are likely to be wrong. Specifically, your estimate is very likely to be optimistic because you forget about all of the details that consume most of the time. For this reason, the person who eventually must do the work is not likely to be very committed to the time you have specified. If he misses the mark, he is likely to say, "It was your number, not mine. I knew it couldn't be done that fast."

No project can succeed when the team members have no commitment to the plan, so the first rule of project planning is that the people who must do the work should help plan that part of the project. Not only will you gain their commitment to the plan, but you will most likely cover all of the important issues that you personally may have forgotten.

I want to point out that one reason for this mistake (or trap) is that we confuse the thought process with documentation. I explained in Chapter 1 that my flow chart shows the *thought process* you must follow to manage a project. Even for a project to prepare a meal (it is a small project, after all), you should go through every step in my flow chart. If you don't believe it, try it out. You will find that all of the steps apply.

> The first rule of planning is that the people who must do the work should participate in the planning.

For example, when you get to step 6, where you would prepare a schedule in a large project, do you develop a critical path schedule? No. Do you consider the order in which various steps must be done? You bet. Otherwise the meal will not come together properly. Your steak will be ready, but you'll be sitting around for a half-hour waiting for the baked potatoes to get done.

The Ready-Fire-Aim Mistake

One reason people don't plan projects is that they are convinced that they could have finished the work by the time they could do the plan. The complaint is, "We don't have time to plan, we need to get the job done." However, this is a counterintuitive situation. Especially if you have a really critical deadline, you must have a good plan.

As a simple example, suppose I have flown to Chicago for a meeting, and because of bad weather my plane lands very late. I have never been to Chicago before. I rush off the plane, dash to the rental car counter, and get my car. The agent asks, "Mr. Lewis, do you need a map?"

"I don't have time for that," I say. "I have to get to my meeting. I'm already late!"

Mistake 2: Ready-fire-aim. People are convinced they don't need a plan.

We can easily see the fault in that logic. But we can't seem to see the same fault in the logic that says we don't have time to plan projects!

Another example is the 1983 San Diego Home Builder's Association contest that I touched upon earlier.

> The more important a project deadline, the more important the plan.

The goal was to see how fast a team could construct a 2,000-square-foot (approximately 225 square meters) single-story house, sitting on a cement slab. This was not a prefabricated house. The teams started with raw materials and had to pour the cement slab. They had marked it out and had leveled the building site. Furthermore, they had limited building materials. If a piece of wallboard was damaged and they didn't have enough to complete the job, the competition ended for that team.

The week before the competition, the two teams built two houses for practice. They did an after-action review, learned from the practice session, and tweaked their plan. According to their estimates, teams should be able to build the house in roughly three hours and forty minutes, using 350 workers on each site.

The winning team actually completed the house in two hours and forty-five minutes! It was fully wired, with plumbing and appliances installed, landscaped with sod and bushes, and ready for occupancy.

I know it sounds incredible. Even impossible. How did they get the cement to harden that fast?

They put exothermic chemicals in the mortar so that it would cure in 45 minutes. You could see steam coming off the concrete. The joke was that, if the foundation hardened too fast, they would have a workman permanently cemented into the house.

No doubt one of the first thoughts that comes to your mind is, "I wouldn't want to live in it." Of the four constraints (P, C, T, S), the one you are concerned with is quality (performance). They must surely have done shoddy work to get it finished so fast.

Well, they covered that concern by having professional San Diego building inspectors on site, inspecting the work as it progressed. If it didn't meet the building code (which is fairly rigorous in the earthquake-prone area), they made the crew do it over.

You really have to see it to believe it. If you are interested, you can get a video of the competition by calling the San Diego Builder's Association at (619) 450-1221.

This example illustrates a project in which the planning time far exceeded the execution time.

Planning in Too Little Detail

One major cause of project failures is that ballpark estimates become targets. For the benefit of my readers outside the United States who may not understand the idiom "ballpark estimate," the expression comes from baseball. If the ball is hit over the wall, it is out of the ballpark. If it does not go over the wall, then it is in the ballpark. So we use the term ballpark estimate to mean that it is approximately correct. (It is within acceptable boundaries or limits.)

The problem is that a ballpark estimate is done by comparing one project to another similar one, adding a bit for this, taking off a bit for that, then inserting some money for unknowns (called contingency). The tolerances on ballpark estimates can be extremely large. Imagine being asked what it would cost to develop a vaccine for AIDS, as an example. A person could only offer a guesstimate with a huge range. There are simply too many unknown factors to be able to give a precise number.

Mistake 3: Broad-brush planning.

This is an example of planning a project in too little detail. If a better estimate is desired you must identify the major tasks to be performed, and probably some of the subtasks as well.

I once worked with a defense contracting company. Their projects were bid at a fixed price. To estimate the cost to do the

Principle:
If you aren't careful, ballpark estimates become targets.

job, the person preparing the bid would ask various individuals how much his or her part would cost. Each person would do a ballpark estimate. They would then be awarded the bid (based on being the low bidder) and would lose money on the job.

I explained that they were planning in too little detail. They needed more detailed project planning in order to get a realistic estimate.

Three years later, in a follow-up interview, I asked, "How are your projects going now."

The response was very positive. "We don't get as many jobs as we used to," said my contact, "but when we get one, we make money on it."

Isn't that the name of the game?

As a way of indicating the level of detail that you should incorporate into a final project plan, consider a client I worked with who had never done very much project planning. Most of their planning was done on the backs of envelopes. Nevertheless, they had been very successful.

A new manager inherited the company and explained to everyone that they had to do a better job of planning. The reason was survival. A Japanese competitor had just entered their market and was selling their product at a lower price than my client. The new manager explained that he didn't know the cost to develop his product, so in order to ensure that the company would make a profit, he had to sell at a higher margin than the Japanese company, who had a fairly accurate measure of their development costs. That being the case, they could charge a lower profit margin, because they knew how many units they had to sell to reach breakeven, and therefore when they became profitable. His point was that good project management could give them a competitive advantage in the marketplace.

His proposal was met with considerable resistance. The engineers had never had to do this "administrative stuff" before and saw no need for it now. In part, they were afraid of being held accountable for estimates that might not be correct. This seemed to be "policing" them.

The frustrated manager told them he at least wanted them to give him a bar chart schedule. They responded by giving him a schedule that had bars 26 weeks long for individual tasks. His response was that they would never complete a 26-week task on time. They would back-end load it and ultimately fail.

His reasoning was that they would delay starting on time, fully convinced that they could always make up one day. After all, they had 26 Saturdays to make up the lost day. Next day, still busy, they would convince themselves that they could always make up two days, then three days, and so on, until they had slipped an entire week. It is incredibly hard to make up a week of lost work.

The term "back-end loading" means that they were going to push their work out toward the end of the task, and then if they encountered technical problems, they would ultimately fail.

It is incredibly hard to make up for lost time.

He suggested that they should always follow the rule that no task ever have a duration greater than 4 to 6 weeks. So a 26-week task should be subdivided or "chunked down" to increments of about 4 weeks. Furthermore, they needed a marker that told them they were actually finished, and such markers can be difficult to apply to knowledge work. Another term, "exit criteria," also refers to some way of knowing that the work is complete.

Rules for Planning

- No task should have a duration greater than four to six weeks.

- Engineering and software tasks should have durations no greater than one to three weeks.

- All tasks must have markers that enable everyone to tell that the work is actually complete.

Had I known then what I know now, I would have told him that engineering and programming work should be chunked down even further, so that durations fall in the range of one to three weeks. Otherwise you find that such work gets to 90 percent complete and stays there forever.

Planning In Too Much Detail

Unfortunately, the reverse of too little detail causes problems. Some people get carried away and microplan. I know. I did it myself once, and lived to regret it.

Mistake 4: Microplanning.

The basic principle is that you should never plan in more detail than you can actually control. In engineering software, that means no more than the nearest day. You simply can't control much better than that.

However, people who do maintenance work can sometimes control the work to the nearest hour. It is common practice to schedule jobs to refuel nuclear reactors or over-haul a power generator to the nearest hour. The schedules will be re-vised at the end of the shift, or once a day when they need to be. These jobs would not be scheduled to the nearest 15 minutes, however, because they can't be controlled that closely. If you make the mistake of scheduling in too much detail, you will spend all of your time keeping your schedule up to date, and that is a waste of time.

> **Never plan in more detail than you can control.**

Apparently people sometimes fall into the microplanning trap because their scheduling software permits them to plan down to minutes. If you *can* do it, goes the thinking, then maybe you *should* do it.

Failing to Plan for Risks

A "can-do" attitude is far preferable to a "can't do" attitude—up to a point. That point is when the person ignores probable risks. I once had a manager tell me he didn't want me to suggest that his people pad their schedules. He wanted their schedules to be *aggressive.* I appreciate his concern, but there is a difference between aggressive and foolhardy.

> **Mistake 5:** Failing to plan for risks.

If you are doing construction work, and that work may be delayed by weather, it is common risk management practice to allow for weather delays by padding your schedule. If the weather delay doesn't happen, you get ahead. If more delay oc-curs than you anticipated, you will have to work hard to re-cover. But to ignore the possibility of weather delays altogether is foolhardy.

To ignore probable risks is not a "can-do" attitude but a foolhardy approach to project management.

Murphy's Law states that whatever can go wrong will go wrong. Stated in terms of probability, this means that there is a higher probability that things will accidentally go wrong than that they will accidentally go right. And of course, we know that even Murphy was an optimist.

> There is a higher probability that things will accidentally go wrong than that they will accidentally go right.

Risk management is an integral part of good project management, and will be discussed later in this chapter.

DEVELOPING THE WORK BREAKDOWN STRUCTURE

At the beginning of this chapter, I showed that we are now down to step 6 of my overall flowchart. Step 6 actually consists of a number of substeps, as shown in Figure 8.3.

F I G U R E   8.3

Step 6 of The Lewis Method Expanded

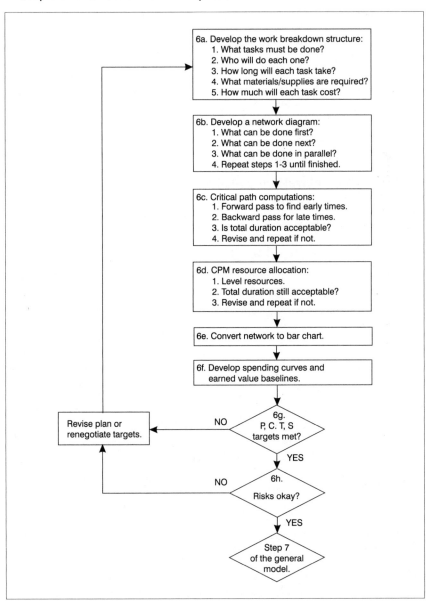

As we saw earlier, implementation planning answers the questions shown in step 6a of Figure 8.3, and repeated here:

1. What must be done?

2. Who will do each task?

3. How long will each task take?

4. What materials, supplies, and equipment are required?

5. How much will each task cost?

> The first step in implementation planning is to answer the question, "What must be done?"

Notice that we don't worry about the order in which tasks will be done until we get to step 6b. This is the scheduling problem, and will be fully covered in Chapter 9.

For now, we will concentrate on the first question: What must be done? The tool of choice for doing this is the work breakdown structure (WBS), which is constructed in step 6a. An example of a very simple WBS, a small project in your yard, is shown in Figure 8.4.

As you can see, there are five major tasks to be done: Cut the grass, do trim work, and so on. Some of these tasks also have subtasks underneath. The terminology will be explained shortly.

But what use is this? First, one of the major causes of project failure is that something is forgotten until the project is underway, and then it is discovered. The forgotten work has a serious impact on the project, either in terms of schedule or cost. The WBS is one device that helps us ensure that nothing significant has been forgotten.

As a matter of fact, I consider the WBS to be the most valuable tool of project management, as it ties the entire project together. This position is contrary to popular belief that project management is just scheduling. There are some projects so small

Work Breakdown Structure for Yard Project

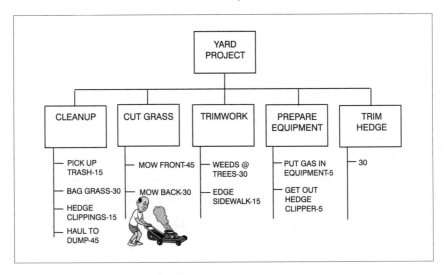

that developing a schedule would be a waste of time, but a WBS is *always* useful. Here's why:

1. It identifies all work to be done in the project graphically, so it can be reviewed by all stakeholders to ensure that nothing has been forgotten.

2. It provides a graphical representation of the scope (or magnitude) of the job. This is important because people are sometimes surprised at the cost estimates you give them, and this helps them see why the job is going to cost as much as you have said.

3. The WBS provides the basis on which resource assignments are made.

4. This allows you to estimate working times for each task.

5. Knowing the working time then allows you to calculate labor costs for all work, so that you develop a *labor*

budget for the project. The times also provide the basis for developing a schedule.

6. You can also identify material, capital equipment, and other costs associated with each activity (such as insurance costs).

Terminology

Now let's discuss terminology. In Figure 8.5 you will see that each level of the WBS is given a name. The first level is called program, and the next is called project. This explains the difference between program management and project management. A program is a very large job that consists of a number of projects. A good example is a program to develop a new airplane. A partial WBS for such a job is shown in Figure 8.6.

The engine design is a project in its own right, with a project manager and project team. The wing design, avionics design, and so on, are also large projects. In fact, the wing design would probably be done by the aircraft company, and the engine and avionics would be contracted to other companies such as General Electric, Rolls Royce, and Collins Radio.

> Don't worry about the sequence of tasks while constructing the WBS.

The program manager has responsibility over the entire job. The project managers do not report to him or her on a solid-line basis, but do report on a dotted line. Note that an airplane such as Boeing's 777 or an Airbus 319 has wing-mounted engines. Somewhere in the engine design project will be a task to design the mountings for connecting the engine to the wing. And in the wing design there will be a task to design the corresponding engine mounts.

Clearly, these tasks will be interactive in nature and will have to be coordinated between the two project teams. The program manager must see that this is done. However, when the WBS is

F I G U R E 8.5

Names of Levels in a WBS

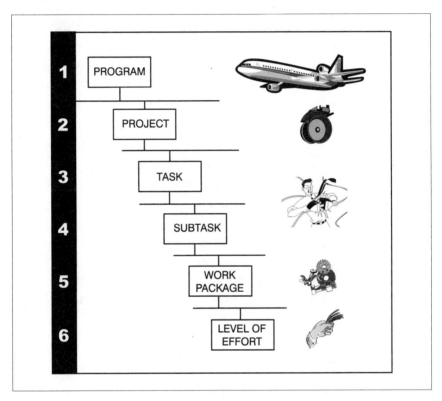

F I G U R E 8.6

WBS for an Airplane Development Program

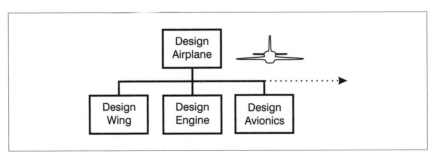

drawn, we do not worry about the sequence in which these tasks are done. This will be worked out when the schedule is developed.

I make this point because there is a strong tendency for people to think about sequence while constructing the WBS. "You can't do that until you have done this," they say. You have to keep telling people, "That's true, you can't do this until that is done, but we're not trying to work that out yet."

Work Package

What exactly does "work package" mean? It is simply a label that identifies a specific level in the structure. If I ask you about a work package in the engine project for the airplane, you would know it is something at level 5 in the structure. Whether something goes at level 5 or 6 (or whatever) can only be known by breaking work down in progressive steps until you reach a point of diminishing returns. And wherever an activity falls, it falls. It is not a matter of something absolutely being a level-3 subtask. It is a function of how the work is actually structured. You will see this in the example that follows later in this chapter.

The Steps in the Process

How do you go about developing a WBS? I'm going to use a simple example. We're planning a family camping trip. It is a family of four—two adults, a boy who is 12 years old, and a girl who is 8. They have set aside a two-week period for the trip and have already arranged with their employers to be away during that time. Furthermore, they have a budget. They don't want to spend more than a certain amount for this trip.

Now notice what has been specified so far in terms of the PCTS constraints. We have specified time and cost. Scope and performance are undefined.

What would scope mean in a camping trip? Things like what the family wants to do while away; that is, a list of activities in which they want to engage. It may also involve whether they are tent camping or taking a Winnebago. As for performance, remember this is the quality of work done. In the camping example, it means the quality of the family's experience. If they try to cram too much into the trip, like people sometimes do when they go abroad and want to see 12 cities in three days, they will sacrifice quality in the process.

The family makes a list of everything they want to do. It doesn't appear that quality will be sacrificed, but when they add up the costs, they realize that they will exceed their budget. What do they do?

Two possibilities exist. First, they can decide that this is a once-in-a-lifetime trip, and they will just put a little more on the credit card than they had intended. Or they may decide that the budget is very important and delete some activities from the list.

The importance of this example is that you can never escape the PCTS constraints in *any* project—not even a simple thing like a family camping trip. Tradeoffs are always being made to balance project requirements.

The First Step

When I draw a WBS, I begin by identifying major tasks. My first pass would look like the one shown in Figure 8.7. As I continue, this may change. For that reason, it is convenient to do this on a white board or to use PostIt™ notes so things can easily be moved around.

Once I have listed all of the tasks, I begin breaking them down. For example, "Select Site" can be broken down as shown in Figure 8.8.

Now note that the task to list activities during the trip can be a stand-alone task, or it may be part of the family meeting. That is, if they are going to make the list during the family meeting, we can remove it as a task and put it there as a subtask. This is shown in Figure 8.9.

First Pass on a WBS for a Camping Trip

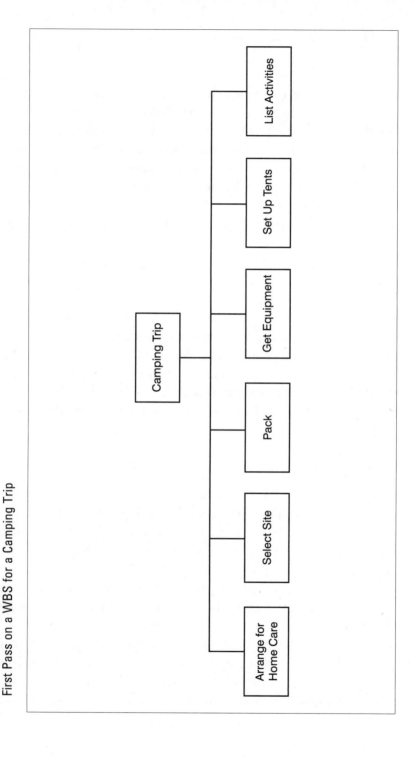

WBS with *Select Site* Broken Down

WBS with *List Activities* Moved under *Family Meeting*

Furthermore, I can expand the subtask "Research," as shown in Figure 8.10. This process would continue with all tasks and subtasks until I have reached a point where I think everything has been covered. When this process is done with a team, you are likely to think of everything. If you do it by yourself, you may miss something, so if it is a one-person project you are planning it is a good idea to have someone else review your WBS before going any further.

Your completed WBS might look something like the one shown in Figure 8.11. This is by no means the only possible solution. Most projects are open-ended problems, in that there is no single way to go about the work.

I suggest that you pause at this point and draw a WBS for something you are currently doing. It can be a home project or work activity. Just sketch it out to satisfy yourself that you have done it correctly. (If you have any questions about the procedure, send me an e-mail at jlewis@lewisinstitute.com, and I'll try to help you.)

Some Things Worth Noting

If you compare the camping trip WBS with the one for the airplane, you will notice a significant difference. The projects in the airplane program all produce tangible deliverables. In the camping trip, however, very few tasks produce deliverables. "Get Supplies" is one that does. "Arrange Home Care" does not. You have cut off the newspaper, asked the post office to hold your mail, and arranged for someone to come over and water your plants. There are no deliverables here, so how would you know the activities have been taken care of? The simplest way is to use a checklist for tasks that have no deliverables.

I consider this WBS to be primarily process oriented. The airplane WBS is deliverables oriented at the top level. However, as you get further down into the structure, you will find a number of process-oriented activities. As an example, you will have to test

F I G U R E 8.10

WBS with *Research* Expanded

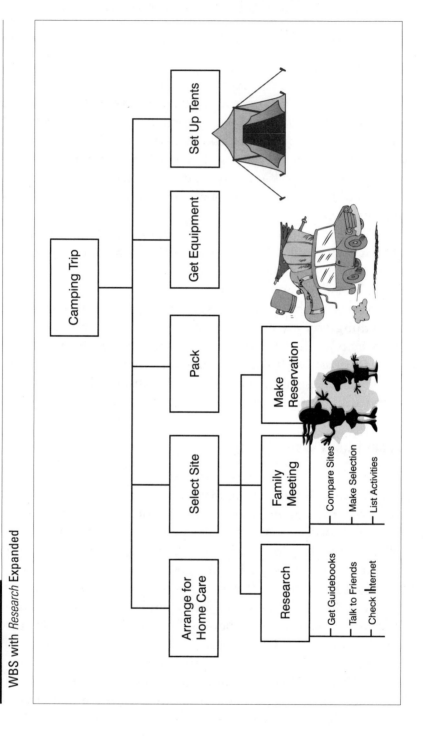

FIGURE 8.11

Completed WBS for Camping Trip

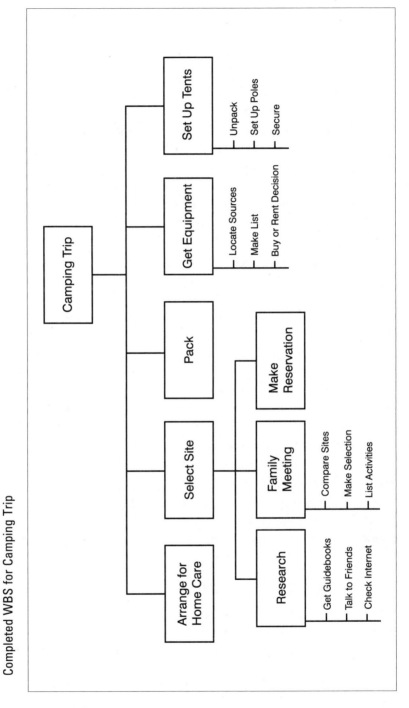

the engine. There is no hardware deliverable, but you will produce a test report. That is your deliverable, and it is evidence that the test has been conducted.

In many cases, you don't even produce reports, so how do you know the work has been done? You use exit criteria. As a simple example, if you change the oil in your car, and I ask if you are sure you've done it correctly, you could show me that the dipstick registers "Full" and shows clean oil. One of these is *quantitative* and the other is *qualitative*. I would also look under the car and inspect to see whether any oil is dripping out, which would mean that the plug had not been correctly reinstalled. Another qualitative exit criteria.

I know of a situation where a company produced a prototype product and called one of the vice presidents out to examine it. He didn't like a major feature of the product and insisted that it be redesigned. The prototype had been built with tooling, which had to be scrapped. The total cost to redesign the product was huge.

In this case, the exit criteria was that the vice president approved the product. Knowing that, it would have been best to get him to look at preliminary drawings, rather than wait so late. In fact, I wouldn't be surprised if they tried to do so and were unable to get him to review the design because he had a heavy schedule and felt that he couldn't afford the time. The lesson is that corrections should always be made as early in a process as possible, because each succeeding step magnifies the cost to correct an error by about 10 times; the progression goes 1, 10, 100, 1,000, and so on.

Suggestions on How to Proceed

When you develop a project plan, you are determining the who, what, when, and how, as I have previously explained. It may be helpful to approach a WBS by answering questions in this order:

1. What must be done? Example: The house must be cleaned. This would be the project.

2. What must be done to clean the house? Wash the windows. Clean the floors. Put everything in its proper place. Dust the furniture. Carry out the garbage. These would be major tasks in the project.

3. Who will do each one? Mom will clean the floors. Tommy will put everything in its place. Sue will dust the furniture. Dad will carry out the garbage. Donnie will wash the windows. This assigns roles and responsibilities.

4. How will each task be done? Mom will clean the floors by vacuuming the carpets and mopping the tile floors. Sue will dust the furniture using furniture polish. These will be subtasks.

5. What is needed to do each subtask? A vacuum cleaner. Furniture polish. Rags. Paper towels. Garbage bags. Identifying these allows you to develop costs for equipment and materials. This is a major part of the budget.

6. How long will each subtask take? These estimates provide the basis for the labor budget (see step 8) and for developing the schedule.

7. What is required for each subtask to be considered complete? This will constitute exit criteria for each activity.

8. In a normal work project, how much will each subtask cost for labor? This gives you the labor budget, which, when combined with the equipment and materials budget, yields the total project budget.

Guidelines to Follow

Following are some guidelines that you should follow in developing a WBS:

- Up to 20 levels can be used. More than 20 is considered overkill.

- All paths on a WBS do not have to go down to the same level. One path may go down five levels and another only three levels. When you have reached a point that allows you to manage the work, you stop. Don't force the structure to be symmetrical.

> A work breakdown structure *does not show the sequence in which work is performed!* Such sequencing is determined when a schedule is developed.

- The WBS does not show sequencing of work except in the sense that all level-5 work packages hanging below a given subtask must be complete for the subtask to be complete, and so on. However, work packages below that subtask might be performed in series or parallel. Sequencing is determined when schedules are developed.

- A WBS should be developed before scheduling and resource allocation. Identify the tasks first, then come back and decide who will do them, and estimate how long they will take.

- The WBS should be developed by individuals knowledgeable about the work. Different parts of the WBS will be developed by various groups. Then the separate parts will be combined. Remember, the first rule of project planning is that the people who will ultimately do the work should develop the plan.

- Break down a project only to a level sufficient to produce an estimate of the required accuracy. This should be explained. One of the big advantages a WBS offers is greater accuracy of cost and time estimates than you would get by simply comparing one project to another. A project-to-project estimate is called a ballpark estimate, as was mentioned previously, and we saw that its accuracy is lacking.

If you break a project down to the level that can be controlled, you can develop a working estimate. But what does this mean? Ask yourself what level of detail you can control in your work. Can you predict to the nearest hour when a task will be finished? The nearest day? Nearest week? If you break work down into such small units that they take hours to perform, but you can't control work to that degree, you will spend all of your time updating your schedule and get no work done! I know. I've done it.

It isn't any fun. So when you reach a level that you can control, stop there.

It may be that an estimate is needed to decide if a project should be done. It may be possible to make that decision if the accuracy of the estimate is ± 50 percent. You may only have to break the project down two levels to achieve that accuracy. Going further at this point would be a waste of time if the decision is to not do the work.

- A WBS is a list of activities, not a grocery list. Imagine that I am doing a home project—some yard work, some repairs, and some grocery shopping. I draw a WBS like that in Figure 8.12.

> A WBS is a list of activities. It is not a grocery list.

As you can see, I have put my grocery list on the WBS. That is not what you do. You identify the activities that must be perform in order to buy groceries. It would look like the WBS in Figure 8.13.

F I G U R E 8.12

WBS for Home Project

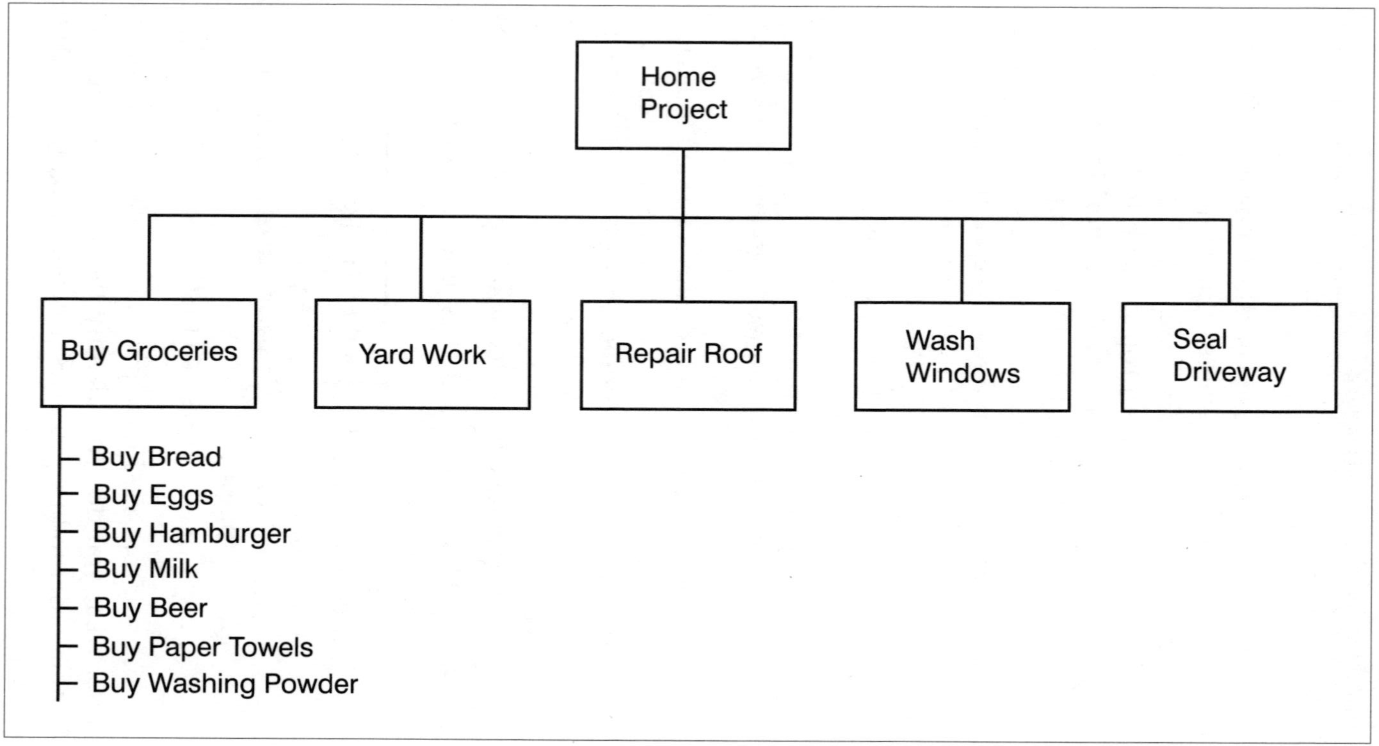

WBS with Proper Activities Shown for Buying Groceries

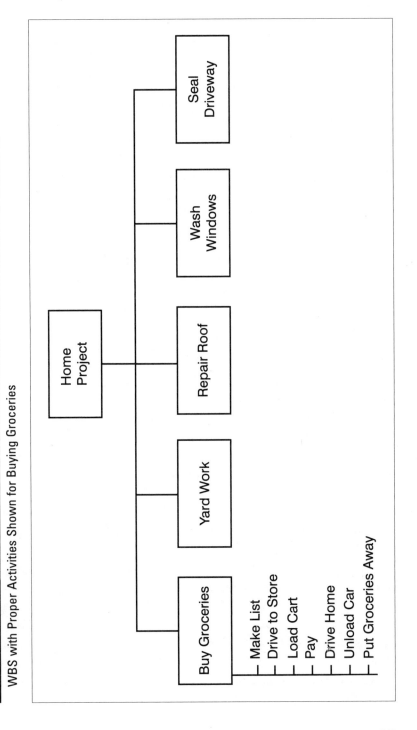

This is a very easy trap to fall into. Here is a test to help you decide if you have made this mistake. In Figure 8.13, if I have done all of the activities listed, the task to buy groceries will be complete. In Figure 8.12, however, if I have bought eggs, milk, and bread, I am still standing in the grocery store. The activities in Figure 8.12 are not predecessor to "Buy Groceries"; they *are* the components of that task listed in detail. When they are all done the task above will be complete. This is your test.

Using MindManager® Software to Develop a WBS

If you have ever developed a mind map®, you know how useful they are for thinking about an issue, especially brain storming. Mindjet software has a program called MindManager that allows you to create a mind map on the computer and then export it directly to MicrosoftProject, Microsoft Word, Outlook, and PowerPoint. Being able to export directly to Microsoft Project saves you entering the data twice and also allows you to proceed with project planning in the correct sequence. That is, you develop your WBS first, then export it to the scheduling software. Trying to create your schedule and WBS simultaneously by just entering data into Microsoft Project is not a good way to go about it.

Figure 8.14 provides an example of a mind map developed with MindManager. This is a simple example of a yard project, shown previously in Figure 8.4.

Using a computer projector, you can develop a mind map with a group in brainstorming mode and everyone can see what you're doing. In addition, if you decide you don't like where you placed something, you can drag it to another location without having to retype it. The program can be downloaded for a 30-day evaluation by going to www.mindjet.com. (I am not receiving a fee for this endorsement; I just think the program is a great tool for project planning.)

Mind Map Using MindManager Software

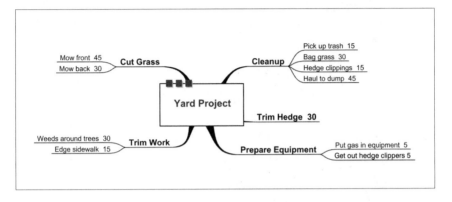

ESTIMATING TIME, COST, AND RESOURCE REQUIREMENTS

Once you have your WBS completed, you are ready to use it for estimating. This step scares the daylights out of a lot of people. They don't know how long something will take, but they know if they give their manager a number they will be held to it. So they try to waffle or avoid committing to a number altogether. As I pointed out earlier in this chapter, people think you can't schedule creative tasks, but you can.

You *cannot,* however, schedule pure discovery work, and you should always separate discovery from development in a product development environment. As an example, the CFO at Merck Pharmaceuticals wrote an article in the *Harvard Business Review* reporting that they examine approximately 10,000 compounds before one makes it as a drug. There's no way you can schedule such work.

That does not mean that you can't plan research projects, however. I've been told that by a number of scientists. What confuses them is that research projects have conditional branches.

You do a series of studies or experiments, and, depending on the results you get, you go in one direction or another. This is shown in Figure 8.15.

You may not know which branch you will ultimately take at the beginning of the project, but you can plan everything up to that point. Furthermore, as you near that branch, you must begin considering what you will do once the outcome is known. If you don't, you will waste valuable time deciding later on. (And you may have no idea what to do next; it isn't a simple thing!)

What Is Estimating?

In simple words, estimating is *guessing!* Yes, there are kinder, gentler ways to put it, such as forecasting or predicting. But the truth is that an estimate is a guess based on something. It is best when it is based on experience. But what if you have no experience—if it's the first time something is to be done?

F I G U R E 8.15

A Project with a Conditional Branch

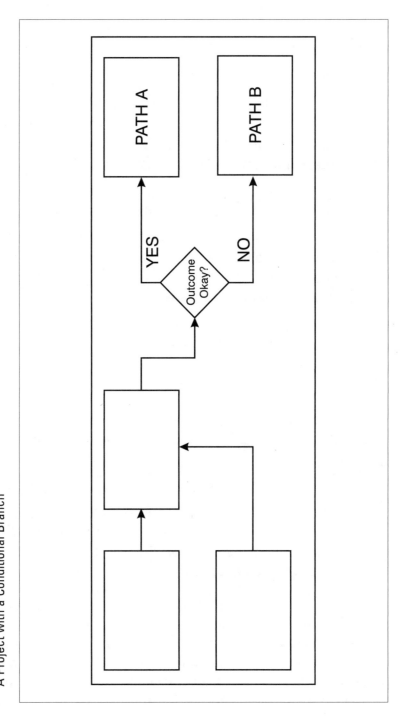

In that situation you have to use another approach. There are two primary ones that we will discuss later. However, it should be clear that, no matter how much experience you have, estimating is guessing. Why? Because

> Estimating is *guessing!*

all activities are probabilistic, not deterministic! There is a probability that a task can be completed in a certain time, given a fixed level of effort. If you want to guarantee that the task is finished in a fixed time period, then you must vary effort, reduce

> All activities are probabilistic, not deterministic!

scope, or sacrifice quality. You can't have it all. Therefore, "exact estimate" is an oxymoron.

I said that estimating is best done when you have experience, or history, with an activity. Let's see what that means. You have history on an activity that you perform regularly—namely, driving to work. If I ask you how long it takes, you can give me three (and possibly four) numbers. One is the typical driving time. It happens most frequently. Another is the best case. You have never been able to get to work any faster. And finally, there is the worst

> "It's a poor sort of memory, that only works backwards," the Queen remarked.
>
> — Lewis Carrol
> *Alice's Adventures in Wonderland*

case, where traffic tie-ups delay you. This worst-case time happens often enough that you are well aware of it.

There may also be a "worst-worst" case. Just once, you got caught in a traffic tie-up that caused you to take three hours to get to work. However, it only happened once, and you don't expect it to happen again. The "normal" worst-case time does happen fairly often, so it is the one you should use.

T A B L E 8.1

Driving Times Reported by Many People

Typical time	45 minutes
Shortest time	30 minutes
Longest time	60 minutes

When I ask people for their driving times, I usually get numbers like those shown in Table 8.1.

Notice that the worst-case time is skewed upward. The driving time is not normally distributed. A normal distribution is shown in Figure 8.16, and a skewed distribution is shown in Figure 8.17.

The question is, what do we do with historical data when we have it? To illustrate, write down your own driving times, and then answer this question: If I ask you how long you estimate it will take you to get to work on a random day (you don't know what day of week or what the weather is doing), what will you tell me? Most people give me the typical time. Now, if you have a very skewed distribution, this is probably the modal time. If the distribution is a normal distribution, then the typical time would be an average. For an average, the probability that you could get to work in that time or less would be 50 percent. This is shown in Figure 8.18.

Most people don't feel uncomfortable with a 50 percent probability of driving to work, but they do feel uneasy if the probability of completing project work is that low. So they tend to pad the number to increase the probability of success. As you can see in Figure 8.18, if you go only one standard deviation above the mean, you increase the probability to 84 percent.

F I G U R E 8.16

Normal Distribution

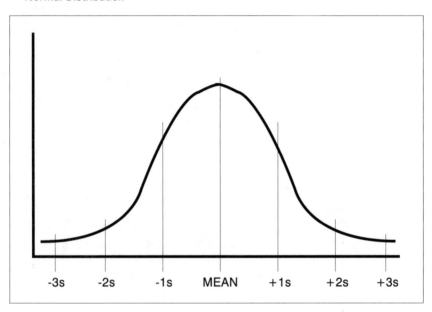

F I G U R E 8.17

Skewed Distribution

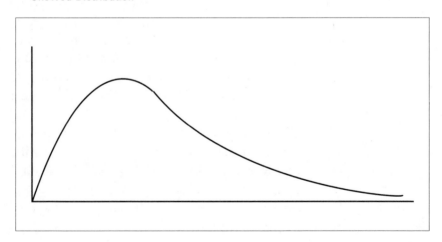

Normal Distribution with Probabilities Shown

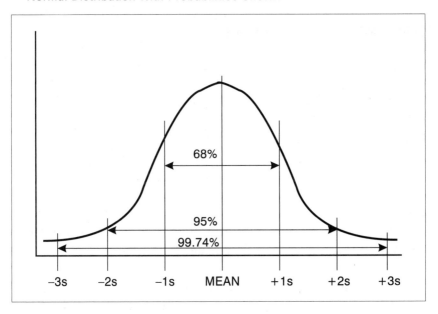

I often ask people, "If the president of your company wanted to have a meeting with you first thing in the morning, and it was career suicide to be late, how much time would you allow yourself to get to work?" Most of them go to the worst-case time—or higher—and raise their probability to 99.9 percent.

Because there is a significant penalty for being late, they reduce their risk by padding the schedule. They will

> As the probability of project success goes toward 100 percent, the probability of funding goes to zero.

do the same thing with projects. And when they do, the cost of the project goes sky high, and it will most likely not be funded.

I can promise you, however, that if it gets funded, it will cost what we have budgeted, and possibly more. This is based on Parkinson's Law: work will always expand to take as long as has been allowed. The project will never finish early.

> **Parkinson's Law:** Work will expand to take the time allowed.

Why? Because if you finish early, everyone will think you padded the schedule, and next time they will cut your time and budget accordingly.

Now this is organizational insanity. A sample of one has created an expectation for all future work!

I am convinced that everyone should have to study statistics, because they would then understand that all processes vary. Your driving time varies. The amount of time you need to get dressed in the morning varies. The time it takes to write a 10-page document varies. Why? Random noise.

All kinds of things affect driving time, for example. The exact time that you leave home. The weather. Road construction. School buses. You name it. These are factors outside your control, and they must be accepted.

Can we reduce variation? Yes, up to a point. That is what all process improvement is aimed at doing.

Can you eliminate variation altogether?

Absolutely not.

Yet we have two rules in organizations that show that we don't understand this. One is, "Thou shalt not go over budget."

The other is, "Thou shalt not come in under budget."

This is plain stupid. It is insisting that people violate a law of nature—namely, to achieve zero variance in their spending to budget. This is possible only if you finagle, so everyone plays games to achieve the impossible.

The problem is, this is easier to do with a department than with a project. You budget a department based on head count. You can control spending to a much tighter tolerance than you can a project, because a project is budgeted based on a bunch of guesses.

We simply must reach a point where everyone understands that variation is a fact of life and must be accepted. We waste millions of dollars every year attempting to make variances approach zero, when it is counterproductive to do so.

Imagine now that you finished a task ahead of schedule and passed it on to the person who is next in line. What would happen? Would she start work on it immediately?

Of course not.

She doesn't have to start until a few days later, according to the schedule, so she won't.

Goldratt (1997) calls this the *student effect*.

Remember when you were in school, and the teacher announced on Monday that there would be a test on Friday? Everyone moaned and groaned. "I already have three tests this week," says one student. "This is going to kill me."

So the teacher relents and says, "Okay, we will have the test Friday of next week, instead of this week."

Everyone sighs in relief.

When will the students start studying for the test?

You guessed it. They will start studying on Thursday night the following week! They won't have any more study time than they would if the test had been left on this Friday.

> **Goldratt's Principle:** A project will accumulate delays but will never accumulate gains.

Goldratt concludes that, when you combine Parkinson's Law with the student effect, a project will accumulate delays but will never accumulate gains. This means that they almost always cost more than necessary and take longer than they should. There is a plenty of room for improvement.

You can't solve
a problem with
the same thinking
that created it in
the first place.
~ Albert Einstein

How do we solve this problem? We must change our thinking. We must accept variation, and in doing so eliminate penalties
for being either early or late on a task-by-task basis. As Goldratt
argues, it doesn't matter that there is some variation in task completion. What matters is that the project finishes on time.

If you allow task completion dates to vary, some will finish
early, some will finish a bit late, and the variations will average
out. Otherwise, you will always finish late.

In other words, this means that estimates should be based on
that typical driving time, rather than the worst case.

Consensual Estimating

What do you when you have no history? You could hold a wet
string up and see how long it takes to dry, multiply the result by
33 and divide by six. That is called an estimating algorithm.

Of course, I'm joking.

A lot of people are now using consensual estimating. It
works like this. For all of the tasks in your WBS, you ask several

individuals who know something about a given task to estimate how long it will take, independently of each other. Then you have a meeting in which you compare estimates. Suppose that for a single task you had a result like that shown in Figure 8.19.

Notice that there are three individuals in fairly close agreement, and one whose number is considerably lower. It would be tempting to throw out the low number and go with the majority. But that's not a good idea. What you want to do is understand why the difference exists, so you discuss the issues affecting the task. In doing so, the person who estimated low may revise his estimate upward.

Conversely, the majority may realize that they missed something the other individual thought of, and they may revise their estimates downward.

Whatever the case, they ultimately are asked to choose a number that they can all support. Notice they aren't asked to totally agree with the number. You almost never get total agreement in a group. What you want is that they will all support a single estimate. This is the practical meaning of the word consensus.

F I G U R E   8.19

The Distribution of Several Estimates for a Single Task

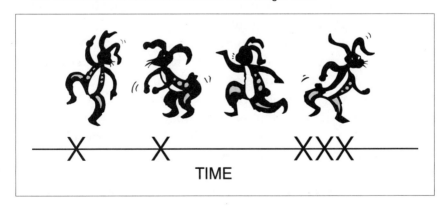

TIME

There are four major advantages of using this approach:

1. No one person is "on the hook" for the estimate. If it turns out to be significantly off, no individual will get chastised for it.

2. Inexperienced members of the team learn from the others, and their ability to estimate improves.

3. Collectively, they are more likely to think of all the factors that may affect the time required to do the task than would be true of any individual.

4. You will have higher commitment to the estimate than would be true if an individual produced it.

The seeming downside is that this will take much longer than if an individual did each estimate. But it isn't true. The cost of taking more time to refine the estimates will be more than paid for by a successful project. When you consider the high cost of a late project, you find that good planning is a bargain.

Calendar-Time Estimates

I have suggested that you use working-time estimates to plan a project. However, if you ask a person "How long will it take you to do a report for me?," the person will most likely tell you, "Oh, I should be able to do that within a week."

She knows it is about two hours of actual work, but because she has a lot of work to do, it will take her a week to get to it. So she gives you a calendar-time estimate.

Do you really care about the actual working time? After all, isn't it the calendar time that is really important?

Actually, you need both. You need the actual working time to work out labor costs, and you need calendar time to predict project completion. In fact, if she tells you the report will be done in a week, and you need it sooner, you will ask her to give it a higher priority so she can do it in a couple of days. You are always

Use working-time estimates to plan a project.

juggling tradeoffs between working time and calendar time, so you have to ask both questions when you ask for estimates.

CLARIFYING ROLES AND RESPONSIBILITIES

I said above that you can't estimate task durations unless you begin with the assumption of a resource, either by name or at least by skill level. Once you have assigned resources to all activities, fill out a responsibility chart like the one in Figure 8.20 so that everyone can tell at a glance who is responsible for each task.

GAINING COMMITMENT FROM RESOURCE PROVIDERS

In many projects, you don't own your resources; they are provided by functional managers on a temporary basis. Once your implementation plan is complete, you should get it authorized (step 8 of The Lewis Method model). The necessary signatures should be obtained in a project plan sign-off meeting, if possible. Circulating the plan through the interoffice mail to be signed almost always leads

F I G U R E 8.20

Responsibility Chart

Linear Responsibility Chart

Project:	Date Issued:	Sheet Number	of
Manager	Date Revised:	Revision No	File: LRCFORM.61

Project Contributors

Task Descriptions															

CODES: 1 = ACTUAL RESPONSIBILITY; 2 = SUPPORT; 3 = MUST BE NOTIFIED; BLANK = NOT INVOLVED to problems—people tend to skim instead of reading, and their commitments don't hold up later on. They should be clear that their signatures indicate their commitment to provide resources *when* they say, in the *quantities* they say.

DEVELOPING THE PROJECT BUDGET

Developing a budget is implied in everything that has been discussed up to now. Once you estimate how long tasks will take, you can multiply these by labor rates and develop your labor budget. When you need materials, capital equipment, or outside services for some part of the WBS, you can estimate these and include them in your budget. If you start at the lowest level in the WBS and add costs for each category (labor, capital equipment, etc.), and continue working up toward the top of the WBS, you will eventually have total costs for the project.

Repeating what I said previously, this shows why the WBS is the most important tool of project management. No other tool provides the means for developing a total project budget. Furthermore, if the budget exceeds what you want to spend on the project, you have a convenient way of analyzing the project to identify components that can be eliminated, thus reducing the scope, so that the project can be completed for the desired amount.

Labor Cost Estimates

Labor cost estimates are also known as budgeted cost of work scheduled (BCWS), or *planned value*. When you start working on the project, you will compare actual costs of work performed (ACWP) to the planned value to determine spending variances. You can also compare earned value (or budgeted cost of work performed, BCWP) to the planned value figures to determine schedule variance. This will be covered in detail in Chapter 12.

Contingencies

In addition to labor, materials, capital equipment, and outside service costs that go into a project budget, you may also include
some buffer or padding to cover risks. These are called contingencies, and the two kinds of contingencies that are normally placed
in project budgets will be discussed in detail in Chapter 11.

Fiscal Budgeting of Projects

Many organizations try to budget projects on a fiscal basis, even
though the job spans several years. This creates a host of problems. The main reason is that these same organizations often practice a ridiculous budgeting system in which a department that
does not spend all of its budgeted funds in a given fiscal year
loses those funds the next year. This practice should have been
outlawed years ago, but it persists. The result is that organizations
try to find ways to spend every penny they have budgeted so they
won't lose it. This creates huge waste. Many of these organizations are in the U.S. government.

Furthermore, as I mentioned earlier in this chapter, project
budgets are based on estimates, whereas department budgets are
based on headcounts, history, and projections. These estimates
can usually be within a few percent. Project budgets typically
have tolerances of ± 10 to 20 percent, so to expect them not to vary
is ludicrous.

Project schedules are dynamic, not static, so as they
accelerate or fall behind, spending likewise varies, making the
total variance of project spending very large. Cutting the funding
of a project because all monies were not spent in the fiscal year
demonstrates a lack of understanding of the dynamic nature of
projects!

9

CHAPTER

Project Scheduling

In previous editions of this book I have demonstrated how to do network computations in the main body of the book. However, with the ready availability of cost-effective scheduling software, almost nobody does such calculations manually any more. I do believe that you should understand how they are done, or else you won't understand what the software is telling you. So, in this edition, an Appendix covers this topic.

This chapter will concentrate on the practical creation of a schedule using software, and on managing resources, which is the major problem you will encounter in developing your schedule.

THE BASICS OF SCHEDULING

Before we go any further, let's make sure you are familiar with all of the terms and concepts of scheduling. If you are absolutely sure you know this material, feel free to skip to the next section. Otherwise, read on.

Until about 1960, projects were scheduled using bar charts. Henry Gantt worked out a system of notation for creating such charts and using them to report progress, so they are commonly called Gantt charts. A simple example is shown in Figure 9.1.

> How does a project get to be a year behind schedule? One day at a time.
>
> — Fred Brooks
> System 360 Chief Designer, IBM

This is the way Gantt charts were drawn before 1960. Notice that the chart gives no indication of whether activities B and C depend on the completion of activity A or whether they just coincidentally start when A is completed. This means that if activity A slips, we can't tell what impact it will have on subsequent tasks.

F I G U R E   9.1

A Simple Gantt Chart

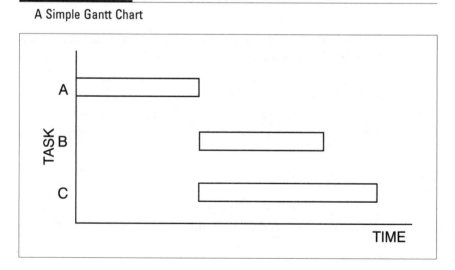

For that reason, a method of showing such dependencies was developed in the late 1950s. The relationships among tasks were shown using arrow diagrams. Two different forms were developed. One was called critical path method (CPM), and the other was called program evaluation and review technique (PERT). The difference between the two systems is that PERT makes use of a calculated task duration and allows you to estimate probabilities of completing work, whereas CPM just makes use of estimated task durations with no regard for probabilities.

Both systems allow you to determine which series of activities (or path) in a project will take the longest time to complete. When the project is scheduled to end at the point where the critical path ends, it will have no latitude. Shorter paths, however, will have latitude, which is called either slack or float. The slack or float provides

> **Critical path:** a path that has no float and is the longest path through the project
>
> **Float or slack:** any path shorter than the critical path will have latitude that is commonly called either float or slack.

some protection from unexpected events or from inaccurate estimates. You never want to have a schedule that has no float, as the risk is extremely high that you won't meet your completion date.

In addition to having two systems, there are two forms of notation. One is called activity-on-arrow (AOA) and the other is activity-on-node (AON). In AOA notation, the arrow represents the work to be done, and the circle represents an event—either the beginning of another activity or the completion of a previous one. This is shown in Figure 9.2.

For AON notation, a box (or node) is used to show the task itself, and the arrows simply show the sequence in which work is done. This is shown in Figure 9.3.

F I G U R E 9.2

Activity-on-Arrow Notation

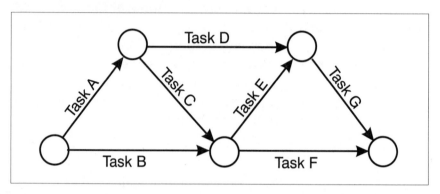

Since both systems get the same schedule results, it makes no difference which one is used. However, most software produces only one of them and it is usually AON. A few programs, such as Primavera, allow you to choose the system you prefer.

Arrow diagrams allow you to determine whether it is possible for a task to start at a certain time. When you create a large schedule using bar charting you may inadvertently show tasks

F I G U R E 9.3

Activity-on-Node Notation

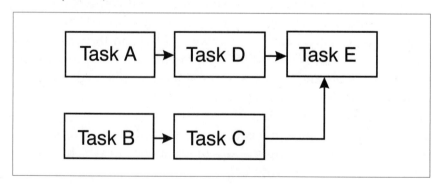

starting before a predecessor is finished, and if this isn't possible, then your schedule won't work. This was one of the main reasons why CPM and PERT were created in the first place. So, if you want to create a schedule that will work, you should always work out the interdependencies among all of the activities in a project.

However, you don't want to give an arrow diagram to people to use as a working tool. They are too hard to read. The bar chart is a much better working tool because it is simple to read. Fortunately, all scheduling software will produce a bar chart for you. Be careful, though. One common error people make is to tell the soft-

> Be careful not to enter too many "must start on" and "must end on" dates into your schedule or you will create a schedule that simply won't work.

ware that every task must start on certain dates and end on certain dates, and if these conflict with what is naturally going to happen based on task dependencies the software will just regurgitate your input, and you may be left with a useless schedule. The software itself is designed to tell you when tasks will start and end, based on their durations, resource allocations, and interdependencies. If you tamper too much with dates, you will have a garbage-in-garbage-out situation.

Furthermore, if you don't enter predecessor or successor information into your software, then

> You *must* enter dependencies in order for your software to work out where your critical path and float are.

it cannot work out your critical path and determine how much slack or float you have on noncritical paths. This approach relegates the software to a presentation tool at best, and only allows you to document your failures.

Although both CPM and PERT find the critical path and float in a project, the emphasis has always been on the critical path. However, in today's world, the objective of project management is universally to complete a project in the minimum possible time, and this is a primary advantage of using arrow diagrams. The shortest possible schedule will be the one in which as many tasks as possible are done in parallel.

> The real advantage of network diagramming is to help you find all the places where work can be done in parallel, thus creating the shortest possible schedule.

This can only be done using a computer, as the resource allocation problem becomes formidable and manual methods are nearly impossible for all but the most trivial of networks.

Before You Use the Software

There is a great temptation to create a schedule by entering data into the templates provided by the software. There is a major flaw in this approach. You can only see a small segment of a large project schedule on the screen, and if activities have predecessors or successors that are off the screen, it can be almost impossible to determine what they are.

> You should construct the schedule on paper before entering it into your computer.

A better approach is to either sketch the network on paper, or use PostIt® notes on a whiteboard to work out the logic. A major advantage of this method is that a group can participate, and members can see possibilities that you may miss if you do the schedule individually. Then, once the logic is worked out to everyone's satisfaction, you can have someone transcribe the network into your scheduling software and let the computer generate dates for activities.

In creating a schedule this way, follow this guideline: if two tasks can be done in parallel from a logical standpoint, draw them that way. It is tempting to consider resource limitations while constructing a schedule, but if you do it takes forever to work out the network, and you may have unnecessarily tied your hands.

For example, suppose I have assigned Mary to two tasks that can logically be done in parallel. When I start constructing my schedule, I decide that it won't be possible to do the work in parallel, since Mary can't do two things at the same time. So I draw them in series instead.

But who says that Mary *must* do them both? Perhaps Jane can do one of them and Mary can do the other. That will produce a shorter schedule than if the two tasks are done in series.

In addition, suppose one task has a 10-day duration and the second has a 5-day duration. They are parallel, but the 10-day task also has 5 days of float. Thus, these two tasks can be done in series without impacting project completion, and Mary can do both of them. This is shown in Figure 9.4.

A little thought reveals that following this rule means that you are adopting a hidden assumption that you have unlimited resources—which, naturally, you don't. So you find that you have double- and triple-scheduled members of your team.

Not a good rule, you say.

True, but think about it this way. An unlimited resource schedule will produce the shortest possible schedule. Since most projects are assigned an end date from the beginning, if you create an unlimited resource schedule and it won't meet the imposed end date, then you are in trouble before you do any work and you may as well know it. You know it will only get worse when you factor in your limited fund of resources.

The important point is that the software enables everyone to see what possibilities exist for a project and to make informed decisions about tradeoffs. Remember, you are always constrained by

F I G U R E 9.4

Schedule with Mary on Both Tasks

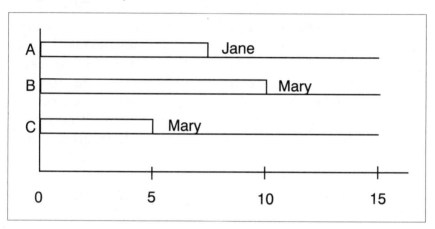

PCTS, and if you can't meet the required time with the available resources (this equates to cost), then you will have to find more help,
reduce scope, or—heaven help you—reduce performance (quality
of work). The latter is generally unacceptable but is what your team
may do if you don't give them relief from time or scope.

SOFTWARE CAPABILITIES

I have mentioned elsewhere that there are lots of people who
think that project management is just scheduling. If they provide
you with a software program, they have made you into an instant
project manager; or, at the very least, into a scheduler. Of course,
this couldn't be further from the truth.

The software can't work out dependencies for you. That is
something you must do yourself. Nor can it tell you how long a
task will take. All it can do is computations. It is a tool, and unless you know how to deal with the various issues in a project all
that tool can do is help you document your failures with great
precision.

The software can't work out dependencies for you.

In fact, we have given thousands of individuals powerful scheduling software without training them how to manage. This is like giving someone a fantastic accounting program when they don't know the difference between a debit and a credit and expecting the software to turn them into a skilled accountant.

Giving a person a powerful scheduling software program, when he knows nothing about project management, just allows him to document his failures with great precision!

One huge advantage of using software is that it will drop out weekends, holidays, and vacation periods for employees, and tell you the actual dates on which activities should start and finish. Doing calendar computations manually is an onerous task, and the software is worth its weight in gold just for this alone.

A schedule is initially developed under the assumption of unlimited resources.

Resource Leveling

As I have said above, a schedule is initially developed under the assumption of unlimited resources. Once this is done, the software can show you where you have overloaded your resources. If there is enough float in your schedule, it can make use of that float to schedule tasks so that resources are no longer overloaded and the end date can be met. This is called *time-critical* resource allocation. The software is instructed to level resources without slipping the already determined end date. It will then make use of task float to delay activities until resources become available, but it will only delay a task to the point at which it runs out of float. To delay it any further would cause the end date to be missed.

However, if there is insufficient float in the schedule to level resources completely, the software can be instructed to relieve the overloads, even if it means sliding out the end date. This is called *resource-critical* allocation. Under this condition you may find that a schedule that was going to end in December 2006 under the unlimited resource assumption is now going to end in the year 2013 because it is starved for resources.

Clearly, this is an unacceptable solution. Nobody is going to accept a schedule that is going to take so long to complete. So what good is the resource-critical method?

Simple: it creates a *moment of truth.*

It alerts everyone to what is going to happen to a project if something isn't done. More help is needed, scope must be reduced, or performance requirements must be relaxed; otherwise the project will take forever.

The advantage is partly psychological. In the days before software, when we had this problem we had no credibility with our managers when we told them about the problem.

"I need more help," you would tell your boss.

"Quit whining and get the job done," the boss would snarl.

And all too often, you pulled it off.

And shot yourself in the foot in the process.

Why?

Because they expected you to pull it off the next time. After all, you've just proven that you didn't need all the help that you claimed you needed. You were just whining.

Please don't misunderstand me. I have no objection to pulling off a miracle once in a while. But I don't want it to become the expectation for all time to come. After all, how did I pull it off this time? Through blood, sweat, and tears. Every member of the team put in extraordinary effort to meet the end date. You don't want them to have to do that on every project, because it may not work next time. So if I get shot in the foot, my company may be set up for a fall next time around.

Using software to do a what-if schedule gives you more credibility. We all know that computers simply output garbage when we input garbage, but it is *calculated garbage,* and thus more believable! That is a psychological advantage that you never had in the days before software.

Guidelines for Minor and Major Increments in a Schedule

You may fall into the trap of scheduling work in more detail than you can manage. This is especially tempting when you are using scheduling software. After all, the software can compute virtually any kind of network you create.

Sure, but can you do the work as scheduled?

I know about this trap. I have made most of the mistakes you can make in managing projects. I got carried away and scheduled work in increments of days. The only problem was, we couldn't control the work that accurately, so before I could get the schedule published it was off, and my boss was on my back because I had already missed a scheduled date. The net result was that I spent all my time managing the schedule rather than letting the schedule help me manage the project.

The first guideline, then, is to never schedule work in more detail than you can control. For some people, this means you can schedule to the nearest hour. Projects to overhaul power genera-

Conduct lessons learned reviews in a timely manner.

tors are sometimes scheduled to this level of detail, because they have enough history to know how long each step will take, and also because getting the generator back on line as quickly as possible is very important.

For others, scheduling to the nearest day is all that they can control, and in some cases, the nearest week is adequate. In very large projects that last several years, you may find work being scheduled to the nearest month.

As for major durations, the first rule is that no task should have a duration greater than four to six weeks. Furthermore, you must have a marker that indicates when the task is actually complete, and this can be very difficult with nontangible tasks; that is, those that have no tangible deliverables. When there is no specification or deliverable that indicates task completion, then you must use some kind of exit criteria. As an example, the work is examined and a "pass-fail" judgment is made. This is totally qualitative, but it is the only thing you have where aesthetics are involved.

> **Guidelines**
> No task should have a duration greater than four to six weeks. For knowledge work, the maximum duration should be one to three weeks.

The rule about four- to six-week increments applies to long-duration tasks. It is especially useful to apply to outside vendor projects, such as long-lead capital equipment. It is a good idea to require your vendors to report progress on their projects in minimum increments of four to six weeks, and the progress report must go beyond an affirmation that the work is on schedule. You must require that they report progress using some such method as earned value tracking (see Chapter 10) or, if this is not possible, then they should use exit criteria to ensure that progress is really what they say it is.

The next rule applies to engineering, programming and other knowledge work, in which there may be no tangible deliverables. For such work, the rule is that work should be scheduled in maximum increments of one to three weeks. This is very important to enforce, or you can bet that such work will reach 90 percent completion and stay there forever. The progress report for knowledge work invariably looks like the graph shown in Figure 9.5.

This is actually a universal graph. Here's how it is generated. Suppose the work is supposed to take 10 weeks to complete. This is by agreement with the person doing the work. At the end of the first week, you check on progress.

F I G U R E   9.5

Progress Graph for Knowledge Work

"How's your project work going?" you ask.

"Fine," says the person.

"I can't plot 'fine,'" you say, "I need to know what percent complete the job is."

Now what do you think she will tell you?

You guessed it. It's the end of the first week on a 10-week job, so she must be 10 percent complete.

And at the end of the second week?

Right again. It will be 20 percent complete.

This is called *reverse-inferential* progress reporting, and is a method used when people can't tell exactly how much they have actually done.

Now you notice that when the work reaches around 80 or 90 percent complete, the graph turns horizontal. One of two things happens. Either the person has an existential crisis, which means that she discovers the part of the iceberg that's underneath the water (that is, all the work she has to do that she has forgotten), or she is in the debugging phase of her design work. If it is an iceberg problem, she would have to show that she is really only perhaps 50 percent complete—which would mean that she would have to report negative progress. This is shown in Figure 9.6.

However, we know we can't report negative progress because senior managers get very agitated if we do this. The best alternative is to report only that progress is stalled.

In the situation where debugging has started, it is common to pass the deadline and then find the solution to the problem, so that the work is completed in one simple step. This is shown in Figure 9.7.

RESOURCE ALLOCATION

If you are going to manage resources in a project, you have to specify who is working on each task and at what allocation level. When you do this, be careful. Microsoft Project operates

F I G U R E 9.6

Graph Showing Negative Progress

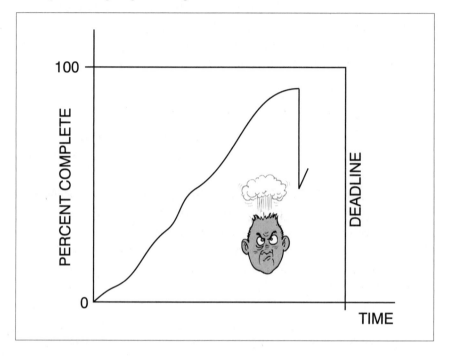

differently than other scheduling software in how it treats allocation level and task duration.

If you specify that a task duration is 10 working days, and that Ron is working on the task half time (50 percent would be what you specify), most software programs will leave the task duration at 10 days. The calendar duration is treated as *fixed*, or as being the same as the working time minus any weekends or holidays that may intervene. With MS Project, however, you get a different result. Project will change the duration to 20 calendar days. The assumption is that duration of the task is *variable*, meaning that the calendar duration depends on the rate at which the person works on the task. You can change the default so that Project

F I G U R E 9.7

Graph Showing Progress Being Completed in One Step

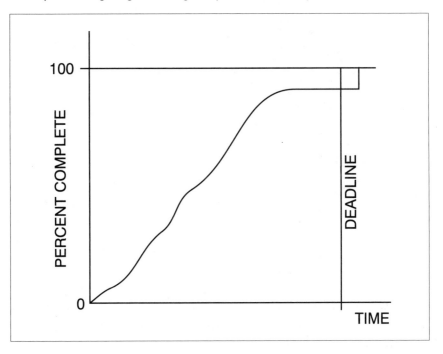

works like other programs, treating task durations as fixed. However, there is a certain logic to the Project default. Ideally, you should always estimate working time and convert to calendar time in exactly the way that Project does it.

In any case, be careful that you assign the correct resource availability or you will get an invalid result. For example, I had a fellow tell me that his company had always assigned people to tasks on the assumption that they were working about 80 percent of the time on projects. When they continuously missed project deadlines, they did a time study to determine what was really happening. To do this, people logged their time once an hour for two weeks and then analyzed the logs. To their surprise, they

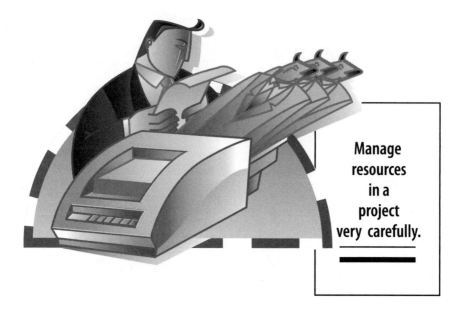

**Manage
resources
in a
project
very carefully.**

found that people were only working on projects 25 percent of the
time, not the 80 percent that they had assumed! This meant that
their schedules were off by a factor of three because of their incorrect allocation assumption.

This is a common cause of problems. The only time you ever
get 80 percent availability from people is when they are tied to
their workstations, and the only people for whom this is true are
factory workers. You may get close to 80 percent availability from
them, but for knowledge workers—who aren't tied to their work
stations—you'll never get such a high level. It is more likely to be
around 50 or 60 percent.

The thing is, you have to know what that number is if you
are going to correctly schedule work. So it helps to do a time
study, as was described above, to determine that level. Have people log their time once an hour—it need not be more often—to discover their true availability. If the number seems too low, then
you have to remove the causes.

**Knowledge
worker productivity
is never more than
50%–60%**

Major Causes of Reduced Availability

There are two major causes of reduced resource availability. One is having people work on too many projects at the same time. The other is overallocation of people to their work. When people have to work on more than one project at the same time, they constantly have to shift back and forth between them. This is called multitasking. The trouble is, every time a person "shifts gears," to use the normal expression, it takes time for them to remember where they were, get their work in place, and so on. This added time is called setup time in manufacturing, and, remember, we learned years ago that setup time is total waste. Setup time adds no value to the product. So, in manufacturing, an effort has been made to reduce setup time as much as possible or to eliminate it altogether by running a process continuously.

Think about it this way. Suppose you are sitting at your desk working and the phone rings. You answer it. The person says, "Sorry, I have the wrong number," and you hang up.

"Now where was I?" you think.

You have completely lost your train of thought. Time management experts say that you will typically lose 10 to 15 minutes every time you get interrupted, so if you get four phone calls in an hour, you may easily lose the entire hour!

So let's assume that each time you switch from one project to another you add 15 minutes setup time to each task. As an example, suppose you had planned to work on a single project task all day. You could finish the task in that single eight-hour day if you could just work on it continuously.

However, if you are working on several projects, you will be expected to share your time between them, and if you get no more than one hour of uninterrupted work at a time, your eight-hour task will take at least nine hours and forty-five minutes. This is shown in Figure 9.8.

We assume that all tasks have some setup time built in, so we add 15 minutes for each time the task is stopped and restarted. That is seven increments above the single eight-hour block, so it adds one hour and forty-five minutes of setup time, rather than two hours.

I can almost guarantee you that this task will actually take 10 to 12 hours to complete, rather than the original 8 hours. The 15 minutes of setup time is a very conservative number.

F I G U R E   9.8

Eight-Hour Task Performed in One-Hour Increments

Queuing and Resource Availability

The second major cause of reduced availability is from overallocation of people to their work. To understand this, we need to understand the basics of queuing theory. You may never have studied queuing theory, but I can assure you that you have experienced it. Every time you try to get onto a busy highway at rush hour, you experience the effects of queuing.

As an example, Raleigh, North Carolina, has a beltway around the city. At rush hour, you can bet that the beltway is packed with cars, all doing 60 to 70 miles an hour. In fact, let's assume that the cars are packed so tightly that you couldn't put another car on the road if your life depended on it.

No problem. Everyone is happy.

How can this be?

No one wants on the beltway and no one wants off.

Of course, you realize that this is a fictitious condition, which could only exist in a steady-state universe. One that may have

The second major cause of reduced availability is from overallocation of people to their work.

been approximated about 1800, when people weren't in as much of a hurry as they are today.

Today, we live in a turbulent universe. Everyone wants to be where they are going ten minutes ago.

So suppose someone wants on this bumper-to-bumper beltway. If no one gets off, how long will it take this interloper to get onto the beltway?

You guessed it. It will take forever!

Queuing theory shows how long you must wait to get access to a system as a function of how fully it is already loaded. The curves look something like the one in Figure 9.9. Notice that, by definition, a system can't be loaded beyond 100 percent. It doesn't matter. At 100 percent, you have to wait forever to get access to the system, just like our driver has to wait to get onto the beltway.

F I G U R E 9.9

Waiting Time as a Function of System Loading

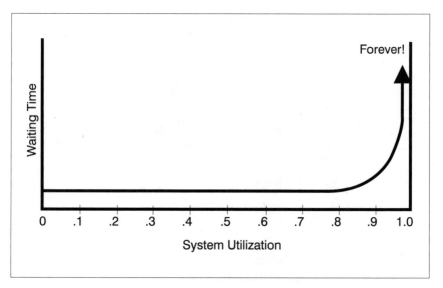

Okay, what does this have to do with projects?

First, let's think about a practical application of queuing theory. Manufacturing people have known for a long time that you shouldn't load a factory more than about 85 percent on the average. You may exceed that level occasionally, but if you consistently stay higher than 85 percent, you are asking for big trouble, because if anything happens out of the ordinary—a machine breaks down, or someone calls in sick, or a supplier is late delivering materials—you are already so high on the curve that your waiting time goes to forever in a heartbeat.

However, we don't load people to 85 percent. We load them to 120 percent. We know that if we only loaded them to 85 percent, they would sit around and do nothing during that 15 percent free time, and that would be costly, so we make certain that they have no free time. This is commonly called "being lean and mean"—a biological metaphor. The question is, do you want to get rid of all of your body fat? No way. You want some for reserve energy. The same is true of an organization. Carrying lean and mean too far is short-sighted.

When you have no reserve capacity, you can't respond to surprises, glitches, or even opportunities. And since Murphy's Law

> No system should be loaded beyond 85 percent capacity for very long.

guarantees that there will be some glitches in every project, you can also be sure that there will be delays caused by queuing, and that the result will be a late project.

Every organization should have some reserve capacity if it is going to respond to turbulence. But tell that to senior management, who believe that lean and mean is the correct way to fly!

A few people are beginning to realize that the lean-and-mean paradigm has gone too far. Downs (1996) was a downsizing consultant until he realized this. His book *Corporate Executions* goes into far greater detail about the pitfalls of going too far with cutting fat from an organization than is possible in this chapter.

And what do you do about setup time?

You reduce it by prioritizing projects.

As a general rule, no one should be working on more than two or three projects. Ideally, a person would be on a single project until it is completed, and then would shift to the next job.

Can this really be justified?

You bet.

When I first realized this, I was working with a company that was having difficulty getting new products released. They would go along for most of the year and nothing would be released. Then headquarters would call and ask why no new products had come out the back door.

"We're working on them," would be the response.

"Well, we want to see something get to market by the end of the year," headquarters would tell them.

> You can do *anything*, but you can't do everything!
>
> — From the cover of
> *Fast Company Magazine,*
> May 2000

So there would be a big push to release all of the products that were in various states of completion, and they would turn out 10 or 12 new products near the end of the year.

Do you know what happens when you release that many products in December?

Absolutely nothing.

Manufacturing can't get set up to make them, and even if they could, the salespeople couldn't sell them.

But let's pretend that they could both make them and sell them, and let's assume that they were able to sell all of those new products during the entire month of December. If that happened, you would have a sales graph like the one in Figure 9.10.

F I G U R E 9.10

Sales for All Products in December

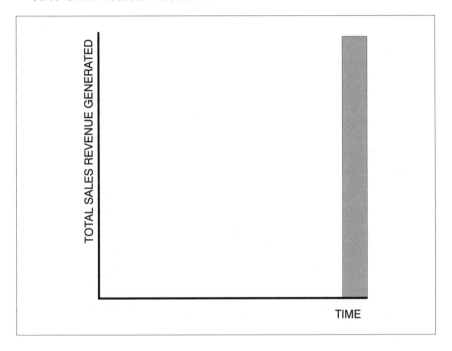

I said to the managers at this company, "You need to prioritize your projects. Work on them one at a time and get them out the back door so that they start selling sooner."

It took nearly three years to make it happen, but by that time they were releasing a new product every month or so. That is, they had a steady stream of new products entering the market.

The result can be shown in another graph, superimposed on the one from Figure 9.10. As you can see, if a new product comes out at the beginning of the year, and we assume flat sales, you get the rectangle labeled Product 1. The next month, Product 2 is released, again with flat sales throughout the year. Then Product 3 comes out, and so on. This is shown in Figure 9.11.

F I G U R E 9.11

Sales for a Constant Stream of New Products

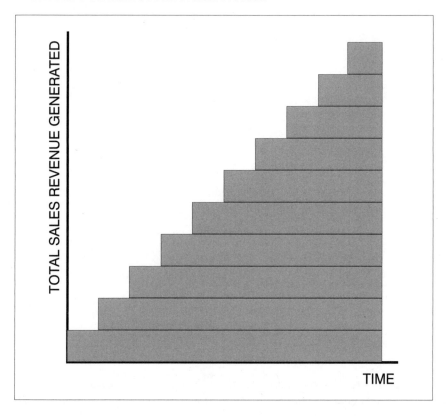

As the graph indicates, the sales for the year approximate a triangle. The area under the triangle shows the units of money multiplied by time. This is called the *time-value of money*, or interest or cost of capital. So which figure has the greatest area, the rectangle for the month of December or the triangle for the entire year? It's a no-brainer. The triangle has considerably greater value to the company than the rectangle.

This demonstrates that the only economically viable approach that a company can take is to prioritize its projects. To have "all the balls in the air" at once is to confuse activity with progress. When you ask a manager what must be done first, and she tells you "It all has to be done," she is overlooking the time value of money and its impact on the organization.

Think of this in reverse: when you are late to market with a new product, you have lost both the revenue that would have been generated by sales during that period and the cost of capital associated with it. That is why it is so important to complete projects on time.

CONCLUSION

In closing, let me say that if you follow the guidelines in this chapter your schedules will be more workable. The only thing that you have to worry about is whether your estimates of task durations are realistic, and these can usually be improved through consensual estimating.

Whatever approach you follow, the schedule should be used to help you manage the project, not make you a slave to software.

10
CHAPTER

Managing Project Communications[1]

According to the PMBOK, "project communications management is the Knowledge Area that employs the processes required to ensure timely and appropriate generation, collection, distribution, storage, retrieval, and ultimate disposition of project information" (PMBOK 2004, p. 221). Communications management has to do with determining who needs information, when they need it, and how it will be transmitted. It does not include the act of communicating itself, although this is certainly an important area with which every project manager should be familiar. The art of communication is not specific to project management, and it deals with such things as how to write effectively, whether to communicate orally or in writing, sender-receiver models, such as barriers to communication, and so on.

Every project plan should contain a communications plan that addresses these questions. The importance of such a plan can-

---

[1] Note: This chapter is largely taken from Lewis and Dudley, 2005.

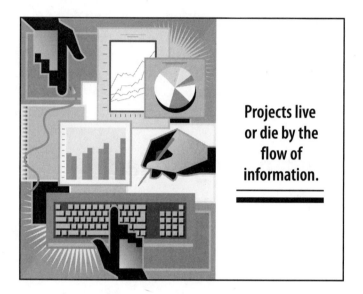

Projects live or die by the flow of information.

not be overstated. Projects live or die by the flow of information, and many problems occur simply because various stakeholders are not kept informed. John Cashman, who flew the first 777 airplane, told me that the team developed a communications plan early in the program. The result was people saying, "Oh, that's why they're doing that. I wondered about that." Furthermore, they referred to the big jet as our airplane. Being kept constantly informed gave them a sense of belonging to the entire team and a sense of ownership.

COMMUNICATIONS MANAGEMENT PROCESSES

There are four primary processes listed in the PMBOK for communications management:

1. *Communications planning.* As stated above, determining the information needs of all stakeholders: who needs what information, how frequently they need it, and how will it be given to them.

2. *Information distribution.* The process of making needed information available to those who need it in a timely manner.

3. *Performance reporting.* Collecting and distributing information on progress. This includes measuring progress, reporting status, and forecasting future results.

4. *Administrative closure.* This includes gathering information and generating and disseminating information about a phase or final project closeout.

Communications Planning

Not all stakeholders to a project have the same needs for information. The first step in communications planning is to identify all stakeholders and then survey them to determine their information needs. This will be discussed below. Communications planning is often tied to organizational planning, since the organization structure of the project will affect how information is disseminated. In addition, while it is not specifically covered by the PMBOK, as the size of a project team grows so does the overhead cost of communication. This overhead can, in fact, be very substantial and can tax the project manager to keep everyone informed of what is going on. This is because the number of channels of communications is given by the following equation:

$$C = N (N - 1) / 2$$

Inputs to Communications Planning

Communications Requirements   There is often a temptation to communicate everything to everyone (or nothing to anyone), but this can quickly become a significant burden. As was shown above, as the number of participants in a project grows so does the number of channels over which information flows, and if the amount of information also increases, it can overwhelm the communications

The methods used to convey information among all project stakeholders can vary considerably.

network. People then begin to suffer from information overload. It is therefore important that only information necessary for the correct functioning of the project be disseminated, and only to those stakeholders who actually need it. Another way to think of this is that the only information that should be communicated is information that contributes to success, or that could lead to failure if it is not communicated. To determine communications requirements, you should consider the following:

- The project organization and stakeholder responsibilities.
- Disciplines, departments, and specialties involved in the project.
- The number of individuals involved at a project and at what locations.
- External parties that want information, such as the media.

Communications Technology

The methods used to convey information among all project stakeholders can vary considerably, from brief, face-to-face encounters in the hallways, to formal meetings, to e-mail, Internet accessible databases, and video conferencing. Some factors that may affect the communications plan include:

- Immediacy needs of stakeholders. That is, do some individuals need almost real-time information about the project, or can they use simple, periodic reports?
- Availability of technology. Are the systems already in place, or would they have to be developed?
- Skills of project team members. Will team members already have required skills to operate required technology, or must some training be provided?
- Project duration. Will technology change over the life of the project, and if so, must it be incorporated into the project?

Constraints

Constraints are factors that will limit a project team's options for communicating. For example, projects in which work is contracted out will require different communications than those in which all work is done internally.

Constraints are factors that will limit a project team's options for communication.

Assumptions

We have discussed assumptions in Chapter 8, so these will not be considered in this chapter other than to say that all projects involve assumptions, which must be clarified to avoid later problems.

Tools and Techniques for Communications Planning

Stakeholder Analysis   It is important to understand the information needs of all stakeholders and ensure that they receive that information in a timely manner, using the appropriate technology. Discussion of stakeholders is contained in Chapter 6.

Outputs from Communications Planning

Communications Management Plan   Obviously the purpose of communications management planning is to produce documents that prescribe how communications in the project are to be handled. This document will, of course, be a communications management plan. It should specify the following:

- How information will be collected and filed, and in what format. What procedure will be used to update documents and ensure that everyone has the latest revision? This is very important, as failure to control revisions can lead to some members of the project team working with obsolete schedules, and so on. Usually a revision number is attached to a document, together with a date, so that you can quickly determine if the document is the most recent version.

- The information to be collected and the format in which will it be distributed. What level of detail will be provided? Are there specific terms to be used in specific ways? If so, these should be identified.

- Who receives what information, and how it will be distributed. Not all stakeholders need all information. There

**Not all
stakeholders
need all
information.**

must be a distribution matrix that specifies this. Examples
of how information is distributed include written reports,
meetings, and face-to-face verbal communication. In the
event of widely dispersed teams, this may be supple-
mented by e-mail, teleconferencing, and so on. Documents may also be distributed electronically, using either
PDF files or native files (doc, xls, msp, etc.)

- A production and distribution schedule. How often will
  each kind of information be collected and distributed? In
  some projects, project status data is collected and distributed weekly. Others may use a monthly schedule.

- A method of accessing information in between scheduled
  distributions.

- A procedure for actually revising the communications
  plan itself as the need arises. An example would be that
  when stakeholders change, the distribution list must
  change.

The communications plan may be very formal or informal,
highly structured or not, as the needs of the project dictate.

Information Distribution

Perhaps it is obvious, but information has no value unless it reaches the appropriate individuals involved in the project. Furthermore, that information must be in the proper format and must be timely. Often, because of flaws in the communications system, information reaches a person too late for him to act on it in the required manner. Also, even though the PMBOK does not discuss it, people in today's world tend to suffer from information overload, which can result in project communications being overlooked or ignored by the intended recipient. Information distribution involves implementing the communications plan and also responding to nonplanned requests for information.

Again, the PMBOK does not discuss distributing anything but information about work results. Nevertheless, stakeholders are concerned about events that may affect the work, organizational changes, and other events that could impact the project either positively or negatively.

Tools and Techniques for Information Distribution

Communications Skills   Communication is a two-way street. In involves not only the dissemination of information but the receiving of it as well. The PMBOK says that the sender is responsible for ensuring that information is clear, unambiguous, and complete, and that the receiver is responsible for making sure that information is received in its entirety and is understood correctly. I disagree with this, but if it is asked on the exam, give the PMBOK answer.

Here is the problem. The receiver cannot be held responsible for communication. Only the sender has that responsibility. I must ensure that the intended message was received and understood. An example of this is seen in air traffic control. I was flying into Chicago's O'Hare airport on a United flight, and at the time they had an audio channel on which you could listen to air traffic. The controller told a pilot to descend to a certain altitude and fly 300 knots exactly. The pilot responded, "Roger. Descend to 6000 and fly 300 or better." The controller replied, "Negative. 300 exactly!"

This is a system in which the receiver of the communication is expected to repeat back what he has heard, so that the sender can ensure that it was received correctly, and in this example the message was misunderstood. Had the controller not detected the misunderstanding, the plane would have been flying too fast, overtaking traffic ahead, and this could have been a disaster.

To make the point a little more strongly, how can the recipient of a communication know that she has misunderstood it? Clearly, she cannot. So the basic premise that we must remember as project managers is that responsibility for communication rests with the communicator, not with the recipient!

There are several dimensions to communications, and all of them can affect the ultimate outcome. These include:

- Written and oral, listening and speaking
- Internal (that is, within the project) and external—to the customer, the media, the public, and so on
- Formal (written reports, briefings, review meetings) and informal (casual memos, conversations in the hallway, and so on)
- Vertical (up and down the organization hierarchy) and horizontal (with peers)
- Information retrieval systems

Many of us share the problem of trying to find information that we have filed away somewhere. Information can be shared in projects through a number of methods, including manual and electronic filing systems, databases, project management software, and other information systems. Some of the information that project stakeholders may need includes technical drawings, design specifications, test plans, and personnel data. An information retrieval system should be designed so that people can access such information in a timely manner.

Marvin Patterson, in his book, *Accelerating Innovation* (1993), has argued that a reference librarian can be a big help to a project team that relies on processing information to develop new products. Such an individual can provide that information in a just-in-time (JIT) manner, thus improving the performance of the project team.

Information Distribution Methods   The ways in which project information can be distributed are almost endless. Though not used (much) any more, smoke signals, carrier pigeons, and telegraphy are all possibilities. On a serious note, the conventional methods include formal meetings, the grapevine, document distribution in either electronic or hard-copy format, e-mail, the project intranet, and so on.

Outputs from Information Distribution   Outputs from information distribution include project records, project reports, and project presentations.

Project records include memos, progress and status reports, purchase requisitions, correspondence, and various documents describing the project, including revisions to the plan, and so on.

Information can be shared in projects through a number of methods.

These must be maintained in some organized fashion. A project notebook (which may actually comprise a number of binders for large projects) is one way to do this. The advantage of a notebook is that you have everything in one place, and it can serve as a convenient resource when doing lessons-learned reviews later on.

Project reports are, of course, formal documents that detail project status and/or issues that need attention or have been dealt with.

Project managers are often asked to make project presentations to various stakeholders to keep them up to date on what is happening with the project. In fact, research has shown that projects are often judged negatively when stakeholders are not kept informed and when the project is not presented in a good light. It is therefore useful to "sell" your project; that is, present it in the best possible light to key stakeholders. The downside is that stakeholders can make heavy demands on project managers to keep them informed. I remember a project manager over a very large government project telling me that he spent about 60 percent of his time doing such presentations to members of congress and several other stakeholders, so that, if he had not had a project administrator who handled the day-to-day management of the job, it would have gotten into serious trouble.

Performance Reporting

Performance reporting involves the development and dissemination of documents and exhibits that show the status of the project at a given point in time. Typically, these are used to measure schedule and cost, but any number of other indicators—such as training, testing, or other project objectives—can be included.

The process of performance reporting generally includes:

- *Status reporting.* Where does the project currently stand?
- *Progress reporting.* What has been accomplished since the last status report?

- *Forecasting.* What is expected to be accomplished in the next period?

Tools for performance reporting include:

- *Performance reviews.* These are typically meetings set up so that you can present the current status of the project. They can be formal or informal, and the depth of the content will depend on the audience. Senior management reviews can be more general that those for the engineering manager, although my experience is that senior managers cannot resist getting into the details, so be prepared.

- *Variance analysis.* This involves comparing the actual value of an item to what that value should be at this time. The list of items to be measured should have been developed during project plan development (covered in Chapter 8).

- *Trend analysis.* This is tracking performance over time to see if things are improving or deteriorating. An example might be the number of bricks laid in a shift. Trend analysis could point out problems with material supply or quality. Note that trend analysis extends over time, while variance analysis focuses upon a given point. You can, of course, track the variance over time.

- *Earned value analysis.* Earned value analysis (also called earned value management in the PMBOK) is a method of tracking schedule and cost variances together. (I cover earned value analysis in great detail in Chapter 12, so I will not go into it here.)

The result of performance reporting is the actual documentation that will be distributed and archived for future use. Other outcomes might include:

- Change requests: it may be that a change in direction or emphasis might result from your review. Perhaps more staff will be needed. This will improve schedule at the expense of the budget. On the other hand, maybe things are going too well, and companion parts of the project will not be ready when you are finished.

- Budget adjustments.
- Scope additions or deletions.
- Firing the project manager.

Performance reporting should be done routinely and continue through administrative closure.

Administrative Closure

This is the process of documenting the results of your work to ensure that you have met all requirements and specifications. It should be done whenever a phase of the project is complete, and at the end of the project as well. This is valuable, since near the end of a project team members are often re-assigned and are thus not available to participate. Some items to be considered during administrative closure include:

- Collecting and archiving all project documents, including final cost and schedule information.
- Updating records and specifications to reflect what actually happened on the project.
- Revising employee databases to reflect current skills and anticipate future training needs.
- Developing the final project report, which will assess just how the project went, and review the results of the project as it relates to the resulting product. Remember, well run projects can produce lousy products!
- Performing a lessons-learned review that includes all stakeholders and team members.

11

CHAPTER

Managing Risks

When I first started teaching seminars in 1981, there were many managers who objected to discussions of risks because they considered this "negative thinking." They believed that people should always think positively. What they didn't understand is that there is a difference between being *realistic* and being either overly positive or negative.

> There is a greater probability that things will accidentally go wrong than that they will accidentally go right.
> —Murphy's Law

A risk is anything that may happen that could create an adverse effect to your schedule, costs, quality, or scope.

One of the single most important things you can do to ensure a successful project is *manage* risks. A risk is anything that could adversely affect your schedule, costs, quality, or scope. That is, a risk may impact your PCTS targets. Simply put, you either manage risks or they will manage you.

A supermacho mentality still exists that doesn't understand this. "Damn the torpedoes, full speed ahead" is an approach that sounds glamorous, but it can wreck your project.

A manager once told me that he didn't want me to suggest to his people that they pad their schedules. "I want

> Damn the torpedoes—full speed ahead!
> —Admiral David Farragut

them to be aggressive," he said. As I have remarked, there is a difference between an aggressive schedule and a foolish one. To reiterate a previous example, if you are doing construction work, and are certain that weather could delay your project, you would be derelict in your duty as a project manager to not address potential delays. You'd do so by allowing a bit longer for work to be completed than it would take if there were no weather delays. This is called padding the schedule, and is proper risk management in construction.

> What we anticipate seldom occurs. What we least expect generally happens.
> —Benjamin Disraeli

In step 4 of The Lewis Method you are asked if SWOT and risks are okay. This was discussed briefly in Chapter 6. You will note that step 6 also asks if risks are okay. So, there are two specific places in a project where risk management is important—in planning strategy and in implementation planning. Actually, it is important that you constantly ask "What

There is a difference between threats and risks.

might go wrong?" so that you can anticipate and deal with risks, even in the execution phase of the project.

Also in Chapter 6, I pointed out that there is a difference between threats and risks. A risk is something that you can do yourself, such as having an accident, or that can happen to you in an impersonal way, such as bad weather. A threat, on the other hand, is something that will usually be done to you by some entity, whether a person or an organization. As an example, a threat to project success is that a competitor beats you to market with a new product. In practice, it is okay to lump the two together for the purpose of analysis and contingency planning.

THE RISK MANAGEMENT PROCESS

There are three steps in the risk management process:

1. Identify risks and threats by asking, "What could go wrong?" or "What kind of threats exist?"
2. Quantify threats and risks by assigning them a risk priority number (RPN).
3. Develop contingency plans to deal with risks that cannot be ignored.

Risk Identification

As I said above, you need to identify risks that may impact your strategy and your implementation plan. To revisit another example, if you are developing a new product using cutting-edge technology, the possibility exists that you won't be able to get it to work. The more unproven the technology, the higher the probability that you will have difficulty. One way to manage such risk is to do a feasibility study to see if you can make the new technology work before you launch a full-scale development effort. If you can't get the results you want, you can fall back on more proven technology.

Conduct
lessons-learned
reviews in
a timely
manner.

If you launch a development program using unproven technology and can't make it work, the consequences are far more serious than if you do a feasibility study and reject the new approach. For one thing, it is more obvious to everyone that a feasibility study is a success regardless of the outcome. If you say yes, we can make it work, that is a success; but so is the negative result, because it will save you a lot of grief trying to make something work that can't be done.

When you get to the implementation planning stage of your project, you again want to identify potential implementation problems. In this case, the WBS can be used to guide your thinking.

I previously used a yard project as an example of developing a WBS. That WBS is repeated in Figure 11.1.

Now, suppose I want to do risk management. For each task in the WBS I ask, "What could go wrong?" Here are some examples for each task:

FIGURE 11.1

WBS for a Yard Project

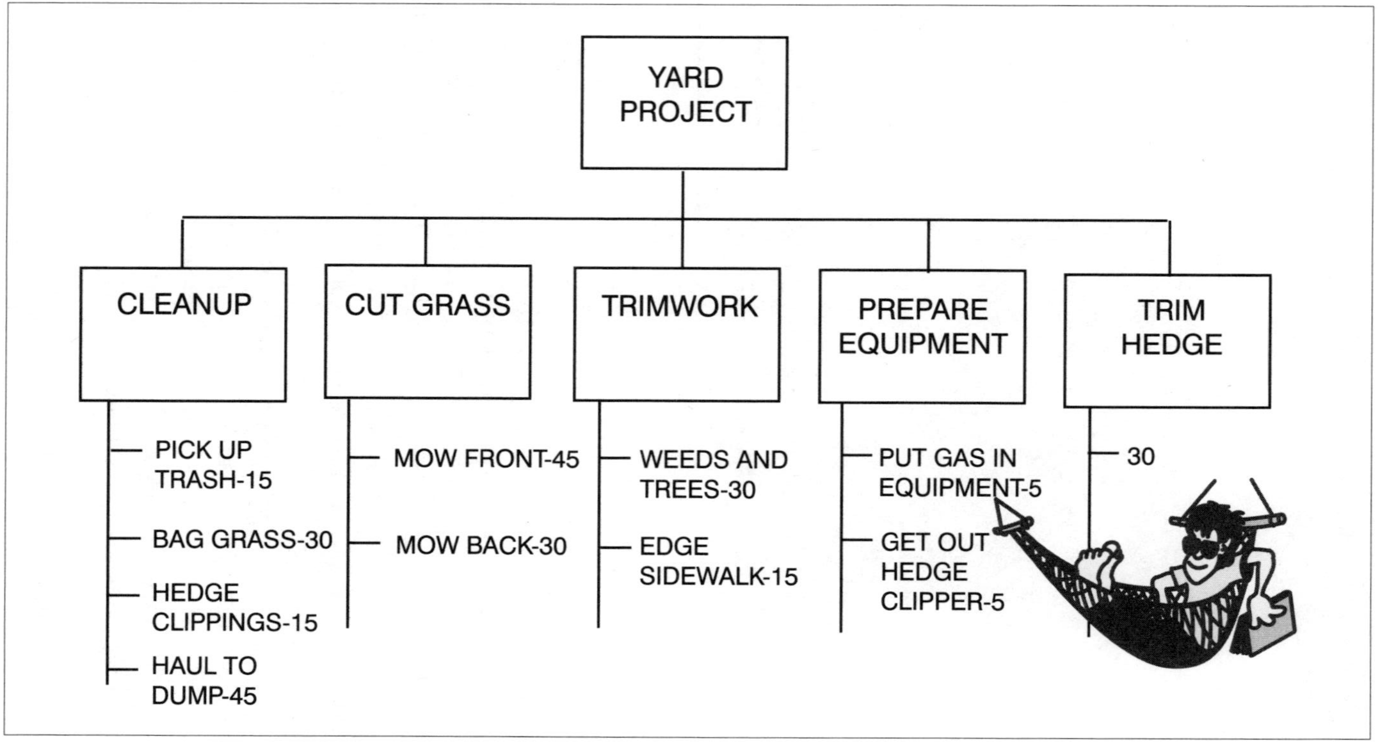

1. *Cleanup:* The dump may be closed when we get there, so we have wasted time driving over there. The contingency would be to call and see if the dump is open.

2. *Cut grass:* It might rain while we are cutting grass. The contingency would be to check the weather forecast and schedule the activity on a day when good weather is forecast.

3. *Trimwork:* You run out of string for your string trimmer. The contingency would be to keep a supply of string on hand.

4. *Prepare equipment:* Your mower runs out of gas. The contingency would be to make sure you have plenty of gas before you start.

5. *Trim hedge:* You might trim unevenly, and the yard would look bad. The contingency would be to have someone do the trimming that is more skilled at it.

I have listed only one risk for each task. Clearly, more than one thing could go wrong on complex tasks, so you list all of them, then quantify them and deal with the more serious ones.

Be careful at this stage in planning that people don't go into "analysis paralysis." You are likely to identify the most likely risks fairly quickly. Trying to find every single thing that could go wrong is unproductive. However, you should be careful not to reject a risk simply because you consider it highly unlikely to occur. As you will see in a subsequent section of this chapter, there are low-probability events that have a very severe impact on the project if they do occur. These should never be ignored.

RISK QUANTIFICATION

We know that all risks are not equal in their impact on a project. The question is, how do you decide which ones you can ignore and which ones you should manage? The desired approach would be to find some way to prioritize the risks. This can be done by calculating risk priority numbers (RPNs) to them. Three factors contribute to the RPN. First is the *probability* that the risk may occur. Second is the *severity* of the effect on the project if it should occur. And third is the question of whether you can *detect* the risk before it hits you.

This risk management methodology was worked out in an engineering discipline called failure mode effects analysis (FMEA). When designing a product, an engineer is supposed to identify possible modes of failure for various components, then ask what the severity of that failure may be and whether it can be detected. As an example, your dome light may burn out in your car, and you could have your transmission seize up. The probability of both occurrences may be very low. However, the severity of a dome light burning out is far lower than if the transmission seizes. Further, you will know immediately if your transmission seizes, but you may not know until you open your door at night that your dome light has burned out, since you may not notice it during the daylight.

To calculate RPNs, we use three tables. The first assigns a rank of 1 to10 to probability, based on a logarithmic probability scale. The second table assigns a similar rank to severity, and the third does the same for detection.

In the original FMEA approach, detection means that you may or may not be able to tell a failure has occurred in a product. For example, if you have manufactured a car that has a crack inside the engine block, you may not be able to detect that crack before the car leaves the factory. On the other hand, if a tire goes flat, that is easy to spot and correct before the car is shipped. If a fault can be detected with certainty, the number assigned is 1. If it absolutely can't be detected, it gets a rank of 10.

The problem with this mode of detection is that it usually yields a 1 when used in project risk analysis, and so loses its utility. I think a more helpful way to consider detection is to ask whether a failure mode can be detected *before* it happens.

Table 11.1 is used to quantify risk probability.

T A B L E 11.1

Probability of Occurrence

Probability of occurrence	Possible occurrence rates	Rank
Very high: occurrence is almost certain	≥ 1 in 2	10
	1 in 3	9
High: repeated occurrences possible	1 in 8	8
	1 in 20	7
Moderate: occasional occurrences	1 in 80	6
	1 in 400	5
	1 in 2,000	4
Low: relatively few occurrences	1 in 15,000	3
	1 in 150,000	2
Remote: occurrence is unlikely	≤ 1 in 1,500,000	1

Table 11.2 is used to quantify the severity of the failure. Finally, Table 11.3 is used to quantify detection capability.

Examples of RPN Calculation

An example that I find helpful for illustrating risk management is to assume that you are riding a bicycle from the East Coast to the West Coast of the United States. You identify several risks that could affect your trip, and estimate the numbers shown in Table 11.4.

You will see that having a flat tire and being hit by a car both have RPNs of 200 points, which would imply that they are equal in importance. However, they are *qualitatively* very different. The RPN for having a flat tire is 200 points because the probability is high and detection capability is poor. Getting hit by a car has a very low probability, but high severity and poor detection. These two risks demand very different responses. This is why we talk about risk *management,* not just risk *identification.*

T A B L E   11.2

Severity of the Effect

Effect	Criteria: severity of effect	Rank
Hazardous—without warning	Project severely impacted, possible cancellation, with no warning.	10
Hazardous—with warning	Project severely impacted, possible cancellation, with warning.	9
Very high	Major impact on project schedule, budget, or performance; may cause severe delays, overruns, or degradation of performance.	8
High	Project schedule, budget, or performance impacted significantly; job can be completed, but customer will be very dissatisfied.	7
Moderate	Project schedule, budget, or performance impacted some; customer will be dissatisfied.	6
Low	Project schedule, budget, or performance impacted slightly; customer will be mildly dissatisfied.	5
Very low	Some impact to project; customer will be aware of impact.	4
Minor	Small impact to project; average customer will be aware of impact.	3
Very minor	Impact so small that it would be noticed only by a very discriminating customer.	2
None	No effect.	1

As a general rule, *any time severity is in the range of 8 to 10 points* you should require that some step be taken to deal with the risk. This is especially important to consider when probability is low. People tend to ignore risks when they think there is a very low likelihood of occurrence.

The Challenger space shuttle disaster is a good example of this. Many of the members of the team responsible for the launch believed that the probability of failure of the O-ring seals was very

T A B L E   11.3

Detection Capability

Detection	Rank
Absolute uncertainty	10
Very remote	9
Remote	8
Very low	7
Low	6
Moderate	5
Moderately high	4
High	3
Very high	2
Almost certain	1

T A B L E   11.4

RPNs for a Bike Trip

Identified Risk	P	S	D	RPN
Flat tire	10	2	10	200
Get hit by a car	2	10	10	200
Bad weather	10	2	2	40

low. Perhaps it was. Nevertheless, the severity of failure was a 10, as demonstrated by the fact that the explosion killed all of the astronauts aboard. Had the team considered severity and followed the rule, they would have delayed the launch until the temperature rose.

That particular disaster is also a good example of groupthink, and CRM Learning (see the resources listed at back of book) offers a video that discusses this. Groups are particularly prone to ignore risks when they are under pressure to get a job done, as was the case with Challenger. If you don't remember the history, Christina McAuliff was supposed to address congress from space. This was a big political event, so the team felt pressured to launch on schedule. For more on groupthink and how to avoid it, see Chapter 15.

> Regardless of the value of the RPN, when severity is high, you must do something to manage the associated risk.

Develop Contingency Plans

As I stated earlier, it is not enough to identify and quantify risks. The idea is to manage them. There are a number of responses to risk:

1. Risk avoidance.
2. Mitigation (reduction, such as using air bags).
3. Transfer (as in loss prevention through insurance).
4. Accommodate: accept and live with the risk.
5. Ignore the risk (very dangerous).

Risk Avoidance

As my colleague, Harvey Levine, has said, it is better to avoid a risk than to have to manage it. Delaying the Challenger launch would have been risk avoidance. This is a trap for the obsessive "can-do" manager. He drives on in the face of a risk and pays the consequences later on.

Risk *prevention* is a special case of risk avoidance. Japanese manufacturing has for many years employed "foolproofing" as a risk avoidance strategy. The idea is to set up the assembly process so that it cannot be done incorrectly. One example was the auto plant that, on occasion, when installing a gas tank in a car, would find that one of the four mounting

> The mouse that hath but one hole is quickly taken.
>
> — George Herbert

brackets had not been welded onto the tank. The solution was to set up a fixture to hold the tank while the brackets were being welded onto it. Feelers were attached to detect the presence of the brackets. If all four brackets were not in place, the welding machine would not weld any of them.

> It seems reasonable to say that it is always better to avoid risk than it is to manage it.
> ~ Harvey Levine

In construction projects we pad the schedule with rain-delay days, based on weather history for the area and time of year. This way we avoid the risk that we will be delayed by bad weather. In engineering design, I mentioned the use of parallel design strategies to avoid the possibility that the deadline might be missed because one strategy proves difficult to implement. In any project, risk aversion or avoidance might be the most preferable strategy to follow.

Mitigation or Severity Reduction

If we can think of contingencies in the event that a risk takes place, we may be able to mitigate its effect. Placing airbags in cars is an attempt to reduce the severity of an accident, should one occur. Stafford Beer (1981) has argued that seatbelts and airbags in cars actually give drivers a false sense of security. We have defined the problem as protecting the driver from being harmed if she is in an accident. Beer argues that it would perhaps be better to redefine the problem as how to keep a driver from having an accident in the first place (risk avoidance). He suggests that if we lined the dashboard of the car with spikes, making it very clear that an accident has serious consequences, we might give drivers incentive to be more careful. His suggestion is not without merit.

In projects that involve procurement, sole-sourcing is a risk to consider. The alternative is to second-source all procured parts or equipment. That way, if a supplier can't deliver on time or at the specified price, the second supplier might be able to step in. This can be thought of as either risk avoidance or risk mitigation.

Temporary workers are used as backups for critical personnel who become ill or are injured. Overtime is used as a contingency when tasks take longer than estimated. This is one reason why overtime should not be planned into a project to meet original targets, if possible. Rather, it should be kept in reserve as a contingency.

Another possible contingency is to reduce scope to permit the team to meet the original target date, then come back later and incorporate deferred work to finish the job.

Having a fire evacuation plan in a building can be thought of as a contingency and also a loss-prevention plan.

Transfer or Loss Prevention

Insurance is one way of protecting against loss in the event that a risk manifests. Having alternative sites available into which a group can move in the event of a disaster is a loss-prevention strategy. Backup personnel can also be thought of as loss avoidance. When a key person falls ill, If someone else can do the work there will be no loss to the project. Of course, this is difficult to do with highly skilled personnel.

Cost Contingency

Cost contingency is also called management reserve. Unfortunately, it is misunderstood. Too often it is believed that management reserve is there to cover poor performance. This is incorrect. Management reserve is a fund that is part of a project budget to cover the cost of unidentified work. All projects should have a work budget to cover the cost of identified work, and a management reserve to cover work not yet identified. In addition, on projects that are paid for by a customer, there will be a component of the total job cost called *margin*. This is the intended profit for the job. Poor performance eats into margin, not management reserve.

The management reserve account is not touched unless we identify new work to be done. This is a change in scope, of course. At that point money is transferred from the management reserve account into the work budget, and performance is subsequently tracked against the revised budget. A log should be maintained of all scope changes and their effect on the work budget, manage-

**Insurance is
one way of
protecting
against loss.**

ment reserve, and margin (if the change has such an effect). In
customer-funded projects, the customer may be required to pay
for scope changes, and in that case there is no impact on the management reserve account.

Accommodate

Sometimes we just accept the fact that risk is present, and we
take our chances. All of us do this when we drive a car or fly in
an airplane. We know that there is a chance of an accident, but if
we refused to accept that possibility we would never get into a
vehicle or plane. This is not the same as ignoring a risk, which is
covered next.

Ignore

This is different than accommodating a known risk. It is like putting your head in a hole in the ground and pretending that the risk does not exist. People do this when they practice unprotected sex with partners whose past sexual histories they do not know.

CONCLUSION

Risk management makes good business sense. Failing to account for factors that may sink a project is not aggressive management; it is being derelict in one's duty as a project manager. Banks won't insure homes or cars unless the buyer carries insurance to protect against loss from fires or accidents. Risk management is an important aspect of being effective project management.

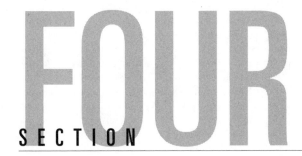

EXECUTION AND CONTROL

12

CHAPTER

Project Control

The only reason for doing a project plan (including the schedule) is to achieve control of the project. Remember the definition of control? If you have no plan, you can't possibly have control, by definition! So now we are ready to deal with how control is actually achieved in a project.

MEASURING PROGRESS

If you are going to control a project, you need to know two things: where you are supposed to be, and where you are. The plan tells you where you are supposed to be. As for where you actually are, that comes from your project information system—which in many organizations is nonexistent.

**Predicting the
future is easy.
It's trying to figure
out what's going
on now that's hard.**
~ Fritz R. S. Dressler

This system must provide information on all four project constraints. Remember, the relationship between them is given by the formula:

$$C = f(P, T, S)$$

So, if you want to know the true status of the project, you must know what costs have been incurred to date, whether the work meets functional and technical requirements (that is, performance), whether the work is on schedule, and whether the scope of work done is at the right level.

> To measure progress you must know the value of all four constraints.

Again, remember that cost is for labor only in this equation. As I have said before, you care about materials, capital equipment, and other project costs (such as travel or insurance), but they do not enter into this particular equation; they are tracked separately.

The easiest of the four variables to ascertain is cost. You may not have a system in place to provide that information, but if you wanted to get it you would be able to do so by having everyone record the hours spent on the project, multiply those hours by the hourly labor rate that they are paid, and then add them up.

It is harder to obtain data on the right side of the equation. To illustrate, let's begin with a simple example. Say you are building a brick wall. It is supposed to be a foot thick, 10 feet high, and 100 feet long by today's date. When it is finished it will be a foot thick, 20 feet high, and 200 feet long.

The nice thing about brick walls is that you can measure them. So you take a scale out to the wall and determine that it is indeed 1 foot thick and 100 feet long. You inspect the mortar between the bricks and it looks nice and clean and uniform. In addition, you check to see if the wall is perfectly vertical, and it is. This tells you that the quality of work done (functional and technical performance requirements) is okay. Next you measure the height of the wall and find that it is only 8 feet high. This tells you that scope is not correct—the workers have accomplished only 80 percent of what they were scheduled to do up to now.

That being the case, we also know that they are behind schedule. How far behind? Well, if you assume work is linear over time (which it isn't, but we will assume that it is for now), and they have been working for 10 days on the job, then they have accomplished what they should have done by day 8. Therefore, they are about two days behind schedule.

This isn't totally correct, because work is almost never linear. But it is a fair approximation for a wall of this height. This is tangible work, which is much easier to measure than knowledge work.

For example, if you were checking progress on a software task, and the programmer had estimated that she would have written about 10,000 lines of code by today's date, but she has only written 8,000 lines, is she 80 percent complete?

Who knows? She may find that the code she has written won't work and she'll have to start over completely. Or she may actually be finished because she found a way to write the code using fewer lines than she originally anticipated.

In addition, knowledge work usually proceeds along a progress curve like the one shown in Figure 12.1. Note that very little progress is made for a long period; then the work accelerates quickly, and then near the end it slows down again.

This is sometimes the source of great anxiety for senior managers who do not understand the nature of this progress curve. They expect work to be more linear, so when a knowledge worker seems to be "going nowhere" for a long time, they get very concerned and start putting pressure on the person to get the job done. The net result of this pressure may very well be to slow the person down. As one of my engineers told me once, when our manager was putting pressure on him to speed up, "Putting two jockeys on one horse won't make him run faster."

F I G U R E 12.1

Progress Curve for Knowledge Work

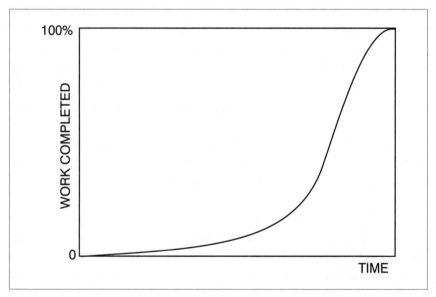

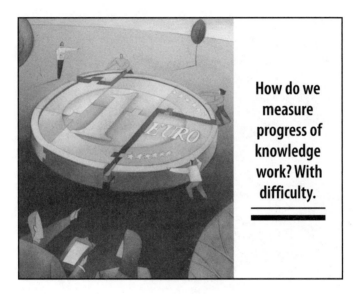

How do we measure progress of knowledge work? With difficulty.

So how do we measure progress of knowledge work? With difficulty.

If you remember the chunk-down rules that I presented in the scheduling chapter (Chapter 9), they establish that knowledge tasks should have durations no greater than one to three weeks. Furthermore, I said that the chunks must have markers that tell you they have been completed. These markers are called exit criteria. For software or engineering design, the exit criteria may be that the design has been reviewed by one's peers, who have reached consensus that it should perform correctly once it is completed. Of course this is a judgment on their part, and they could collectively be wrong, but it is the best we can do with work of this nature.

If the task is to conduct a test, the exit criteria may be raw data that verifies that the part meets the technical and functional specifications. Or, in an environmental cleanup project, we may have a situation where oil has seeped into the ground and at this stage of the project the oil in a certain area has all been removed. That makes it binary. It has or has not been removed.

**We simply
must recognize
the limitations
in our ability to
measure where
we are.**

In some cases, the exit criteria takes the form of a checklist (such as pilots use to ensure that all of their instruments and controls are functioning correctly before they take off). In others, it is a judgment by someone in the organization, as when a marketing vice president approves the aesthetics of a design.

It is really hard to know if P and S are correct, and if these cannot be determined then you don't know how you are doing schedulewise. For that reason, I have been told that there is no point in trying to measure progress in knowledge work.

I can't agree with that. If you don't know where you are, you can't have control. My suggestion is that we simply must recognize the limitations in our ability to measure exactly where we are. If we are building a brick wall, we may hold tolerances of ± 5 percent.

For knowledge work, the tolerances are more typically ± 20 to 25 percent, and if there is a lot of research involved, we could have a situation where the tolerance may be −100 to +20 percent on schedule. In other words, we must accept very large tolerances on poorly defined or intangible work.

THE PITFALLS OF REPORTING SCHEDULE ONLY

Estimates are that over two million individuals have purchased some form of scheduling software. So far as I know, all of the major programs allow you to report progress using a bar chart schedule. The reports typically look like the one in Figure 12.2. Small bars are run through the larger schedule bars to show how far along the work has progressed. For noncritical tasks, the smaller bars are black, and for the critical path, which is usually shown with a solid black bar, the progress bar will be white.

In Figure 12.2, weekends are shown by vertical shaded areas indicating that no work is done on these days. If a project is scheduled to work seven days a week, the shading would be removed. The 'time-now" date is shown as a vertical dotted line between the 19th and 20th. You will note that the 20th is a Monday. Usual convention is to report progress on Monday morning for the previous seven days.

According to this report, Activity A, which is a critical path task, is behind schedule by one day. This immediately tells us that the project is in jeopardy of slipping a day unless something can be done to get this activity back on track, since a delay on the critical path will delay the completion date correspondingly.

Activity B cannot be seen, as it is scheduled to start at a later date than this report shows. Activity C is complete, D is one day ahead of schedule, and E is right on target. So says the report.

What is missing from this report is information about cost, performance, and scope. We must take for granted that performance and scope are correct if schedule is where it is reported to be. But there is nothing we can infer about cost.

To see why this is a problem, assume that Activity D is a software development task. The work was supposed to take 40 hours (we will assume 100 percent productivity of the programmer). The person doing the work, call him Dave, says that he is right on schedule. He has given you this information at 8:30 on Monday morning. You feel very comfortable with his work. You

F I G U R E 12.2

Schedule Showing Progress

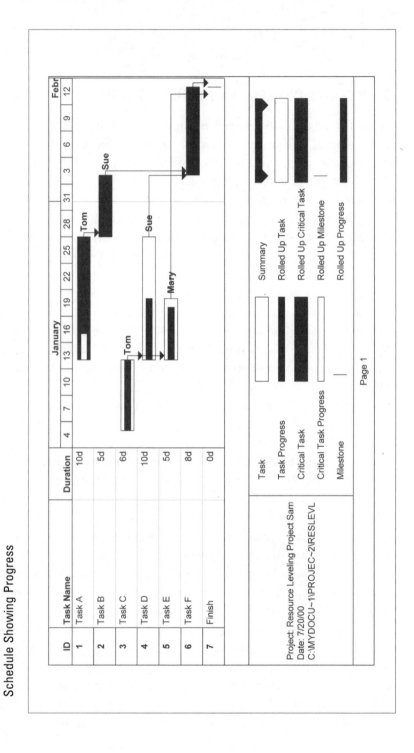

are concerned only about that critical path activity. Something has to be done about it.

At 8:45 a.m., Tom comes by and has a brief conversation with you. "I really felt sorry for Dave last week," he confides.

"How so?" you ask.

"Oh, didn't you know? He had a terrible time with the code he was writing. Instead of the 40 hours he expected the work would take, he actually put in nearly 80 hours to get the job done."

"Really?" you say, pondering the situation. "Well, I'm sorry to hear that he had so much trouble, but he's salaried so it doesn't affect my budget. Everything is fine."

Wait a minute! Is that really true?

No way!

If Dave missed his estimate by 100 percent last week, perhaps his estimate for subsequent weeks is off in a similar way. If so, how many 80-hour weeks can he work before he burns out and starts making errors and missing deadlines? This is a sure sign of potential trouble, and you have to do something about it right away.

So you go talk to Dave.

"I understand you had problems with your code this last week," you say.

Dave seems a bit surprised that you know about this, but he agrees. "Yes. It turned out to be a lot harder than I expected."

"Well, do you think this will continue to be true?" you ask.

There are two possibilities—yes or no.

If he says yes, then you must do something right away. There are only a few possibilities. You can get some help for him, if that is possible. You can reduce the scope of the remaining code that must be written. Or you can accept that the task is going to take a lot longer to complete than the original estimate, in which case it may use up all of its float and end up on the critical path. You may also decide between you that Dave is not the right person for this job and replace him.

**Principle:
Unless you know
both cost and
schedule, you
have absolutely
no idea where
your project
actually is.**

If he says no, it was a one-time occurrence and he is confident that the remaining work will go according to plan, then you tell him to keep you posted. If the work does turn out to be as difficult this week as it was last week, you want to do something before Dave gets himself—and your project—in serious trouble.

Notice what happens here. Without knowing how much effort (cost) Dave put into the work, you have no indication that there is a problem. This leads to an immutable law of tracking progress: unless you have an integrated cost-schedule tracking system, you don't have a clue where your project is! It is simply not enough to let people report schedule progress alone.

Knowing cost allows you to figure out what is going on. If the work is on schedule, and fewer hours were required than estimated, then people are working more efficiently than you expected. If work is on schedule and more hours have been expended than planned, this is a sign of trouble. If work is behind schedule and total hours worked are less than planned, then people are not doing what they are supposed to, and you need to find out why. And so on.

We still do not have any good way to measure scope or quality, so these will have to be estimated or evaluated using the best approach possible for the work in question. This means that the accuracy of our control system will not be very good, but we must have some way of tracking progress, and this is the best we can do.

TRACKING PROGRESS USING EARNED-VALUE ANALYSIS

The earned value system is actually derived from standard cost systems used to measure performance in manufacturing. An industrial engineer determines how long a manufacturing procedure should take and multiplies the time by the labor rate for that operation. This becomes the standard cost for that operation. Work is then tracked, and the time required to do the step is multiplied by the existing labor rate at the time the step is done. This is the actual cost of the operation. Note that the labor rate could change from the time the standard cost is established until the operation is performed, so you could have a variance caused by a change in labor rate. You can also have a variance because the actual time required for the step is different than what was determined by the industrial engineer in the beginning. Finally, we measure what proportion of the work is completed in the standard time. If it is exactly what should have been done, the operation is 100 percent efficient. If the time taken is less, then efficiency is greater than 100 percent, and conversely.

The earned value system was adopted by project management practitioners as a way of measuring progress, and it is considered to be the best system designed to date. The earned-value system for tracking projects has a number of detractors. The most common complaint is that you can't measure knowledge work, and I wholeheartedly agree. You can't; but you must pretend you can or else you can't possibly achieve control of knowledge projects, and this category probably is the largest in the world at present. As I have said previously, we simply must accept that the precision of our measures will be much worse than is possible for well-defined or tangible work, but at least we have some indication of how we are doing before a disaster occurs.

As I just stated, the earned value system provides three measures that allow us to determine project status. These are measures of what is supposed to be done, or planned value (PV), what has actually been done, or earned value (EV), and the amount of effort or cost that has been expended to do the work, or actual cost (AC). (I should say at this point that the original system used four-letter acronyms for these measures, but a few years ago there was an attempt to simplify this by changing them to two letters, as I've used above. Unfortunately, numerous books and articles use the four-letter versions, so that you may find it hard to follow these other sources unless you know how to translate. So, as I continue this discussion, I will provide translations for you.)

To see how earned value works, we will start with a very simple example.

Assume for a moment that you have guests coming to stay with you for a few days, and you want to make a good impression by having a spotless house. You don't have time to do all of the cleaning yourself, so you call a cleaning service and ask what they will charge to clean the house from top to bottom. They come out to your house and give you a quote.

"We should be able to thoroughly clean your house with one worker in 40 hours," the agent tells you.

"How much will that cost?" you ask.

"Our billing rate is 20 dollars per hour," says the agent, "so it will cost you approximately 800 dollars."

"Is that a fixed price?"

"No, we charge by the hour. If it takes a little less, you will pay less, and conversely."

"Okay, let's do it," you say.

The agent agrees to have someone at your house by eight o'clock Monday morning. You make a note that the job will cost about 800 dollars, and this number is called the budgeted cost of work scheduled (BCWS) to be done—or, to use the new term, this is planned value (PV).

On Monday morning, around 7:00 a.m., the phone rings. It is the agent.

"I have a problem," she tells you. "The guy we were going to send over to clean your house had an accident this weekend and can't make it. However, I have another person available, but we bill him at 22 dollars an hour. Is that okay?"

"You have me at a disadvantage," you say. "I have to get the house cleaned, so go ahead and send him over."

So the alternate worker comes out to your house and starts the job. You have to leave town for a job, so you don't talk with the worker until you return on Friday. He is just wrapping up for the week.

"How did it go?" you ask.

"I'm afraid I didn't quite finish," he says.

"Well, how much did you get done?" you ask.

He thinks for a moment. "As near as I can tell, I got about 80 percent of it done," he says.

Notice those words. *As near as I can tell.*

In other words, he is *estimating* where he is!

As former president George Bush used to like to say, estimating is one of those kind, gentle words that really substitutes for the fact that you are guessing. That's right, an estimate is a guess.

Let's get this straight. Control is exercised by comparing where you are (which you only know by guessing) to where you are supposed to be (which is another guess) and then taking action to correct for differences between the two. Does this sound like witchcraft and magic to you? It does to me.

Nevertheless, as I've said above, even though it's not precise it's better than doing absolutely nothing.

Most importantly, the example shows the difficulty of measuring progress even in tangible work. How do you know how

Is witchcraft involved?

much of the house has been cleaned? Can you measure it on a square-foot basis? What about cleaning walls or dusting furniture? The truth is, you have no choice but to estimate progress, compare it to the scheduled work (also estimated), and do your best to correct for deviations.

Fine. How do we assign a value to what has been done?

Well, if we compare what has been done to the original target, how much should it have cost you to do 80 percent of the total job? The BCWS (PV) was $800 worth of work. If the worker has only done 80 percent of that, it *should* have cost me $640, calculated as follows:

$$BCWP = 0.80 \times BCWS = 0.80 \times 800 = \$640.$$

This number (BCWP) is the earned value (EV). The worker has contributed $640 of value to cleaning the house. Of course, he was supposed to have done $800 worth of work, so he did not perform according to plan. Using the two-letter codes, and repeating the calculation, we have:

$$EV = 0.80 \times PV = 0.80 \times 800 = \$640.$$

The fact that the worker did less than was supposed to be done is bad enough, but then it occurs to you that he has actually worked 40 hours at a higher labor rate ($22 per hour) than you originally budgeted for, so the actual cost of the work performed (ACWP, or AC) is $880.

$$SV = BCWP - BCWS = EV - PV$$
$$CV = BCWP - ACWP = EV - AC$$
$$BV = BCWS - ACWP = PV - AC$$

This is not good. Not only did you get less than you were supposed to get, but you have paid more for it as well.

The status of this task is determined using the following equations:

Schedule variance = BCWP – BCWS (or EV – PV)
Cost variance = BCWP – ACWP (or EV – AC)
Budget variance = BCWS – ACWP (or PV – AC)

Using these formulas, we arrive at the following variances:

Schedule variance = 640 – 800 = – $160 worth of work.
Cost variance = 640 – 880 = – $240.
Budget variance = 800 – 880 = – $80.

In conventional accounting practice, a negative variance is unfavorable, so this means that the job is behind schedule by $160 worth of work. To convert that to time, you divide by the original $20 per hour labor rate, and you see that the person is eight hours behind schedule. That makes sense. If he only did 80 percent of the work and it was supposed to take five days, he has done what should have been done in four days, so he is one day (or eight hours) behind.

But notice the cost variance. Why is it $240? Because you have spent $80 more for the work than originally budgeted and gotten $160 less work done than you were supposed to get. So your cost variance in this case is the sum of the budget and schedule variances, and since the number is negative, you are overspent by $240.

Here is an important point. We have already seen that if you look only at schedule, without knowing cost, you have no warning that a project may be heading for trouble. In the same manner, if you were tracking only your budget variance you would know that you were spending too much, but that alone does not show the true picture. Not only are you spending too much, but you are getting much less than you should for what you are spending. This also confirms the need to know both cost and schedule in order to form a true picture of project status.

It is also instructive to notice how this job got into trouble. You failed to check on progress through the week. Rather, you

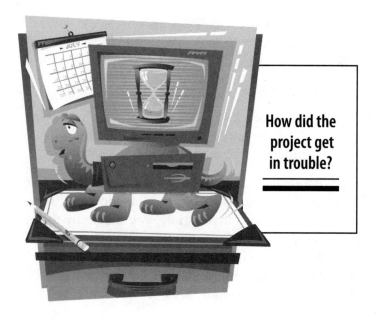

**How did the
project get
in trouble?**

waited until Friday afternoon to find out that the worker was not on target. Had you checked progress around midweek, and found that the work was already falling behind, you might have been able to get the worker to spend some overtime to get it finished by Friday afternoon. Now all you can do is pay for work on Saturday or have the person come back next week to finish the job.

This suggests a guideline: The rate at which you monitor progress must be proportionate to the total time the work will take. A task that is supposed to take a week should probably be monitored daily. That doesn't mean that the project manager should do this—the individual(s) doing the work should monitor their own progress and should be told how much leeway they have to take steps to get back on track.

RESPONDING TO DEVIATIONS

In tracking a project, you must always ask three questions. What is the status? When there is a deviation, what caused it? What should be done about any deviations that exist?

If we apply these to the housecleaning example, the answer to the first question is that you are behind schedule and over-spent. When it comes to question two, however, is it clear that you don't know the cause of the deviations? It could be that this person is not as efficient as he should be, or it could be that the estimate was wrong in the first place.

How would you figure it out?

Suppose you bring back this same worker week after week to clean the house, and he can never get it all done in 40 hours. Does this prove it is the person?

No. It could be impossible for anyone to do the work in 40 hours.

Then suppose we alternate between two workers. If neither of them can clean the house in 40 hours, we are pretty certain the estimate was optimistic. However, if one can clean the house in 40 hours and the other cannot, then it is clearly the person.

Or is it?

Well, clearly, one person can work faster than the other, but it is important to remember what we said about estimating back in Chapter 7. All estimates are person-specific. It makes no difference what someone else can do. If you want to know when a project will end, you have to estimate for the individuals doing the tasks.

Simply put, there are a very few runners who can run a mile in less than four minutes. So it would be totally unreasonable for you to expect an average person to run the mile in four minutes just because somewhere there is *someone* who can do it.

Given these facts, you can't answer the second question at the moment. All you can do is move on to the third one, which asks what you want to do about deviations. To answer this question, you'd actually have to look at your options: ignore the deviation, take corrective action to get back on track, or change the plan to accept the deviation.

In the housecleaning situation it would seem that you have only a limited number of choices—have the person work overtime

---

Monitoring Progress

When you monitor progress, you ask three questions, as follows:

1. What is the actual status of the work?
2. When there is a deviation, what caused it?
3. What should be done to correct for any deviation that exists?

To answer question 3, note that there are only four responses you can make to a deviation. They are:

1. Ignore the deviation.
2. Take steps to get back on track.
3. Revise the plan to show that the deviation cannot be recovered.
4. Cancel the project.

No matter
how far
you've gone
on a wrong
road, turn
around.
~ Turkish Proverb

on Saturday at premium pay or return on Monday to finish the job at regular pay. If you can wait until Monday, that will be the cheaper option. Otherwise, you may have no choice but to pay premium wages. Of course, there is a third option, which is to leave the 20 percent as is, but that isn't a very attractive choice. Neither of the preferred options fits with the second choice. Both are examples of changing the plan. And of course, it is too late to ignore the deviation.

When would it be okay to ignore a deviation? When it is smaller than the tolerances you can hold and does not show a trend that will eventually take it out of bounds. Consider the deviation chart in Figure 12.3. This chart is showing a project in which tolerances of ± 20 percent are the best that can be maintained. During the first few weeks of the project, the deviations vary randomly within those boundaries. Then there is a definite trend that suggests the project will break the 20 percent boundary if nothing is done to get it back on track. Corrective action must be taken, or, if nothing can be done to get back on track, the plan may have to be revised.

F I G U R E   12.3

Deviation Graph for a Project

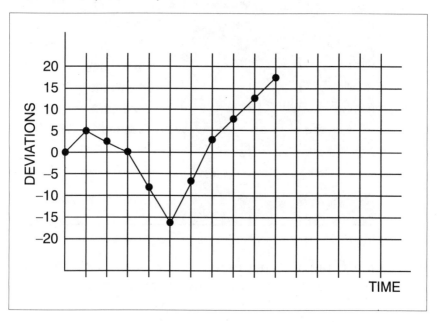

In examining deviations, you must always go back to the equation that relates the constraints to each other, namely:

$$C = f(P, T, S)$$

If you are trying to get back on schedule, you can increase costs (add labor), reduce scope, or reduce performance requirements. All of these can actually be considered a change to the original plan, except that you may not formally revise the published plan. In the case of reducing scope or performance, you probably have no choice but to revise the plan. In the event that you can increase resources without going over budget, you may be able to leave the plan alone.

Let me reiterate once more, just so no one misses it. There are *only* four responses you can make when a project is off track. You can ignore the deviation. You can take corrective action to get back on target. You can change the plan. And you can cancel the job altogether. This would be done when the project has slipped so much that it is no longer viable—it will be too late, too expensive, or nonfunctional.

> **When a project is offtrack, you can:**
> 1. Ignore the deviation.
> 2. Take corrective action to get back on target.
> 3. Revise the plan to reflect the deviation.
> 4. Cancel the project altogether.

Now, before we continue to the next section, here to recap are the two-letter and four-letter acronyms:

BCWS = PV

BCWP = EV

ACWP = AC

Because the two-letter versions are now used by PMI on their PMP® exam, we will use these throughout the remainder of this chapter.

USING GRAPHS TO TRACK PROGRESS AND FORECAST TRENDS

To get an overall assessment of project status, we can plot earned value data graphically. These graphs will also allow us to forecast where the project will end up in terms of both schedule and spending.

Consider the bar chart in Figure 12.4. There are only three activities. As you can see, Activity A spends $800 a week for labor, B spends $2,400 per week, and C spends $3,000 a week. On the first line below the bar chart you see the weekly spending figures, which are obtained by summing the spending on each bar for the week. The final line shows the cumulative spending for this project

F I G U R E 12.4

Bar Graph for a Small Project

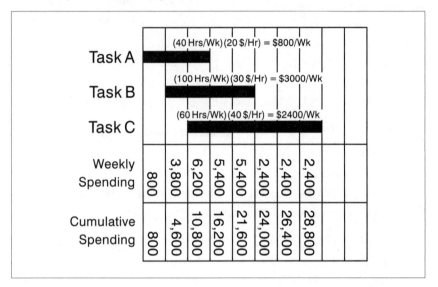

to be $28,800 at the end of the job. Note that these figures represent the PV for the project. If these are plotted, we simply transform the bar graph into a line graph, which shows the cumulative work to be done over time, in dollar value. Since the bar graph is a major component of the project plan, the line graph is also, and is, in fact, called a *baseline plan*. This plot is shown in Figure 12.5.

Once this curve is plotted we can compare progress to it so that deviations from plan can be spotted. To show this, I am going to use a new curve, one for a larger project than the simple three-activity example.

First Case: Behind Schedule and Overspent

For this project, I have total cumulative spending of about $90,000. To show progress, I need to find out how much has been accomplished and how much it has cost. To do this, I go around and find

F I G U R E   12.5

Cumulative Spending for the Three-Activity Project

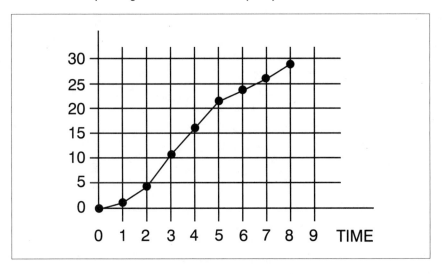

out from everyone how much work they have done, expressed as EV, and I add up the total value of their work. As you can see from the graph in Figure 12.6, they were supposed to do $50,000 worth of work by the date in question. This was supposed to be 1,000 hours of work at a loaded labor rate of $50 per hour. When I total what they have actually accomplished, I find that they have only done $40,000 worth of work. In addition, when I collect their time reports, they have put in 1,200 hours of labor at a loaded labor rate of $50 per hour. Thus the AC for the project work is $60,000.

Returning to our progress questions, we first ask, what is the status of the project? We saw previously that the schedule variance is given by:

$$SV = EV - PV$$

I suggest that you begin with schedule variance, because cost variance doesn't always make sense until you know what has happened to your schedule.

Plot Showing Project Behind Schedule and Overspent

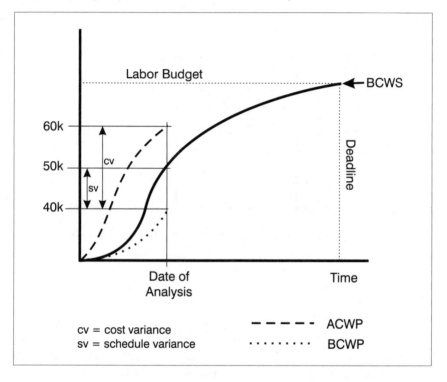

For this project, the schedule variance is – $10,000 worth of work. This is calculated as follows:

$$SV = 40{,}000 - 50{,}000 = -\$10{,}000$$

If you divide $10,000 by $50 dollars per hour, you find that the project is 200 hours worth of work behind schedule. What this means in calendar time depends on the number of hours per day that are scheduled to be worked. However, you can tell the schedule variance by looking at the horizontal axis. This is shown in Figure 12.7.

F I G U R E   12.7

Schedule Variance Shown on Horizontal Axis

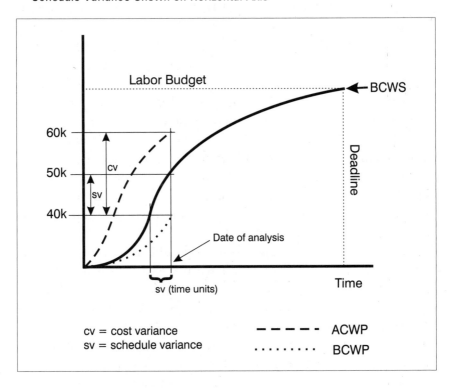

Notice that the schedule variance is shown both as a – $10,000 deviation on the vertical axis and also as a time devia- tion on the horizontal axis. We have done $10,000 less work than was scheduled. We have also spent $60 to do the work, so the cost variance is $20,000. This is calculated as:

$$CV = EV - AC$$

$$CV = 40,000 - 60,000 = -\$20,000$$

Since a negative variance is unfavorable, we are $20,000 over- spent. That is, we have spent $60,000 to accomplish only $40,000 worth of work. As you can see from the graph, the cost variance is the sum of the budget variance of $10,000 and the schedule variance of $10,000. We have spent $10,000 more for labor than scheduled and gotten $10,000 less work done than scheduled. This is the worst state in which a project can be, but unfortunately it happens.

The second question we must answer is, what is the cause of the deviation? As was true for our housecleaning example, we don't know. It could be that people weren't as efficient as they should have been, or it could be that the estimate was optimistic to begin with. And, since we don't have the ability to compare this project to another one, we can't answer the question as we could by comparing workers. All we can do in this case is do a review to determine if there were any factors that caused work to take longer than expected, then try to project from there. We can also ask what to do based on those projections.

This is the third question—what should we do about the deviation? To answer that question we need to have some idea of what is going to happen to the project. That is, where will it end up? If we had some way to extrapolate the EV and AC curves in Figure 12.7, we might be able to determine the end state.

You might do a linear regression to extrapolate these curves, but if you are on the very steep part of the PV curve, fitting a linear projection to the EV and AC curves can be very misleading. It would be better if you re-estimated where the curves are heading, but I am going to pretend that we can fit a nonlinear projection to each curve, which would give the result shown in Figure 12.8.

To extrapolate these curves, assume that if all the work is to be completed, the EV curve must eventually hit the BAC line (budget-at-completion). As you can see from the figure, it will do so at a later time than originally targeted, so the project will be late. Secondly, the AC curve must hit the finish point for the project, so extrapolating it gives a new estimate at completion (EAC) as shown in the figure. Note that the difference between this new EAC and the original BAC indicates how much the project will go over budget.

Project with BCWP and ACWP Extrapolated

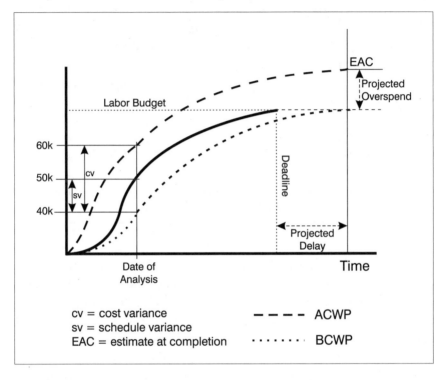

Based on these projections, the project is going to be *seriously* late and overspent unless something can be done to get it back on target. What to do?

First, consider the worst case—that the project can't be salvaged. It is going to be late and overspent. The question in this case is whether it is still viable. If it is product or software development, and we estimate lost sales (because it is late) and increased development costs, we may find that the return on investment (ROI) no longer meets an acceptable level. If that is the case, and unless something can be done to get it back on target, it may be prudent to cancel the job and get on with another project

When you're
riding a
dead horse,
dismount.
~ Sioux Proverb

that will bring an acceptable return. If the ROI is unacceptable, the only reason we would continue the project would be if it is mandated by contract. If the product were a loss-leader, or one needed for position in the marketplace, then ROI wouldn't be a factor and we might continue the job in spite of the projections.

But is there anything that can be done to recover? Perhaps. Notice that if the scope were reduced, the project could be finished by the original completion date, although it will still be overspent. This is shown as SR in Figure 12.8. If that is an acceptable tradeoff, we would agree on a scope reduction, meaning that the plan would be revised and we would continue.

Suppose, however, that you are told it's unacceptable to reduce scope; nor is it permissible to be late. You must bring this project in on time.

This means that you must somehow make the EV curve turn upward so that it intersects the PV curve at the deadline. This is shown in Figure 12.9. Also note that you will most likely incur even greater cost to make this happen, because you'll probably have to throw resources at the project to complete it on time.

F I G U R E 12.9

Project Ending on Time but Overspent

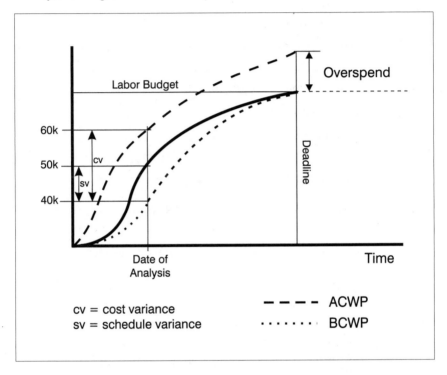

Of course, you can finish the project on time and on budget if you are dealing with salaried people who don't get paid overtime. That is, you can *appear* to do so. But is that really true? Is nonpaid overtime really free?

You can be sure it is not. You will pay in terms of lost productivity, increased rework, field failures, employee absenteeism, stress-related illness, or turnover. In a job market in which unemployment is only a few percent, people can fairly easily find new jobs and may very well leave if unpaid overtime hours mount. And the cost to replace professionals in the United States today is in the range of $100,000 to $200,000. So your unpaid overtime can turn out to be very expensive!

As a final question, you may ask if there isn't something that can be done to get the project completely back on track without going way over budget.

I can assure you that it would take a miracle.

I'll cite the 15 percent rule: If you are 15 percent of the way into a project on the horizontal time line and you are in trouble, you are going to stay in trouble. This means that if a project is supposed to take 100 weeks to complete, and you are in trouble at the end of week 15, you are going to stay there. Period!

> If you are 15 percent into a project on the horizontal time line and you are in trouble, you are going to stay in trouble!

How can I be so confident of this? Aren't there any exceptions?

To answer these questions, consider a study several years ago that found that, of 800 defense contract projects that were in trouble at the 15 percent mark, not a single one ever recovered (Fleming and Koppelman, 1996).

I know, I know. You're thinking that's typical of defense contracting.

But I can assure you that it applies to your projects as well, even if you aren't in defense contracting.

How can I be sure?

Easy. Where did the PV curve come from?

The bar chart schedule.

Where did the schedule come from?

Forecasts—which are, in reality, estimates. And we all know that if the weather forecast for *tomorrow* can't be trusted, there is no need to believe the forecast for six weeks out. In other words, if the near-term forecast (just 15 percent into the project) isn't right, why would it be any better at the end of the job?

This is a good-news, bad-news story. The good news is that you can forecast a losing project very early, so that you can perhaps cancel it and cut your losses early on. The bad news is that, even if it is doing well at the 15 percent point, it won't necessarily continue to do so.

Second Case: Ahead of Schedule, Spending Correctly

To illustrate another combination, consider the situation shown in Figure 12.10. This time the EV curve shows that $60,000 worth of

F I G U R E   12.10

Project Ahead of Schedule, Spending Correctly

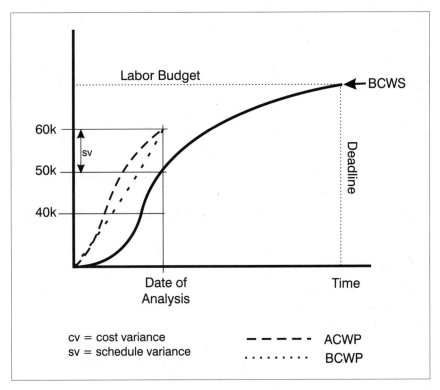

cv = cost variance
sv = schedule variance

work has been done and that the AC is also $60,000. The PV target on this date was $50,000. The status is ahead of schedule, and the cost variance is zero.

Be careful to distinguish between *budget* variance and *cost* variance. The project is above budget by $10,000, but that is because it's ahead of schedule. In words, the workers have done $60,000 worth of work (EV) and spent $60,000 (AC) to do it. A simple way to keep this in mind is that, when EV is larger than PV, you have done more than scheduled, so you are ahead of schedule. If you have done less, you are behind.

The second question we must answer is, what is the most likely cause of this variance? Unlike the first one, where the project was behind schedule and overspent, this variance has a generic cause. Remember, this is labor cost. When you are ahead of schedule and spending correctly, it means that you have more resources applied to the project than you had intended, but they are working at expected efficiency.

In a shared resource environment, that should raise a red flag. Where did you get extra resources? You don't exactly have them sitting around in the hall waiting for something to do.

There are two possibilities. Either you stole them, or somebody got into trouble and couldn't use some people and so sent them to you.

In a construction project, there is another possibility. The schedule had some weather delays built into it for safety, but the weather has been beautiful; so the work has been progressing ahead of schedule.

Now, before I refer you to the third question, I must tell you that I can predict your response. You are going to think, "Is he crazy?" Let's see if I'm right.

The third question is, what do you want to do about the deviation?

See. I was right. You're thinking, "Wait a minute. I'm ahead of schedule and spending correctly, and he wants to know what

I'm going to do about it? Like nothing, man! Hide it maybe. I'm sure not going to slow down."

Before you go too far with that thinking, you have to ask if being ahead of schedule can cause problems later on. And the answer is yes.

Suppose you deliver a product to a customer before they are ready for it. You may have to pay to warehouse it. You may also have to wait to get paid for it.

Speaking of pay, suppose the project is a construction job. Contractors usually want progress payments for their work, so they send you bills totaling $60,000. Your controller may kill you. Your plan said you were going to do $50,000 worth of work, but the contractors have done $60,000. Although the difference may be small, the controller may have cash flow problems and tell you to slow down.

Darn. What a thankless job! Just when you thought you were doing something good, everyone starts trashing you.

It's a matter of degree, you understand. If you are a little bit ahead, nobody will get excited. In fact, we all know it is always better to be ahead than behind. But there are definitely situations where being ahead can be a problem. I know of a company that finished some equipment ahead of time and shipped it. It was delivered to a new facility—where they hadn't finished building the loading dock. The manufacturer had to temporarily warehouse it and pay the rental charges.

Third Case: Behind Schedule, Underspent

The next scenario is shown in Figure 12.11. In this case, EV is at $40,000, and so is AC. The target PV is still $50,000. What is the status? The project is behind schedule but has no cost variance. What is the most likely cause? Lack of resources. You may be waiting for supplies, or too little labor is being applied to the project.

F I G U R E 12.11

Project Is Behind Schedule and Spending Correctly

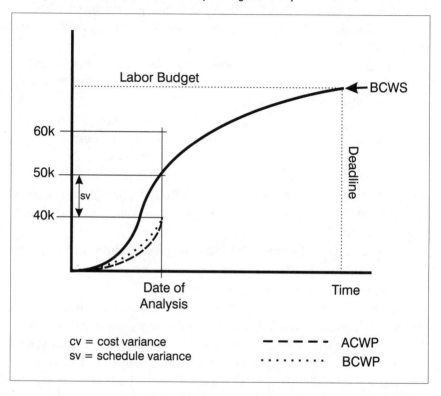

What do you want to do about it? Usually you want to catch up. However, you can almost be sure that to catch up you will blow your budget. It is usually better to stay on schedule than to try to recover once you get behind.

Final Scenario

Examine Figure 12.12. What is the status?

The project is ahead of schedule and underspent. How much? The work is $10,000 ahead (EV is at $60,000) and spend-

F I G U R E   12.12

Project Ahead of Schedule, Underspent

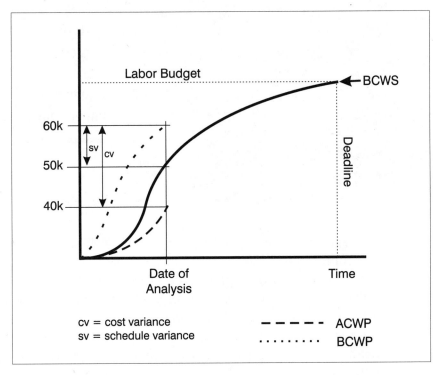

cv = cost variance
sv = schedule variance

- - - - -   ACWP
· · · · · · · · ·   BCWP

ing is $20,000 less than expected. In other words, you have spent only $40,000 to accomplish $60,000 worth of work. Sounds great, doesn't it?

What is the most likely cause of this variance? There are two possibilities. One is that the estimate was very conservative—to the point of sandbagging. The other is that you had a very lucky break. You can bet that sandbagging is far more likely than a lucky break.

Question three asks you what to do about it. I know what you're thinking. Leave it alone. Hide it maybe. You sure aren't going to slow down, and if you were to give the money back, they

would expect you to do the same thing next time. Nobody in their right mind would do either—or would they?

I submit that you should give some of the money back and reschedule the project. If you don't, the organization will loose the opportunity to make good use of the money until the project ends, and that opportunity cost can be significant.

Remember our first project scenario, in which the job was behind schedule and overspent. We said that the project could be canceled if it is no longer viable; but it could be viable and still be canceled simply because there is no money to fund it. However, there would be money to fund that project if we freed it up from this one, which is under budget.

Notice that I said you should give *some* of the money back. As I have explained elsewhere, all work varies. There is some tolerance that we must accept as normal variation. If it is plus or minus 15 percent, then give all but 15 percent of the money back. Keep some in reserve to cover the variation. This is proper control of variance.

Again, I know what you're thinking. If you give it back, and then hit a rock later on, you won't be able to get it back. It is true in many organizations. What I am advocating is that the organization must change the way it treats project budgets. They must all be examined once a quarter, and adjustments made in either direction. That way, people will be willing to give back extra money, as they know they can get it back later if they need it.

In more companies than I care to count, the solution to this problem is to simply tell members of the overspent project to quit charging time to it. They are told to charge to the underspent project instead. That way, both projects will come in on budget.

In defense contracting, if you get caught doing this you could go to jail. It is illegal, because earned value is used to determine when progress payments should be made to a contractor, and if you charge for work you haven't done it is lying and it is illegal.

Most seriously, this tactic destroys our ability to detect a troubled project and do something to help it. Or, if it is too far gone to be saved, we could cancel

> Cross-charging contaminates databases. The proper approach is to rebudget aboveboard.

it. But we can't tell it is really bad off if no one charges time to it.

In addition, this practice, called *cross-charging*, contaminates both history databases. Next time you do similar projects, you will underestimate one and overestimate the other. And you will be in trouble again.

Instead, an aboveboard adjustment to both project budgets should be made. The funds are transferred from one to the other. This does not contaminate your databases, and is acceptable.

USING SPREADSHEETS TO TRACK PROGRESS

The graphical method of tracking progress is effective at showing trends and visually presenting an overview of a project, but it is not very effective at actually determining the true state of the job. The reason is that the graph presents composite data for the project, and that data is not good for seeing problems that exist with individual tasks.

Consider the situation shown in Figure 12.13. There are three tasks going on in parallel. One is $100 overspent, the second is right on target, and the third is $100 underspent. What you see on the bottom line will be a zero variance in spending, because one deviation cancels the other. This would tell you that the project is fine when it is not. To really track progress, you need to look at every task, and the best way to do that is with a spreadsheet.

Most scheduling programs today allow you to report progress using earned value analysis and present it in spreadsheet format. However, not all of them have one feature that I find very useful, and that is the critical ratio. This is a performance index that is actually the product of two individual indices. One is the schedule performance index (SPI), and the other is the cost performance index (CPI). These are shown as follows:

F I G U R E 12.13

Three Tasks in Parallel

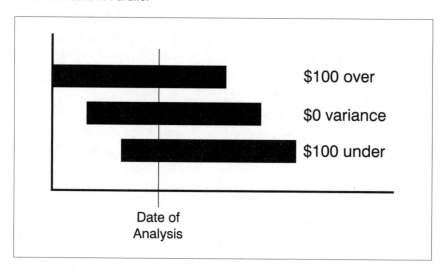

$100 over

$0 variance

$100 under

Date of
Analysis

$$SPI = \frac{EV}{PV}$$

$$CPI = \frac{EV}{AC}$$

Before continuing, I think it is helpful to review the meaning of these equations. First of all, EV, earned value, is a measure of *what you got*. The amount of work you were *supposed* to get is PV. SPI is simply *work efficiency*, or fraction of work done. Finally, AC is the actual cost of work performed, so the CPI can be thought of as *spending efficiency*.

If the two ratios are multiplied together, you get a combined index called the critical ratio (CR):

$$CR = SPI * CPI$$

Like all ratios that indicate performance, these will have values of 1.0 if work is going exactly as planned. If work is going better than planned, the ratios will be greater than 1.0, and if worse than planned they will have values of less than 1.0. When you multiply the two together, one of them may be slightly above 1.0, and the other slightly below 1.0; and the CPI can still be 1.0. This is shown as;

$$CR = SPI * CPI$$
$$= 0.9 * 1.11$$
$$= 1.0$$

A spreadsheet that uses the critical ratio to indicate progress and suggest actions to be taken is shown in Figure 12.14. Note that the critical ratio is calculated in the next-to-last column, and that the last column is headed "Action Required?," which has the following meaning (this spreadsheet can be downloaded from my Web site free of charge).

A manufacturing process can be monitored by measuring the process outputs and plotting those measures on a deviation graph.

FIGURE 12.14

Spreadsheet for Tracking Progress

Earned Value Report

Project No.:
Description:
Prepared by:

Date:
Page____ of____
Signed:

FILE:

WBS # or Name	Cumulative-to-date			Variance		At Completion			Critical Ratio	Action Required
	BCWS	BCWP	ACWP	Sched.	Cost	Budgeted (BAC)	Latest Est. (EAC)	Variance		
				0	0			0	NA	NA
				0	0			0	NA	NA
				0	0			0	NA	NA
				0	0			0	NA	NA
				0	0			0	NA	NA
				0	0			0	NA	NA
				0	0			0	NA	NA
				0	0			0	NA	NA
				0	0			0	NA	NA
				0	0			0	NA	NA
TOTALS:	0	0	0	0	0	0	0	0	NA	NA

NOTE: Negative variance is unfavorable || If Critical Ratio < 0.6, INFORM MANAGEMENT!
( ) = NEGATIVE VALUES

As long as those measures fall randomly around the centerline, the process is in control. When the deviations cease to be random, there is a probability that the process is either out of control or about to go out of control. The tests for nonrandomness are beyond the scope of this book; a good reference is Walpole (1974).

Critical Ratio Greater than One

A similar idea has been developed for keeping track of the critical ratio over time. The control limits are shown in Figure 12.15. If the critical ratio is between 0.8 and 1.2, we consider the deviation to be acceptable. If it falls between 1.2 and 1.3, we are told to check

F I G U R E   12.15

A Critical Ratio Control Chart

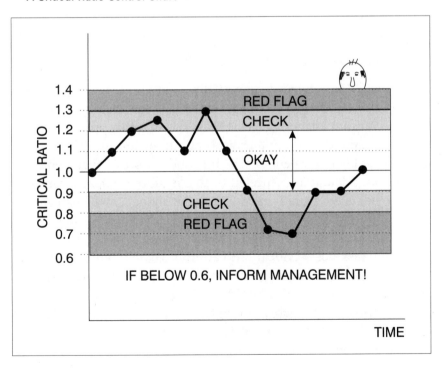

the task (or project), and if the ratio goes above 1.3, we are told to "red flag" it. This means that the ratio is seriously out of line.

However, I said earlier that ratios greater than 1.0 mean that work is going better than planned. So why would a critical ratio above 1.3 be cause for concern?

Have you heard the saying, if something seems to be too good to be true, it probably is? The first concern is whether the data is actually valid or people are deceiving themselves. If the data is valid, then what is going on?

In all likelihood, the project is way ahead of schedule and underspent when the critical ratio goes this high. Wonderful, you say!

Well, maybe.

But this is the last situation we just examined in the section on tracking progress graphically, and we said that the project should be rescheduled and some of the money given back. So the critical ratio is flagging you that something should be done about the project.

Critical Ratio Less than One

When the CR is between 0.8 and 0.9, it is in the check range. If it is below 0.8 it becomes a red flag, and if it drops below 0.6, we are told to inform management. The reason is that this project is really sick, nigh unto death. For a critical ratio to be around 0.6, the project is most likely far behind schedule and seriously overspent. It is a good candidate to be canceled (if that is an option), and cancellation decisions are usually made by senior management—so we are being told to inform them, so that they can decide what to do.

Of course, this only applies to the overall project critical ratio. If a single task has a critical ratio around 0.6, you wouldn't tell senior management about it. It is you, the project manager, who should be alarmed and take action. Chances are that, if this task had any float, it probably doesn't have much left; if it becomes critical and slips any more, it will impact the finish date for the project. You need to take action immediately.

The spreadsheet shown in Figure 12.14 has an "if" formula in the cell to test the critical ratio against the specified limits, and it displays the words Okay, Check, or Red Flag in the cell so that you can scan the right-hand column and immediately see your trouble spots. In addition, you can set up conditional formatting of the cell to highlight it in red, yellow, or green, to correspond to Okay, Check, or Red Flag, respectively. You then can distribute color printouts that make it very easy for people to spot problems.

Forecasting Final Cost and Schedule Results

There are a couple of ways to forecast final results for a project. One is to replan based on what has been learned to date. Another is to calculate forecast results using earned value data. Perhaps the best would be to do both.

The most common and most accepted of the statistical forecasting methods is to use the cumulative CPI estimate at completion (previously labeled EAC on the projection graphs). The formula for making this projection is:

$$\$EAC = \frac{BAC - BCWP}{Cumulative\ CPI} + ACWP$$

If we go back to the first project status example we used, in which the project was behind schedule and overspent, and ask what the EAC will be, we would get the following. The original BAC (budget at completion) is about $90,000. The current EV is $40,000, the AC is $60,000, and the CPI is therefore 0.533 (numbers below are expressed in thousands):

$$\$EAC = \frac{90 - 40}{0.533} + 60$$

This calculates to a EAC of $153,800. If nothing is done to bring spending in line, the project is going to be overspent severely! The only problem with this formula is that it is a more or less linear projection, which depends on the slope of the curve at the present time for its forecast. It is better to re-estimate each task and forecast from those estimates, but this is a quick way to find out how much trouble you are in.

ALTERNATIVES TO EARNED VALUE

As far as I am concerned, there is no completely adequate alternative to earned value tracking. I showed at the beginning of the chapter that, unless you know both how much effort has gone into a project and where the schedule is, you can't tell you have problems. However, there are some approaches that can be used in lieu of earned value if you simply can't find a way to measure EV, for example.

Using Run Charts

One of these is the run chart. You can plot any four of the project variables (P, C, T, S) using this approach. The chart in Figure 12.16 shows a plot of fraction of work completed each week for a hypothetical project called "Echo." To plot fraction of work completed, you divide the amount of work completed to date by the amount of work scheduled to be completed. This could be called percent of scheduled work actually completed, and is equivalent to the ratio EV/PV. From this chart you can see that starting in week 3 there is a downward trend. People are clearly having trouble. Then they somehow begin to recover, and there is an upward trend that peaks in week 15, then falls back a bit. Since work following week 12 is being performed at a greater rate than scheduled, it is likely that the project will finish early, possibly by week 21, rather than as scheduled on week 23. This chart is highly unlikely to occur in reality, because the team is in a lot of trouble early on, but it illustrates the approach.

There are two guidelines for interpreting run charts, to detect meaningful systemic changes:

F I G U R E   12.16

A Run Chart for Project Echo

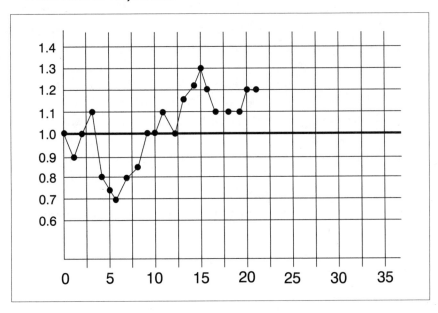

a. Since it is expected that there would be approximately the same number of points above the *average* line as there are below it, a good rule of thumb is that if there is a run of seven consecutive points on one side of the average, something significant may be happening and it would probably be a good idea to call "time out."

b. A second test is to see whether a run of seven or more intervals is steadily increasing or decreasing without reversals in direction. As in (a), such a pattern is not likely to occur by chance, thereby indicating [that] something needs to be investigated (Kiemele & Schmidt, 1993, pp. 2–25).

To track quality, you might want to record rework hours. It is likely that most projects will incur from 5 to 40 percent rework. If you are improving your project management process, you should

see a decline in rework. A run chart that tracks hours spent on rework is shown in Figure 12.17.

If you compare Figure 12.16 with Figure 12.17, you will notice that the curve showing rework hours is almost a mirror image
of the progress curve. This suggests that one reason the team was
not making good progress prior to week 10 is because they were
making numerous errors, which had to be corrected. After week
10 they had reduced the rework significantly, and progress re-
flects this. These figures would be for a very small team.

Other indicators of project quality might be documentation
changes, engineering changes, design revisions, customer com-
plaints, test failures, number of software bugs, and so on.

It is also useful to track the number of scope changes in a
project, but you need to capture the impact of a scope change for

F I G U R E 12.17

A Run Chart for Project Echo Showing Rework

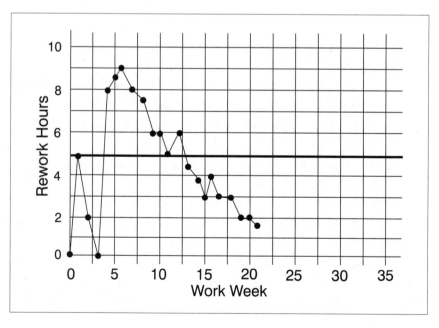

this to be meaningful. You might be able to absorb a dozen small scope changes with almost no project impact, while a single change in scope might nearly sink the project. Since scope changes result in additional work, you can track impact by looking at the dollar value of the extra work required (or the number of working hours if you don't have dollar figures). You can also show impact by any resulting slip in schedule.

The other issue that should be addressed is the cause of the scope change. If the cause was, say, environmental regulations that no one could foresee, then the scope changes are probably legitimate. On longer duration projects, the world is going to move around before you can finish the project. Competitors bring out products that necessitate changes in your design if you are going to continue to compete. This is understandable, although you sometimes should go ahead and freeze a design without the competitive feature, release it, and then start a new project to add that feature. It all depends on how critical that feature is for product sales.

On the other hand, if changes were required because not enough time was spent up-front in defining the project, these are wasteful and should be avoided in the future.

Guidelines on Tracking Progress

Although it seems obvious, there is very little need to go to the trouble of tracking progress unless you keep accurate records. If you don't want the information to be used for control, but rather want to make your project look good, then why bother to collect data? Just write down what you want people to see and save yourself a lot of effort.

There are two major sins committed in tracking progress. One is to let people record their time once a week. I know. I did this 30 years ago when I didn't know any better. We had to record time to the nearest quarter-hour, and we turned the reports in on Monday morning.

There is very little need to track progress unless you keep accurate records.

Even when I was younger, I could never remember what I did the previous Monday. Now I can't remember what I did yesterday. So when my time report was due, I guessed at it the best I could, but you can be sure it was highly inaccurate. That means that the database was a fiction—one which would subsequently be used to estimate future projects. It's useless!

The only reasonable way to record work is to do it daily. It doesn't take that long. If it takes longer than five minutes, you are being obsessive. I don't think it makes sense to record time in increments much less than a half-hour. If you work an eight-hour day, that is 16 entries into your time log. It should take less than 15 seconds to write each one down, so that is about four minutes. (Okay, you're slow; allow yourself 10 minutes, but that's it!)

The second deadly sin is to not track unpaid overtime. In some organizations, salaried personnel are only allowed to report 40 hours a week, because that's all they are paid for. That is a payroll issue, not a project one. For project purposes you need to know exactly how many total hours are spent on a task, so that your database will reflect actual hours for use in future estimating. In addition, if you strip off the overtime, you can't tell that you have problems, as was shown at the beginning of this chapter.

PROJECT CHANGE CONTROL

One major cause of project time and cost overruns is scope creep. Stakeholders ask for "small" changes. They aren't very significant, so you absorb them. The problem is, five-cent changes add up to dollars, and the next thing you know the project has grown considerably larger than it started out to be. Feature creep is also the cause of scope creep. The interesting thing is that the very people who ask for all of the changes develop very convenient amnesia at the end of the project. To protect yourself and everyone else, you have to control changes to the project.

This is done through a formal project change approval process. When someone asks for a change to the project, you should let that person know the impact if the change is made. What will it do to schedule, cost, or performance? Then ask if the individual really wants to accept the impact. If she says yes, then you initiate a formal change procedure.

This procedure requires that changes be approved by more than just the person who asked for it. The change may impact inventory of parts that have already been purchased for the project. It may affect market introduction of a new hardware or software product, which could severely impact sales. It may affect tooling. So a formal change process requires that an approval board review all of these possible effects and sign off on them.

The form shown in Figure 12.18 can be used to control changes to a project. Note that tic boxes are placed in front of signatories, so that, unless the box is checked, that person does not have to approve the change. The rule is that only those individuals who have a need to review the change should sign the form. That way, you cut down on the endless rounds of approvals that can delay the process.

F I G U R E 12.18

Process Review Form

Project Change Approval		
Project Name:	Project Number:	Date:
Project Manager: Requested by:	Department:	Change in: ☐ Scope ☐ Schedule ☐ Budget ☐ Performance

Deviation Information

Description of change being requested:

Reason for change:

Effect on schedule:

Effect on cost (budget):

Effect on performance (quality):

Effect on scope:

Justification:

Class	Distribution of estimated cost deviation	The requested change is:	
Capital		☐ Absolutely necessary to achieve desired results	☐ Scope reduction that will not impact original targets
Noncapital		☐ Discretionary—provides benefits beyond the original target	☐ Scope reduction that will impact original targets

Required Approvals ☐

☐ Project Leader/Manager (type name)	Sign:	Date:
☐ General Manager (type name)	Sign:	Date:
☐ Concerned Dept. Manager (type name)	Sign:	Date:
☐ Controller (type name)	Sign:	Date:
☐ Concerned Vice President (type name)	Sign:	Date:
☐ President (type name)	Sign:	Date:
☐ Other (type name)	Sign:	Date:

13

Conducting Project Reviews[1]

There are three kinds of project reviews that can be conducted: status, design, and process. Each has a different purpose. A status review concentrates on whether the P, C, T, and S targets are being met. Are we on schedule and on budget? Is scope correct? Are performance requirements okay?

A design review only applies to those projects in which something is being designed, such as a product, service, or software. Some of the questions asked during such a review are: Does it meet specifications? Is it user-friendly? Can we manufacture it? Is the market still looking for what we are developing? Are return-on-investment and other product justifications still in line?

A process review focuses on *how* we are doing our work. Two questions are asked: What are we doing well? What do we

---

[1] Some of the material on project reviews has been adapted from my book, *The Project Manager's Desk Reference*, Second Edition.

In the land
of the blind
the one-eyed
man is king.
~ Niccoló Machiavelli,
1469–1527

want to improve? We will discuss how this review is conducted later in this chapter.

During status and design reviews, a project may also be evaluated. An evaluation is usually focused on software or hardware development projects and tries to determine if the total end result that is supposed to be achieved will be accomplished. Will the return-on-investment target be met? Will the product be manufacturable? Can we sell it? The answer to these questions determines whether the project will be continued or canceled. Table 13.1 shows a summary of the three project reviews.

Following are some of the general reasons for conducting periodic project reviews:

- Improve project performance together with project management

- Ensure that quality of project work does not take a back seat to schedule and cost concerns

T A B L E 13.1

The Three Kinds of Project Reviews

Project Reviews and Their Nature	
Status	Looks at the status of cost, performance, schedule, and scope
Design	Examines a product, service, or software design to see if it meets requirements
Process	Reviews project processes and asks if they can be improved

- Reveal developing problems early so that action can be taken to deal with them
- Identify areas where other projects (current or future) should be managed differently
- Keep client(s) informed of project status (this can also help ensure that the completed project will meet the needs of the client)
- Reaffirm the organization's commitment to the project for the benefit of project team members

REVIEWS

Stories abound of projects that are supposed to be within days of completion and are suddenly "discovered" to be weeks behind schedule. This happens because people have been lying to themselves, and to everyone else. When technical problems exist in a project, the experts (i.e., engineers, programmers, life scientists) are inclined to be overly optimistic about how long it will take to resolve the problem. If you ask them how long it will be before they solve the problem, they are likely to say, "We hope to have it solved momentarily." I'm sorry, that answer is inadequate. There

Everyone managing projects should be doing status and lessons-learned reviews.

is a book entitled *Hope Is Not a Strategy* (Page, 2003), and this should be the response to those technical people who are *hopeful*. What approach are they going to use to resolve the problem? What are all the issues surrounding the problem? Do they need outside expertise? And so on.

I'm not advocating beating up people who have problems. Our approach to problems should be helpful. But I am intolerant of people who won't admit the severity of their problems and keep plodding along without asking for help. This is usually caused by egos that won't admit they can have problems like ordinary mortals.

AT&T found years ago that one of the things that differentiated the most successful engineers from the less successful ones was that the willingness to ask for help after they had tried unsuccessfully to solve a problem (I no longer remember the source of this finding). The old saying, "If at first you don't succeed, try, try again," should be amended to, "If after a reasonable number of attempts you can't make it work, ask for help!"

DISPLAYING PROGRESS

We saw in Chapter 12 that the most common method of display-ing progress, using a Gantt chart, can lead to serious problems (see Figure 13.1). This is because the chart shows schedule prog-ress only. It tells you nothing about the amount of effort that was expended to achieve those schedule results. We saw that, if a per-son has worked twice as many hours as originally planned to stay on schedule, this is a sign of trouble to come. Our conclusion was that you must have an integrated cost/schedule tracking system in order to know true project progress. We also saw that you must actually know the value of all four PCTS targets in order to deter-mine true progress, because even if schedule and cost are okay, you may not reach full scope, or the work may have been per-formed poorly, resulting in problems later on.

The preferred system for showing progress is earned value analysis, using spreadsheets, as shown in Chapter 12. However, many managers don't want to wade through all the numbers, so the spreadsheet also performs a critical ratio calculation and com-pares the index to prescribed control limits and displays the result in stoplight format—that is, if everything is okay, you get a green box; if there are reasons for concern, you get yellow; and if you see red there is a definite problem! (The phrase "stoplight format" de-rives from the colors used on a standard traffic light—red to mean stop, green to mean go, and yellow to indicate caution.)

We also learned in Chapter 12 that you can't just display sum-mary data for the entire project because you may have two tasks that have almost equal and opposite variances that cancel, so that a misleading result is obtained in the summary. Stoplight reporting is okay if it occurs at the task level and is backed up by earned value data, so that a person can dig in and analyze that data.

A stoplight report for a project is shown in Figure 13.3. Note that this approach allows you to see what has happened between the previous reporting period and the current one. For example, if status has gone from yellow to red, we know that a task was getting into

F I G U R E 13.1

Gantt Chart Showing Progress (from Chapter 12)

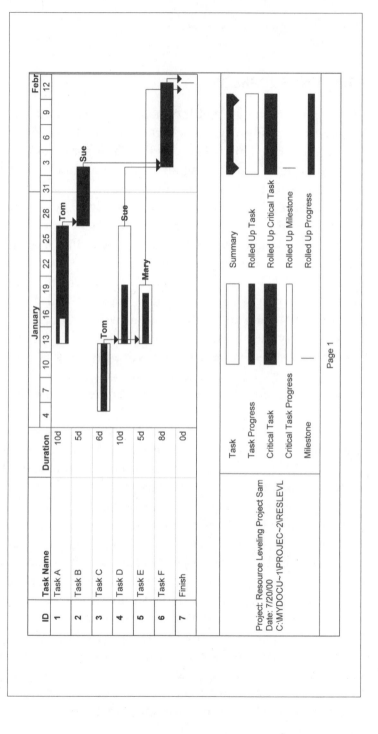

Earned Value Report (from Chapter 12)

Earned Value Report

Project No.:   Date: FILE:
Description: Page____ of ____
Prepared by: Signed:

| WBS # or Name | Cumulative-to-date | | | Variance | | At Completion | | | Critical | Action |
	BCWS	BCWP	ACWP	Sched.	Cost	Budgeted (BAC)	Latest Est. (EAC)	Variance	Ratio	Required
				0	0			0	NA	NA
				0	0			0	NA	NA
				0	0			0	NA	NA
				0	0			0	NA	NA
				0	0			0	NA	NA
				0	0			0	NA	NA
				0	0			0	NA	NA
				0	0			0	NA	NA
				0	0			0	NA	NA
TOTALS:	0	0	0	0	0	0	0	0	NA	NA

NOTE: Negative variance is unfavorable || If Critical Ratio < 0.6, INFORM MANAGEMENT!
( ) = NEGATIVE VALUES

F I G U R E 13.3

A Simple Stoplight Report

Activity	Last Period	This Period
Perform activity one.	Yellow	Red
Perform activity two.	Yellow	Green
Perform activity three.	Green	Green
Perform activity four.	NSTS	NSTS

NSTS = Not scheduled to start.

trouble previously and is now worse off. Conversely, a change from yellow to green shows that the situation has improved.

PROCESS REVIEWS

The objective or purpose of a process review is to improve performance of the team. In reviewing performance, note that we do not ask, "What have we done wrong?" Asking that question simply raises defenses in team members and they will try to hide anything they think is wrong because they assume that they will be trashed for any mistakes that have been made. The purpose of a process review is to learn from experience,

> The purpose of a process review is to learn how to improve performance. If you go on a witch hunt, you will create witches where none existed before.

so that we can avoid those things that were not done so well and continue doing those things that have been done well. It is not a witch hunt. If you go about it in a retributive way, people will hide their faults.

The other reason for not asking what has been done wrong is that the answer may be "nothing," and thus everyone may come to believe that reviews are unnecessary. This is not true. The best-performing team must always attempt to get even better, as their competitors are not sitting idly by maintaining the status quo. They too are improving, and if you stand still for very long they will pass you.

> The ability to learn faster than your competitors may be the only sustainable competitive advantage.
>
> —Arie P. de Geus

It is also a fact that the most dangerous place a team can be is successful. That may sound wrong, maybe even a bit depressing, but it is true. A successful team can easily get complacent. Coaches of sports teams know this. When you have won every game of the season, your very next game is risky because you may

There is a big difference between an excuse and an explanation. Excuses are unacceptable. Explanations are not.

get cocky and careless. For that reason, you can never be satisfied with the status quo.

One favorite expression of some managers is "no excuses." When something goes wrong, they regard any explanation of what happened as an excuse. I find this attitude very dangerous and totally counter to being able to learn. There is a big difference between an excuse and an explanation. Comedian Flip Wilson used to have a wonderful excuse when he did something he shouldn't have: "The devil made me do it," he would quip. That is an excuse.

Saying that El Niño caused so much rain in California one summer that construction of a new plant fell far behind schedule is an explanation, not an excuse. To say that there has been a fire in an auto parts plant, and that parts are not available for production, is an explanation, not an excuse.

You cannot learn from problems or failures if you behave like an ostrich and stick your head in the sand, or you hold your hands

You cannot learn from problems or failures if you behave like an ostrich and stick your head in the sand.

over your ears, refusing to listen to the facts. And those who refuse to learn from history are doomed to repeat their mistakes.

Process Always Affects Task

It is very important to understand that process will always affect task outcomes! That is, the *way* you do something will always affect the results you get. As the old saying goes, "If you always do what you've always done, you'll always get what you always got." And

> Process will *always* affect task!
> —Marvin Weisbord

the corollary is, "Insanity is continuing to do what you've always done and hoping for a different result." In terms of process, these statements mean, "If you aren't getting the results you want, change your process!"

In any project team, the processes we care about include those shown in the "Team Processes" box. One of the most important of these is meetings. Projects cannot succeed without periodic meetings. However, as we all know, the large majority of meetings are badly run, leaving participants drained, frustrated, and

Team Processes
- Leadership
- Decision making
- Problem solving
- Communications
- Meetings
- Planning
- Giving feedback to team members
- Conflict management

wishing they would never have to attend another one. In his video, "Meetings, Bloody Meetings," John Cleese makes a profound comment about meetings: "The essence of management is in how we run meetings." (This video can be purchased from Video Arts, www.videoarts.com.)

Now if that doesn't depress you, you haven't thought about the implications. Meetings typically loose focus, have no clear direction to begin with, go on ad nauseum, and don't accomplish anything. If you can't manage a meeting, how can you manage an organization?

If you want to improve the management of your meetings, read Chapter 16 and follow the model presented there.

CONDUCTING PROCESS OR LESSONS-LEARNED REVIEWS

As I have already said, lessons-learned reviews focus on processes; that is, how is work being done, and can those processes be improved? There are some problems or pitfalls in conducting lessons-learned reviews, so here are suggestions on how to make them effective.

> Lessons-learned reviews focus on processes. If you want to get better results, you have to improve how you do your work.

First, it tends to be hard to get people to open up when you initially do these, especially about issues that might seem critical of people. You have to work on building trust by teaching people how to phrase their comments. For example, if I were a team member I might say something like, "Communication in this team sucks." Now, all that comment will do is make some people defensive. Furthermore, it is very vague. What kind of communication? All, or just some? As a group facilitator, I would first explain to everyone that such comments are not helpful. Rather, the comment would be much better if it were rephrased to be specific, such as, "I did not receive information about slippage in tasks that feed my work until several days after the slip was identified. Because of that, I was unable to react in time to keep my own work on track."

The more specific the comments, the better. Also, the more impersonal they are, the better. One rule is to describe everything in terms that others could verify by direct observation—they can see, hear, or feel it. The second rule is to express your comments in nonjudgmental terms; avoid remarks that can be interpreted by others as attacking them in some way.

> You can't solve problems with processes unless you know exactly what the problem is.

I use two flip charts in such reviews. On one I list things done well. The other is used to list things we want to do better. These are the words I write at the top of each chart: "Done Well," and "Do Better." Note this: I do not like the system of placing a plus mark (+) on top of one page and a minus (–) on top of the other. This still designates good and bad, and as I mentioned earlier, saying that something was done badly makes people defensive and they quit participating. Clearly you can't capture information about problems if people won't tell you about them, so you want to frame the entire process as a way of improving, not ascribing guilt so you can place blame and punishment.

I have two scribes available, who are (preferably) not members of the team, to record entries on the charts. When a person makes a comment (these can be in any order), it is recorded. If I am not clear about the meaning, or the person has framed the comment in violation of the rule, I ask for a reframing before it is written down. I also suggest that each person write notes to himself as the process goes along, so he doesn't forget a thought.

I also make a flipchart page that contains all the processes and issues to be examined and post it in the room to jog people to think about everything. (These were shown previously.) One issue that can be a problem is leadership. Team members can be very reluctant to say anything negative about their leader, so it may be necessary for the leader to leave the room so the group can talk openly about any leadership concerns without fear of reprisal. In that case, a stand-in facilitator should be available who understands the process and can help the group frame their comments properly. Rather than saying, "Doug is a sorry leader," the person would be coached to say, "I sometimes feel that Doug isn't listening to me when I tell him about a problem." That would help the leader change his behavior, perhaps by practicing active listening.

Once all comments are captured, I give each person 10 votes to cast for what they believe are the top items. They can cast all 10 for one item, or distribute them. They do this by simply placing a checkmark on the page beside the item they are voting for. Two checkmarks means two votes, and so on. (This is called "multivoting.")

Votes for each item are then counted. The items with the most votes are selected for resolution. I suggest that no more than three or four items be addressed at once. Furthermore, someone on the team should accept an action assignment to deal with each issue. A target date for resolution should be established. I would ask for a progress report before the target date is reached, and a final report (verbal is fine) on the target date.

I strongly suggest that you publish the findings of the review and circulate them to all team members, as well as parties outside the team, so that everyone can benefit from what has been learned. If you have an intranet on which the review can be posted, that is good too. You can now proceed down through the list that was initially generated to solve next-ranked items, so that eventually you resolve them all.

There is one suggestion. If problems fall into the following categories they should be resolved in the order shown, regardless of the number of votes they receive:

1. Goals.

2. Roles and responsibilities.

3. Procedures.

4. Relationships.

The rationale for this is that if goals are not clear, you are headed for disaster no matter how other procedures are going. Furthermore, it is possible

> Conflict among team members is sometimes caused by lack of goal clarity, uncertain roles and responsibilities, or conflicting procedures.

that other processes are being affected because people aren't clear on goals. Next, people must be clear about and agree on their roles and responsibilities, or there will be significant problems with your team. Given that these are clear, you should then agree on procedures—how things will be done. Some of the items gener-

If there are relationship problems in the team, you can work on resolving these.

ated in the lessons-learned review will point to ineffective procedures that can be taken up for resolution.

Finally, if there are relationship problems within the team, you can work on resolving these. However, to work on these matters when there are problems with any of the first three categories can be a waste of time, because the first three categories can themselves cause relationship problems.

THE PROCESS REVIEW REPORT

When a project is reviewed, the lessons learned should be shared with other teams so they can avoid the mistakes made by the team being reviewed and can take advantage of the things the team did well. The lessons-learned report should contain, at a minimum, the following:

1. **Current project status.** This is best shown using earned value analysis. However, when earned value analysis is not used, status should still be reported with as much accuracy as possible.

2. **Future status.** This is a forecast of what is expected to happen in the project. Are significant deviations expected in schedule, cost, performance, or scope? If so, the nature of such changes should be specified.

3. **Status of critical tasks.** The status of critical tasks, particularly those on the critical path, should be reported. Tasks that have high levels of technical risk should be given special attention, as should those being performed by outside vendors or subcontractors over which the project manager may have limited control.

4. **Risk assessment.** Have any risks been identified that highlight the potential for monetary loss, project failure, or other liabilities?

5. **Information relevant to other projects.** What has been learned from this review that can/should be applied to other projects, whether presently in progress or about to start?

6. **Limitations of the review.** What factors might limit the validity of the review? Are any assumptions suspect? Is any data missing, or suspect of contamination? Was anyone uncooperative in providing information for the review?

As a general comment, the simpler and more straightforward a project review report, the better. The information should be organized so that planned versus actual results can be easily compared. Significant deviations should be highlighted and explained. Figure 13.4 is a form intended to be used for a milestone process review. Note that this form will be inadequate to capture all the data generated for an end-of-project review, but it can be used as a guide for questions to be asked.

Was anyone uncooperative in providing information for the review?

F I G U R E 13.4

Process Review Form

Project Change Approval		
Project Name:	Project Number:	Date:
Project Manager: Requested by:	Department:	Change in: ☐ Scope ☐ Schedule ☐ Budget ☐ Performance

Deviation Information

Description of change being requested:

Reason for change:

Effect on schedule:

Effect on cost (budget):

Effect on performance (quality):

Effect on scope:

Justification:

Class	Distribution of estimated cost deviation	The requested change is:	
Capital		☐ Absolutely necessary to achieve desired results	☐ Scope reduction that will not impact original targets
Noncapital		☐ Discretionary—provides benefits beyond the original target	☐ Scope reduction that will impact original targets

Required Approvals ☐

☐ Project Leader/Manager (type name)	Sign:	Date:
☐ General Manager (type name)	Sign:	Date:
☐ Concerned Dept. Manager (type name)	Sign:	Date:
☐ Controller (type name)	Sign:	Date:
☐ Concerned Vice President (type name)	Sign:	Date:
☐ President (type name)	Sign:	Date:
☐ Other (type name)	Sign:	Date:

DESIGN REVIEWS

A design review is conducted to determine if the product being developed is going to perform according to requirements and whether the company will be able to manufacture it at the intended price. If the answer to either of these questions is negative, then a decision could be made to terminate the project. The answers to these questions become more certain as the project progresses and approaches completion. Unfortunately, by the time the answer is certain, significant expenditures have already been made, making cancellation less helpful than it would be early in the project life cycle. However, canceling a project early based on limited information may be unwarranted.

Since decisions to cancel projects are not usually made by project managers, but by business managers, I will not go into detail about the process. A good reference is Patterson, 1993.

SECTION

OTHER ISSUES IN
PROJECT MANAGEMENT

14
CHAPTER

Improving Project Processes

I have previously cited the saying in psychology that really captures the need for performance improvement: *If you always do what you've always done, you'll always get what you always got.* The corollary to this is: insanity is continuing to do what you've always done and expecting a different result! Clearly, if you have tried something repeatedly and have not achieved the desired result, try something different!

Dr. W. Edwards Deming used to say that there are two kinds of organizations—those that are getting better and those that are dying. If you're standing still, you're dying; you just don't know it yet. Your competition isn't standing still; if you are, they will eventually pass you by. He used this point to argue for continuous improvement in organizations. The same can be applied to companies as a whole, or groups within them. This includes project teams.

If you always
do what
you've always
done, you'll
always get
what you
always got.

As I have said, no sports teams with any credibility would go an entire season without trying to improve—they get better by practicing, watching game films to give players feedback on past performance, coaching players, trying new plays, and changing personnel if need be. They understand that their success can breed a sense of complacency; they believe that nobody can drag them down. The same is true of organizations. Judith Bardwick wrote a book entitled *Danger in the Comfort Zone* that echoes this idea.

Yet project teams seldom stop to ask if they can improve. In fact, this is one of the major causes of project failure. Team building is the forgotten side of project management. We get so focused on the task at hand that we totally forget about process issues. This is a concern for *what* must be done to the exclusion of concern for the *how* it is being done. Remember Marvin Weisbord's observation: process issues will always affect task performance. In Chapter 13, we discussed how to conduct process or lessons-learned reviews. The importance of these cannot be overstated.

Many project managers today are feeling the pressure to get their jobs done faster and cheaper at the same time, while holding performance and scope constant. At first glance, this sounds contradictory, since there is usually an inverse relationship between reducing time in a project and the cost to do the work. That is, as we try to work faster costs tend to escalate. This is shown in Figure 14.1.

However, this curve assumes that the processes of doing work remains unchanged and all we are doing is adding resources to the team. That being the case, you cannot simultaneously reduce time and costs both.

On the other hand, by changing the process by which work is done you can reduce both at the same time. Note also that doing

F I G U R E 14.1

Time-Cost Tradeoff Curve for a Typical Project

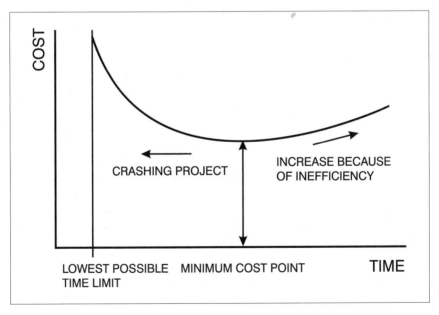

work correctly the first time will help achieve this result. I have shown that the typical rework cost in a project ranges from 5 to 40 percent. Rework is total waste. As one chief engineer said, 30 percent rework in a project is equivalent to having one person out of every three on the staff spending full time just to redo what the other two did wrong. If you reduce the rework, you get the job done faster and cheaper at the same time.

One of the contributors to rework is definitely a process issue: how well the project is defined and planned at the very beginning. The tendency here is to avoid the initial pain of planning. Unfortunately you pay now or pay later, and it is almost always cheaper to pay now than later. As my colleague, Bob Wysocki jokes, "You pain now or pain later." This is shown in Figure 14.2. Good project planning causes a lot of pain at the beginning, but the pain diminishes as the project progresses. With no planning or

F I G U R E 14.2

Pain Curves in Project Management

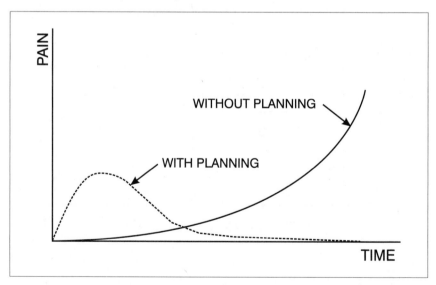

As rework goes up, more overtime is required, which causes greater fatigue.

cursory planning, there is little pain at the beginning, but it grows significantly as the project advances.

You might remember from our discussion of systems issues that one reason for this is that as rework goes up, more overtime is required, which causes greater fatigue, which leads to more errors that have to be corrected (reworked), which means more overtime, and on and on. It is a vicious spiral, getting progressively worse. This is indicated graphically by the exponential increase in pain.

IDENTIFYING PROCESSES

A process is a way of doing something. In Egyptian times, a form of writing called hieroglyphics was invented. Each symbol initially stood for a word or an idea. This same kind of system was used by the Chinese. The problem is that you need to remember about 1,800 characters to have a decent working vocabulary. Eventually, alphabets were invented, which permitted words to be built up from letters, so that with a knowledge of 26–30 characters you could represent any word in the language. This also meant that the way one wrote those symbols changed. Hieroglyphics are often painted with a brush. Alphabetical characters can be easily written with stylus, pen, or brush. They can also be typed. Thus, the invention of the typewriter sped up the process of putting words on paper. More recently, the invention of computers has taken us a step further. All of these steps were refinements of the process of conveying ideas to others through written means.

All process improvements tend to follow an S-curve, as shown in Figure 14.3. Initially, gains in process improvement are hard to come by. Then considerable progress is made. Finally, the

F I G U R E 14.3

Process Improvement Curves

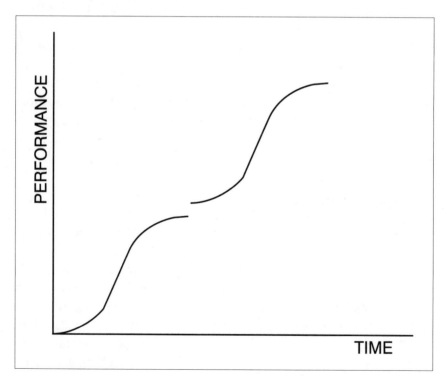

gains become harder and harder to achieve. We sometimes say that we are *pushing the envelope* at either the beginning or end of the process improvement curve.

Notice that, when the end of a process improvement cycle is reached, and the gains become difficult to achieve, it is time to retire the old process and invent an entirely new one. Unfortunately, some managers get hung up trying to improve a process that should be eliminated

> There is no point in trying to improve a process that should be replaced altogether.

because it is at the end of its improvement cycle, but they don't realize this.

Interestingly, organizations that are just getting started with formal project management are down on the low side of the process improvement curve, and they experience significant startup difficulty. This sometimes causes them to throw out the process entirely, because they are experiencing too much initial pain. They don't realize that they will soon cross the peak if they stick with it, and then be in for an easy ride down the right-hand slope of the pain curve (Figure 14.2).

PRINCIPLES OF PROCESS IMPROVEMENT

The first important idea to consider in process improvement is that, if we have learned how to improve processes in one domain, we should be able to apply some of what was learned to other processes. Partly the reason for this is that processes must conform to some of the rules of system behavior, which we discussed in Chapter 9. In that chapter we found that systems that have similar structures can be expected to behave similarly, regardless of the content involved in the system process Thus, since we have had so much experience with process improvement in

If we know how
to improve
processes in one
area, we should
be able to apply
that knowledge
to other areas.

manufacturing, we should be able to adopt some of the procedures used in that area and apply them to improving project
management processes.

Earlier in this chapter I mentioned the pressure to get projects
completed more quickly. A number of books written in recent
years on speeding up the product development process include
Accelerating Innovation (Patterson, 1993), *Developing Products in
Half the Time* (Smith & Reinertsen, 1995), and *Revolutionizing Product Development* (Wheelwright & Clark, 1992), to name just a few.
As I have noted elsewhere, however, product development
should not be confused with project management. Similar pressures to speed up projects are being felt in all kinds of projects, not
just in product development.

One of the first points that must be made about improving a
process is that it should be running smoothly already, or it will be
nearly impossible to tell if it has been improved. If you are familiar with statistical process control (SPC) methodology, you would
say that the process should be in control before you begin changing it. The second point is that it requires good planning to im-

prove a process, and this in turn requires that the process be well understood. We will discuss understanding processes in the next section.

Patterson lists a number of actions that can reduce manufacturing time, and it is instructive to examine these with respect to projects. I have adapted his list, as shown in the box (Patterson, 1993, p. 101).

Improve process quality. Anything that you can do to reduce errors that lead to rework will improve overall process performance, especially speed. Improvements in planning generally reduce errors due to false starts. Time spent planning must be balanced, of course. It is not productive if the team goes into analysis paralysis because they are afraid to make any planning errors.

> ## Actions that Reduce Manufacturing Cycle Time
>
> - Improve process quality (in particular, minimize rework)
> - Implement concurrent processes
> - Add value as rapidly as possible at each step
> - Improve quality and timeliness of incoming materials
> - Eliminate work that adds no value
> - Minimize change-over time (reduce setup time)
> - Eliminate bottlenecks

In Chapter 6, methods of identifying and defining problems were presented. Those methods should be used to help identify and define process problems.

Implement concurrent processes. If we can do as many things as possible in parallel, rather than serially, we can speed up project work. Care must be taken to balance risk with gains in speed. When interdependent tasks are performed concurrently, you definitely increase the risk that costs will be incurred because the work done in one step negates that done in the (normally subsequent) next step.

Add value as rapidly as possible at each process step. In manufacturing, raw materials themselves have almost no value to customers. It is only after they have been formed, shaped, machined, stamped, or molded that they gain value. In projects, the same idea would apply. Every step in the project should increase the value of the final product that will be delivered to the customer. Related to this idea, perhaps as a corollary, is the point about *eliminating any step that adds no value*. Setup time, for example, is an operation that provides no value but may have to be done if a single machine is used for multiple tasks. The longer the run of parts on that machine before a changeover is made, the smaller the setup time as a percentage of the total. The same is true of people. If we can reduce the interruptions and transitions that they experience, the more productive they become.

One example of steps that add no value is the iteration of design to make a product function properly. Elsewhere, I have discussed using design-of-experiments to eliminate the design-test-redesign iteration that creates an endless loop in pro-

Every step in a project should add value to the end "product," or it should be eliminated.

Selection of good vendors and partnerships can greatly improve the quality of incoming goods.

jects. Wherever feasible, this approach is preferable to multiple iterations.

Another subject near and dear to the hearts of many of us is the wastefulness of meetings. Get a copy of *Mining Group Gold* by Tom Kaiser (1995) and practice his model in running your meetings. It will improve your efficiency tremendously. (The model is also available on film from CRM Learning. See the Resources section in Appendix A for ordering information.)

Improve quality and timeliness of incoming materials. A manufacturer who receives shoddy raw materials can hardly produce quality products. Considerable time and money were once spent on incoming inspection of materials. Carefully selecting vendors and forming partnerships can greatly improve the quality of incoming goods and reduce later incurred cost of a poorly manufactured product. In the same way, projects of any kind need good raw materials with which to work. When projects are done primarily by knowledge workers, this means *the right information at the right time*. If the information arrives too late, it will be of no benefit to the current job. If it arrives too early, it may not be recognized as relevant, though if an error is to be made, it should be made in the direction of too early as opposed to too late. A good reference librarian can be an immense help for this issue. Basically, what is needed is a just-in-time (JIT) information system.

Streamline the flow of materials. In manufacturing, modern assembly lines are characterized by the well-planned flow of materials from beginning to end. Good project planning should result in the same smooth flow of information or work from one stage to another. For local project teams, this means that all members of the team have access to information on a timely basis through a local area network (LAN). For dispersed teams, a wide area network (WAN) is needed.

Eliminate bottlenecks. A bottleneck is a point in a process that restricts the flow of materials. In construction projects, bottlenecks are often caused by agencies that must approve building plans or perform environmental impact studies or archaeological surveys. You often can't eliminate these or speed them up, since you have no control over them. About all you can do is work around them.

Eliminate bottlenecks. You have no control over them.

Sometimes a single support group becomes a bottleneck because they are servicing so many teams that they lack capacity to do it well. Bottlenecks are resolved by identifying the root cause of the limited capacity and then investing in the resources needed to bring capacity up to the required level. Needless to say, the economy of keeping a support group "lean and mean" can be greatly offset by time lost by dependent teams. However, since project managers are not always able to influence the powers that be to deal with bottlenecks properly, the best defense is to have work that can be productively done while waiting for other work to clear the bottleneck.

OPERATIONAL DEFINITIONS OF PROBLEMS

I cannot stress strongly enough how important it is that problems be defined correctly so that the right problem gets solved. It should be clear that such a definition must be one that everyone understands and with which all agree. Unless everyone has the same understanding of a problem, there is no way to solve it. An operational definition is needed. An operational definition establishes a language that communicates the same meaning to everyone involved in solving the problem. Since our focus here is on improving processes, this

> Unless everyone has the same understanding of a problem, it is almost impossible to solve it.

language will specifically apply to the processes we are trying to improve. Words such as "defective," "unsafe," or "inadequate," have no meaning unless they are operationally defined.

To illustrate how confusion can be caused by the absence of operational definitions, consider a label on a shirt that reads "75% cotton." What does this mean? Is it three-quarters cotton, on the average, throughout the shirt? Or is it three-quarters cotton applied to shirts over a month's production? Is it three-quarters by linear mea-sure or by weight? If by weight, at what humidity? Does humidity affect the noncotton component the same as the cotton?

Another example: the team says communication is poor. What does this mean? Communication consists of transmitting and receiving. Is transmission the problem, or is it receiving? Is the person talking using precise language? Or are listeners not paying attention? Is the transmission being affected by noise, so that it is not received properly? What are the tangible effects of the communication? Misunderstandings, missed dates, work done in-correctly, or conflicts? Until we arrive at a shared understanding of what is meant by "poor communication," we can't possibly solve the problem.

A given operational definition is not necessarily right or wrong. Its importance lies in its acceptance by all parties involved in dealing with the process. As conditions change, the operational definition may change to meet new needs.

An operational definition consists of:

1. A criterion to be applied to an object or to a group;

2. A test of the object or of the group; and

3. A decision as to whether the object or group did or did not meet the criterion.

The project team is told that they are expected to do their work on time and within budget, while maintaining performance as expected and doing the predefined amount (scope) of work. This statement is loaded with problems. What does on time and within budget mean? Can there be a tolerance? If so, how much? If not, we are expecting the impossible, because all processes vary. To expect people to get work done *exactly* on time is unrealistic. In the first place, where did the time frame come from? It was an es-timate, so by definition it is not exact.

Now, if we know that we can typically achieve schedule and budget tolerances of 10 percent, then we can operationally define on time and within budget as being within this tolerance. By the same token, we must operationally define performance requirements. If the person is writing software, how do you define the performance requirement? The entire program has less than a given number of bugs? It executes at a certain speed? It has no more than x lines of code? All of the above?

Here is an example of actually applying the conditions to arrive at an operational definition. A salesperson is told that her performance will be judged with respect to the percentage of change in this year's sales over last year's sales. What does this mean? Average percentage sales each month? Each week? For each product? Percentage between December 31, 2004 and December 31, 2005? How are we measuring sales? Is it gross, net, gross profit, net profit? You get the picture.

Step 1: Develop a criterion for percentage change in sales.

A percentage change in sales is the difference between 2005 (January 1, 2005 to December 31, 2005) sales and 2004 (January 1, 2004 to December 31, 2004) sales:

Percentage change:

$$(04\text{-}05) = (S05\text{-}S04)/S04$$

where

S05 = dollar sales volume for January 1– December 31, 2005, and

S04 = dollar sales volume for January 1– December 31, 2004

S04 is measured in constant dollars.

Steps 2 and 3. Test the decision on percentage change in sales. This will be done by looking at 2004 and 2005 sales figures and performing the computations.

Example of Identifying a Process Problem

The team has missed the last two project milestones. The project manager is feeling the heat to make sure this does not happen again, as the project deadline is highly critical to the business, and if milestones are slipping it is likely that the end date will be missed. To help identify the possible cause or causes of this problem, you might want to use an Ishikawa diagram, which is shown in generic form in Figure 14.4. The model is also called a fishbone or cause-effect diagram. The problem you are trying to solve is noted in the box to the right, and possible causes are listed on the "bones" of the diagram, grouped according to general categories. This list is usually generated through brainstorming.

Once the list has been created, you classify each variable with a C, N, or X, as follows:

C (Constant) These are variables that we intend to hold constant so that we can achieve the desired response, or possi-

F I G U R E 14.4

The Generic Ishikawa Diagram

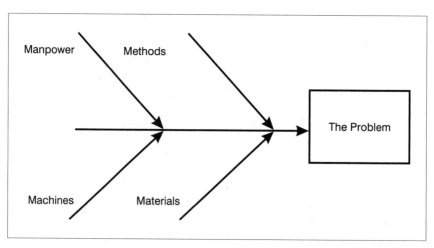

**Make sure
milestones
are not
slipping.**

bly reduce extraneous variation in the response. For each of these variables, we need a standard operating procedure to tell us how the variable is being controlled.

N (Noise) These are uncontrolled variables. They cause "noise" in the system. Although they do affect system response, they are too difficult or too expensive to hold constant.

X (Experimental) If an experiment is to be run, these are the factors to be investigated. Not all cause-and-effect diagrams will contain X factors. However, a variable that is a C today could become an X tomorrow if we decide to investigate the effect experimentally (and vice versa).

In using the Ishikawa diagram, or any other approach, you must take care not to fall into the trap of having people give you causes at too high a level. For example, you ask your group to tell you what problems they think are affecting project team performance, and you get a list like the following:

1. Lack of leadership.

2. Poor communication.

3. Unclear mission and objectives.

4. Inadequate workspace.

5. Lack of training.

The difficulty with this list is that people have concluded that lack of leadership is a cause, based on some lower-level cause. At this point, you don't know what the real problem is to which your team is attributing the causes. To understand the real problem, you now need to ask, "What effect is lack of leadership (or any of the others) having on our team?" The person says, "I think members of the team are demoralized just now."

She is attributing low morale to lack of leadership. But is that true? We would have to look more closely to determine if some aspect of the leader's behavior is causing morale problems. In all likelihood, there may be other factors in the situation that are causing the morale effect.

Once you have identified the root cause of a problem, the solution is often fairly obvious, although not always easy to implement. As examples, if your car is running rough and you find that a sparkplug is broken, then all you need to do is replace the plug and the problem is solved. If sales are down because you are in a recession, however, you can't necessarily solve the problem, even though you know its cause. I also might know that an employee is performing poorly because he has a really rotten attitude, but that knowledge won't necessarily help me solve the problem.

For our example of missed deadlines, here is the procedure you would follow:

1. The project manager calls a meeting to solve the problem of missed deadlines, and the Ishikawa diagram shown in Figure 14.5 is generated. As the diagram shows, there are not many causes under Policies and Machines, but sev-

F I G U R E 14.5

Ishikawa Diagram for Missed Milestones

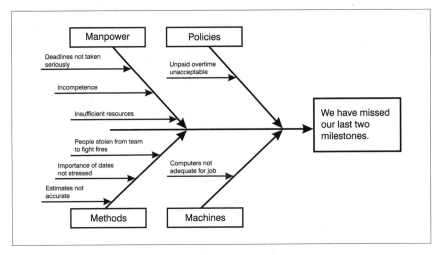

eral under each of the other two categories. The question is, what do you do with these guesses at possible causes?

2. The next step in the process is to allow people time to ponder the causes before evaluating them. Some questions to consider at this time are:

   ◆ Is this cause a variable or an attribute? A variable is one that has continuous measures, such as pounds, feet, and so on. An attribute is present or not present, such as a scratch, dent, or hole.

   ◆ Has the cause been operationally defined?

   ◆ Does this cause interact with other causes?

3. Once people have had time to think about the issue, the next step is to circle likely causes on the diagram. This will always be based on judgment initially. Once this is done, you can rank them in order of most likely to least likely. "Paired comparisons," is a good one to use to rank causes (see Chapter 6).

4. Finally, you need to verify the cause. You can do this in a variety of ways. Begin by gathering data to see if the most likely cause actually has a significant impact on the problem. If not, then look at the next most likely cause, and so on. You can also design experiments to manipulate variables to see if they have an effect, when they are amenable to such treatment. A full survey of such methods is outside the scope of this book. For more in-depth information, consult Gitlow, et. al, 1989, or Schmidt, et. al, 1996.

15
CHAPTER

Closing Out the Project

There is a tendency to think that when all project work is completed the job is finished. You will note that in my model, I don't consider a project complete until a final lessons-learned review has been conducted and documented. This should become a habit, part of an organization's culture. The army calls lessons-learned reviews "after-action" reviews. Their policy is, after anything significant takes place, to pause and learn whatever lessons they can from that event. In the case of military personnel, learning lessons has life-or-death significance. In a way, the same can be said of organizations. You live or die by constant improvement. As has been said, there are two kinds of organizations—those getting better and those that are dying. If you're standing still, you're dying, because your competition is certain to pass you eventually.

Conducting lessons-learned reviews was covered in Chapter 13, so I will not repeat the process here. I simply want to reinforce

The final lessons-learned review should be documented.

what was said in that chapter about the importance of such reviews. In addition, I want to stress that the final lessons-learned review should be documented, and the report sent to all who can benefit from what the team learned. Otherwise, you may find that your team learned valuable lessons about mistakes that are being made by other teams in your organization.

ADMINISTRATIVE CLOSURE

PMI defines administrative closure of a project as the ". . . process of documenting the results of your work to ensure that you have met all of the requirements and specifications" (Lewis & Dudley, 2005, p. 223; PMBOK 2004). While we are primarily discussing final project closeout, administrative closure should be performed at each phase completion in a project. As was pointed out in Chapter 13, lessons-learned reviews (and documentation) should not be restricted to the end of the project only. They should be done at the end of each phase or stage-gate in the project. The final closeout documentation should be a summary of all preceding reports.

Following are some of the issues that should be addressed before the project is considered complete:

- The collection and archiving of all project documents. This includes final cost and schedule data.

- Updating records and product specifications to reflect what was actually achieved, so this can be compared to the original plan.

- Revising employee records to reflect newly developed skills and anticipate future training needs.

- Preparation of a final project report that summarizes the history of the project. The product produced by the project should also be considered. The project may have been kept on track but produced a bad product. Conversely, a good product may have been produced by a troubled project. I have heard it said that a project can be late, overspent, and end with reduced scope, but if the product is successful you will be forgiven. The opposite is not true.

- As already noted, a final lessons-learned review should be conducted with all stakeholders.

THE FINAL LESSONS-LEARNED REVIEW

Unfortunately, in many projects, team members have already been reassigned to other projects and are unavailable to participate in the final lessons-learned review. This should be considered important enough that provisions should be made to bring them together one last time to participate in the review, in spite of their new assignments. The data from lessons-learned reviews should be viewed as one of the most important resources an organization can acquire. It is similar to what Edison said when someone asked if he was discouraged after 1,800 unsuccessful attempts to make a light bulb filament. "No," he said, "I know 1,800 things I don't have to try."

Equally important is knowing what *has* worked. Lessons-learned are not restricted to negative events only. When something worked really well, we want to know about it as well.

PERSONNEL ISSUES IN PROJECT CLOSING

As projects near completion, team members sometimes become very apprehensive about their future with the organization. Will there be work for them once this project is finished? This apprehension can depress performance, and project managers should do whatever they can to protect the jobs of team members and let them know that they are secure. Of course, in matrix organizations there is a limit to what a project manager can do, but whatever the case, failing to attend to these concerns can result in incomplete closure—which will certainly lead to problems in the future.

There can also be strong feelings associated with disbanding project teams. In a project that has lasted for a prolonged period, the project team becomes like a family to some individuals, and losing that family can arouse considerable sadness. Some psychologists specialize in helping members of such teams go through the "grieving" process of losing their "families." This is another of those "touchy-feely" dimensions of human nature that is often not understood by managers, with the consequence that performance deficits accrue. It is important to remember that human beings have an attribute called *emotion,* which differentiates them from computers and machines and actually gives them an advantage over those devices. The root of the words *emotion* and *motive* is the same. People are motivated. Machines are not.

There can be strong feelings associated with disbanding project teams.

And since people form the primary resource in any project, emotion should be considered data to be managed, just like any other information. Failure to do so may result in people not wanting future project assignments.

16

CHAPTER

Managing Multiple Projects

Managing multiple projects is in some ways equivalent to managing a program. We saw in Chapter 8 when we discussed work breakdown structures (WBS) that we begin at the program level and that there will be a number of projects under that level. One example is the development of an airplane, shown in Figure 16.1.

As is shown in the WBS, the engine, wing, and avionics are all projects, and each will have its own project manager. The program manager does not personally attend to all of the project details for each of these projects. It is too much. And this is where people struggle with managing multiple projects.

Just a week ago a fellow in a seminar said he had 20 projects he was trying to manage. With all due respect, I doubt that he is managing them. He is reacting to crises as they arise. Or he is attending to whatever project is most prominent at the moment. He

F I G U R E   16.1

Partial WBS for Developing an Airplane

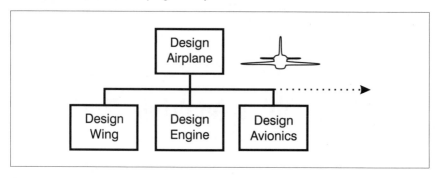

may have 20 projects on a list—and be responsible for them—but he is not really managing.

The human mind can only handle five to nine bits of information at one time. I believe this is the effective range of projects that an individual can actually manage as well. If they are large projects, then the number is probably three to five—and in the extreme case, only one. If they are small, then it may be seven to nine. If you consider also the basic fact of a 40- to 60-hour week, how much time can one person devote to each project? And how much time is required?

> The human mind can only handle five to nine bits of information at one time.

The typical project will require at least two hours of meeting time every week. That means the person trying to manage 20 projects has his entire 40-hour week taken up with project meetings, which means all the other things he must do will have to be handled on an overtime basis.

As I discussed in Chapter 9, my informal surveys reveal that the typical project manager is trying to deal with four to six pro-

The typical project will require at least two hours of meeting time every week.

jects simultaneously. This alone wouldn't be too bad if he or she were actually just managing them, but in many cases the individual is a *working* project manager, which means she must do some of the project work as well as manage it. And we know that this always leads to problems. There is always a conflict between managing and doing the work, and the work always takes priority—meaning that managing suffers.

> There is a big difference between *managing* four projects and trying to do the work itself!

This problem results from a lack of understanding on the part of senior managers about the role of project managers and what can reasonably be expected of them. It is also based on the belief that multitasking is the best way to get productive work out of people, yet we have seen in Chapter 9 that just the opposite is true: multitasking actually results in reduced productivity because of the high level of setup time that it causes.

PROJECT, TASK, PRIORITY?

The other issue in managing multiple projects is whether the person is actually managing projects or just a number of disparate tasks. What I find in many cases is that so-called projects are really tasks. Collectively, they amount to 20 tasks, the equivalent of a single project.

However, even when they are actually projects rather than tasks, what causes all of the headaches is that the project manager's supervisor won't assign priorities. When asked what must be done first, the supervisor says "They've all got to be done." This is true. They all must be done. But unless you have unlimited resources, they can't all be done at the same time. Because no-one will establish priorities for them, they are worked on haphazardly, with the result that they take forever to complete. The solution is to prioritize them, get the high-priority tasks done first, then continue working down the list until they are all done. The net result is reduced setup time, meaning lower cost, greater efficiency, and better utilization of resources.

> If your supervisor won't give you a list of priorities, make your own. If he won't accept this, and insists that they all have to be done, it may be time to look for another job.

When your supervisor won't prioritize for you, the best thing to do is make your own list and send it to your supervisor. Tell him how many hours you estimate each project or task will take, and then point out that even if you work 60 hours a week you can't do all of them at once. For that reason, you've decided to do them in the order indicated on your list, and that this means those at the bottom of the list will be finished by whenever. If your supervisor disagrees with your ranking, then you have forced the issue. If he insists that you must do all of them immediately, he is being totally unreasonable, and you should look for another job. Seriously. If a manager refuses to recognize the reality of human productive capability, then you are headed for a major problem down the road.

PERSONAL EFFECTIVENESS

Trying to do too many things is the mark of ineffective people. Those who are effective have learned to do one thing at a time, do it well, and then to move on to the next task on their list. And they have learned to differentiate between the urgent, the important, the urgent *and* important, and the final category,

> Trying to do too many things is the mark of ineffective people.

those that are neither urgent nor important. This is discussed in all literature on time management, so I won't elaborate on it here.

Effective people have also learned the value of planning. If you are managing several projects—truly managing them—then you should have plans for each project. Trying to manage projects without plans leads to chaos. Furthermore, as we saw in

**Those who are
effective have
learned to do one
thing at a time.**

Chapter 12, if you have no plan, the project controls you rather than you controlling the project.

To return to the question of how many projects a single person can manage, the answer is that it all depends. Many issues affect the answer. Here are some of them:

1. How complex is each project? Highly complex projects require more attention (time) than less complex ones.

2. How many people are working on the job? The Boeing 777 airplane development program had 97,000 people working on it scattered around the world. Do you think the program manager could possibly have managed another program at the same time? I doubt it.

3. Are you managing or doing? If you have to do technical work as well as try to manage the job, you will be lucky if you can manage a single project.

4. How chaotic is your environment? In a shared-resource environment where there are too many projects being done for the available resources, you can't really manage any projects because resources are constantly being moved around. At best you can react to the changes, but you are not really managing.

5. Is the project local or global? Global projects will probably require a lot more time spent communicating with team members than a local one.

6. Do you have a strong role as a project manager or a very weak one?

7. What is your own individual capability to keep up with many things at once? Some of us are sequential thinkers and are very distracted by having to deal with more than one thing at once. Others have no problem with this. So it is a matter of individual disposition, on top of everything else we have considered.

8. How much administrative assistance do you have? If you have a dedicated scheduler, for example, you don't have to sit at a computer all day developing and updating your schedule(s). On the other hand, when you must prepare and type all of your own reports, do your own scheduling, and all of the other administrative tasks, you are limited in how many jobs you can manage.

9. How supportive are functional managers in a matrix organization? If they see projects as an imposition, rather than seeing their job as being to support projects, then you will spend a lot of time negotiating for resources, which means you can't handle many projects.

There are many other issues, such as whether your project team is dysfunctional or cooperative, whether the work is done internally or contracted out, whether it is well defined or not, and so on. All of these combine to determine how many projects an individual can manage.

Is your team dysfunctional or cooperative? This affects the project greatly.

You should keep records, good ones, on how much time you spend on various aspects of each project you manage. You can't tell how many projects you can manage until you have some feeling for where your time goes. In the end analysis, it all boils down to the same issues that are involved in managing a single project. You match the required time with the available time, and that is what you can do. If you want to do more, you must increase your available time or find a way to be more effective and efficient. There are no "magic pills" you can take to solve the problem.

17
CHAPTER

Improving Your Effectiveness

The very fact that you are reading this book—and especially this chapter—indicates that you want to succeed in your career, and no doubt in your life overall. It is very clear that some few individuals are highly successful, while the majority of people are not. Why is this? What differentiates those who are successful from those who are not?

This has been the subject of extensive research, and the answers have been known for at least 20 years, yet not nearly enough people take advantage of this knowledge. Strangely, understanding of how human beings function, which is the domain of psychology, is not widely held, though it is not difficult to comprehend and requires no formal training to acquire. Books, tapes, CDs, and noncredit courses abound that provide this knowledge.

We know that to get maximum benefit from a computer or tool, we need to thoroughly understand how to use it, and it helps

Success is more than money!

a lot to understand how the tool works. Yet, many managers seem uninterested in learning how this most important and prevalent resource—this human resource—works, even though we say that people are "our most valuable resource." Clearly, unless we know how to get the best out of people, we will not do so.

> How can you get the best performance from people if you don't know what makes them tick?

Over the years, I have taught thousands of people how to deal more effectively with others. In particular, the question asked by most managers is how to motivate their followers. Again, this knowledge has existed for about 50 years, but many managers have a total misconception about what works and what does not. In fact, surveys repeatedly find that managers believe that what motivates them personally is different than what motivates their followers. Certainly we all differ in what motivates us individually, but we are all more alike than we are different, so it seems reasonable that managers and employees would not be that different in what "turns them on," and indeed, the research confirms that this is true.

THE PSYCHOLOGY OF ACHIEVEMENT

The desire to achieve is essentially a desire to succeed. As a project manager, you want to complete your projects on time, on budget, with proper outcomes of scope and performance. To do this you have to get your team members to perform at acceptable levels. If you do this, you would most likely consider yourself a success in managing projects. But how do you define success in general? Brian Tracy (1995) says that six conditions must exist for you to be successful. These are:

- Peace of mind. This condition requires freedom from fear, anger, and guilt.
- You must also have good health and high energy.

The desire to achieve is essentially a desire to be successful.

- You should have loving relationships with people.
- Financial freedom is also necessary; you can't have peace of mind if you are always worried about how you will pay next month's rent.
- Finally, you need a sense of fulfillment, or what is called self-actualization.

THE LAWS THAT GOVERN OUR LIVES

As I have said, you need to know the laws that govern your performance in order to achieve. The first of these is the law of control, a sense of being in control of your life. Many people feel that they have no such control, that life is just a series of random events, some good and some bad. This is called having an external *locus of control*. An internal locus of control is having a sense that you control your destiny and the events in your life. I like to call this self-determination.

Get in
control
of your
life!

The Law of Belief

One of the most important laws is the *law of belief*. This law states that our deeply held beliefs become our life's reality. Another way to state this is: what we believe, we make real. For those who have an external locus of control, this law seems difficult to accept. They feel that factors outside their control govern their lives, not realizing that what happens to them is actually

> What we believe, we make real.

the result of what they believe. Furthermore, it is sometimes true that people claim to believe something opposite to what they actually believe deep down inside. We don't always know what we truly believe. However, we can be sure that our behavior is a guide to what we truly believe, because the two will always be consistent.

As an example of how beliefs govern our lives, there was a time when uneducated people believed that the world was flat, and that if you sailed away from land you would eventually come to the edge of the earth and fall into an abyss. Because this belief was so strong, few ventured very far from land, and so they never learned that the belief was false.

Most importantly, once we hold a belief, we filter information in such a way that we maintain the belief. As an example, if employees believe that management has no concern for their welfare, any gesture to the contrary on the part of management will be seen simply as a ploy or an attempt to manipulate them. There are two psychological processes that help people filter information. One is called *deletion* and the other is *distortion*. If evidence is presented that might disconfirm a person's belief about something, that information may not become conscious; the person simply deletes it from his or her awareness. If the information is noticed, then its meaning will be changed to be made consistent

> **Once we hold a belief, we filter information in such a way that we maintain the belief.**

with the belief. An example of this is an employee believing that management is trying to manipulate her.

An example of deletion is that prejudiced individuals don't notice that members of the group against which they are biased actually aren't anything like what they believe them to be. Members of the "out" group are often believed to be stupid or ignorant—to have lower IQs than the "in" group. Actual IQ test scores may prove that this is untrue, but the prejudiced person believes it anyway.

The Law of Expectation

The beliefs that we hold create in us *expectations* for how things will be in the world. These expectations become self-fulfilling prophecies. Rosenthal and Jacobsen (1968) conducted a study that demonstrated how this worked. They administered aptitude tests to grade-school children. They then paired children by race, sex, and score, selected them at random, and assigned them to two groups. Their teacher was told that one group was average, ordinary children. The other group, however, was labeled *late-bloomers*. Teachers were told that these students could be expected to blossom during the school year, to really achieve high academic performance.

At the end of the school year, when performance was measured, the group of late-bloomers was doing significantly better than the "average" kids (using statistical significance as the measure—that is, the difference could not be due to chance alone.). The result indicated that the teacher brought about the expected result, since there should have been no difference.

In a later experiment, the same expectation was created for teachers, but classroom activity was observed through a one-way mirror. The students and teacher could not see the observers; rather, they saw their reflections.

The observers learned that teachers spent more time with the late-blooming children than the "average" children. They encouraged and helped them more. In doing so, they brought about the

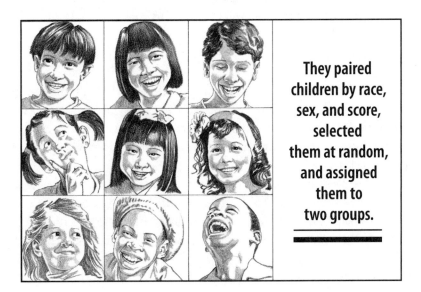

They paired children by race, sex, and score, selected them at random, and assigned them to two groups.

very thing that they expected—one group performed better than the other. There have been many experiments since then that have demonstrated the validity of the self-fulfilling prophecy.

The point is that if you believe that your life is governed by outside influences over which you have no control, that is what you will experience. You will always be tossed around by forces that seem to be luck or chance. On the other hand, if you have an internal locus of control you will experience being in control of your life.

Now, some of you may not believe this. But it doesn't matter whether you believe it or not, the law works just the same. You may not believe in the law of gravity but if you jump off a cliff the law will work anyway regardless of your beliefs—and you know what the outcome will be.

To me, it is empowering to know that I am actually in control, rather than that other forces in the world are controlling me. If you want to demonstrate that the law is true, then you must act as if it is true and you will begin to see results. It may take some time to undo old beliefs and replace them with new, more positive ones, but if you are persistent, you can do this.

SELF-CONCEPT

Perhaps the most important belief a person has is his or her self-concept. This is what you believe about yourself. We have a host of beliefs that form our self-concept. We are smart or dumb, creative or not, strong or weak, assertive or unassertive, good at a sport or a klutz.

The importance of this is shown by research into the effect of attributions on the performance of children in school. The researchers found that American parents are likely to say that a subject is too difficult for their child when that child has difficulty with the subject. Korean parents, however, were more likely to say that the child needed to work harder on the material. That is, the

The most important belief a person has is his or her self-concept.

child simply wasn't trying hard enough. Clearly, you can control trying, but you can't do much about incompetence. So, American children simply give up because there is no use in trying if the subject is too hard for them. Korean children, by contrast, buckle down and work harder.

> When a child has difficulty in school, American parents are likely to say the subject is too hard for the child. Korean parents are likely to say the child needs to work harder.

I remember an engineering student from my college days, who told me his IQ was only 109. Most engineering students have IQs of 125 or higher. This student could easily have concluded that he could never get an engineering degree because he had a lower IQ than his peers. However, he didn't do that. Instead, he worked really hard, and graduated with a 3.85 average. In his entire undergraduate experience, he only made Bs in two subjects—both physical education, in which he was truly limited by physical ability. He went on to get a Ph.D. in electrical engineering. His example convinced me that if a person has an average IQ, he can master virtually any subject that interests him!

> A person of average intelligence can master virtually any subject that interests him.

Because our expectations tend to become self-fulfilling, this applies to our children and our team members. If we have high expectations for their performance, we tend to get it. Conversely, low expectations produce low performance. I personally believe that the most respectful thing you can do for another person is hold very high expectations for that person.

Self-concept consists of three components. One is your concept of your ideal self. This is what you would like to be. Second is your self-image, or what you believe you are actually like. The third element is self-esteem, or how you feel about yourself. If you don't like yourself, you aren't likely to like others.

In transactional analysis, there are considered to be four existential positions. These are shown in Figure 17.1. Theoretically, the two positions "I'm not okay, you are okay" and "I'm okay, you're not okay" are possible, but I don't believe these are actual life positions. Rather, I believe they are momentary. It seems to me that the only two permanent positions are "I'm okay, you're okay" and "I'm not okay, you're not okay."

As you can imagine, the negative position, "I'm not okay, you're not okay" creates expectations for self and others that are pretty low. Individuals who hold this belief tend not to perform well, and often drag down others with whom they interact. They are harsh in their criticism of others as well as themselves.

Contrasted with this position is the "I'm okay, you're okay" outlook. Individuals who hold this belief see themselves and oth-

F I G U R E 17.1

The Life Positions from Transactional Analysis

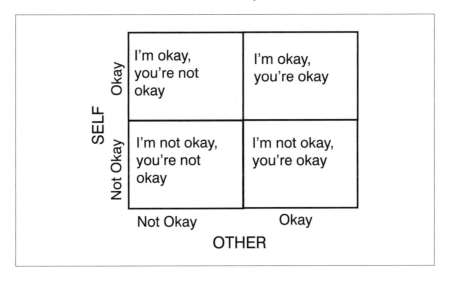

ers as essentially okay. They recognize that we all have defects or flaws, but they don't dwell on these. Rather, they focus on the positive aspects of people and overlook the negative. Because of the self-fulfilling nature of such beliefs, the "I'm-okay-you're-okay" person tends to bring out the best in others and his or her own self.

Charles Sykes, in his book *Dumbing Down Our Kids* (1995), has criticized the self-esteem emphasis in our schools, saying that no studies have shown that high self-esteem leads to high performance but many studies show that high performance leads to high self-esteem. I think he is wrong in claiming that no studies show the relationship between esteem and performance. However, he is right in saying that it doesn't take a child very long to realize that he isn't special because he can ride a bike. Most children can ride bikes. Nor is he special because he can color in a coloring book. Most children can do that as well.

I do believe that high regard must begin with parents and teachers, because children develop their self-concept from the messages these people send them. When adults convey to their children that they love them and have high expectations for their performance in school, then the children are inclined to respond positively. Let's put it in the opposite vein: a child who has a very low self-concept is unlikely to ever perform at a high enough level at anything in order to test her true capabilities. Thus, we must begin by helping children perform well, which will in turn build their self-esteem to ever higher levels.

I must also say that you never want to set an individual or group a task at which they are almost guaranteed to fail the first time out. You should plan small wins for yourself and others. Begin at a level at which you can perform, even though not superbly, and move up from there. I learned this in the 1960s when I taught guitar. Most methods teach beginners the C, F, and G7 chords. The F chord is one of the hardest to make on the guitar, and most beginning students don't buy really good instruments (until they see if they can play), so they have two strikes against them under this approach. I started them with the D, A7, and G chords, which most beginners find relatively easy. This gave them a success experience the first week, giving them confidence that they could move up from there, and most did.

PROGRAMMING YOUR MIND FOR SUCCESS

The most important thing you can do to ensure your success in life is to program your mind for success. You have actually been programming your mind for success or failure all your life, but unconsciously and haphazardly. The result has been that some things you wanted to do you found you were unable to do successfully. If you examine your beliefs carefully, you will find that there was some underlying belief that you could not succeed at that particular endeavor.

The most
important thing
you can do to
ensure your
success in life
is to program
your mind
for success.

Psychologists have found that we become what we think about. It is inevitable, and if you don't like what you are experiencing in your life, you must take charge of your thoughts and change them to bring about the life you desire. There is no other way. You can't just change your behavior because behavior is always consistent with deeply held beliefs. So if you believe you are no good at something—a sport, for example—you will find that you cannot behave inconsistently with that belief.

BEHAVE AS-IF

Here is a major secret to success. Behave as if the thing you want to achieve is already a fact. If you want to be a successful project manager, behave as if it is already true. Take charge of your meetings. Interact with your team members as though you are the team leader (which you are). Do this in a positive way, not in an arrogant, bullying manner.

Observe the behavior of other individuals who are effective.

Observe the behavior of other individuals who are effective, and emulate them. We all learned adult behaviors when we were children by imitating the important figures in our lives. In some cases, these role models were not people we should have followed, but we were too young to judge properly. Now, as adults, we can return to this approach. Select individuals you either know or know about as models for your own behavior. Ask yourself, "How would this person behave in this situation?"

> Here is a major secret to success. Behave as if the thing you want to achieve is already a fact.

MENTAL REHEARSAL

Take time before you approach a situation to imagine yourself in that situation, behaving as you want to behave in actuality. Mental rehearsal has been proven a most effective way to ensure your success at any endeavor. It is used widely by athletes, musicians, and other performers to enhance their success.

Larry Wilson sold a million dollars of insurance when he was only 23 years old. He was inducted into the millionaire's club as a result, and was asked to tell other members how he had done this. The audience was to be about 300 individuals. Larry found himself worrying about his presentation. He had never given a presentation to such a large group. He feared that they wouldn't like him or what he had to say. Fortunately, he caught himself and realized that he was programming his mind for failure.

> Research shows mental rehearsal to be almost as effective as physical practice in sports and music.

He then imagined giving his talk and having the audience give him resounding applause, with some of them coming up and telling him how impressed they were, and how much they had enjoyed his presentation. He practiced this several times a day, up until the time of the event itself. He said that the outcome was almost like deja vu, like seeing something repeated that he had seen before—which he had, of course, in his imagination (Wilson, 1988). He eventually founded Wilson Learning Systems and taught salespeople throughout the world that visualizing success in their sales efforts would improve their sales performance.

Take time to visualize yourself actually performing well, and you will greatly improve your chance of succeeding. If you catch yourself doubting the outcome, immediately reverse this and imagine success.

AFFIRMATIONS AND GOALS

Because the subconscious creates what the conscious mind tells it, without argument or judgment as to whether what you tell it is good, bad, true, or false, you must be careful to obey certain rules.

The most important of these is that affirmations and goals should always be stated in the present tense. If you affirm that "I will earn $50,000 a year," you are affirming something that must occur in the future, and the subconscious keeps it in the future. Rather, you should affirm "I earn $50,000 a year."

The question naturally arises, how can you affirm something that isn't true at the moment? If you have difficulty with this, the affirmation "I have the ability to earn $50,000 a year" may be much more acceptable. Or add to it: "I have the ability to earn $50,000 a year, and I exercise that ability every day in everything that I do." Now, if you visualize yourself earning $50,000 a year, you will find that your mind will create just this outcome for you over time.

If you are still unconvinced, let me ask you: which risk would you rather take—the one that says it's true or the one that says it isn't? It's like believing or not believing in an afterlife. It's too late to change your behavior once you find that hell is a reality.

RELAX

It is important to work continually at changing your thoughts and behaviors to bring them into line with your aspirations. Just don't strain at it. The best results are obtained when you relax and accept that the things you want will come into your life without your forcing it. There is a mental law at work here, and like the laws of physics, you don't have to force it to work. These laws work automatically; if you drop an object, the law of gravity will cause it to fall to earth. You don't have to make it happen. The same is true of the laws of mind. Once you "plant the seeds," you simply add water and fertilizer and await the harvest. It would be foolish to keep digging up the seeds to see if they have sprouted; doing so will only destroy them.

AUTOGENIC CONDITIONING

The most important thing you can do to achieve success is to continually act like the person you want to be. This means you must have a clear mental picture of that person—call it the ideal self-image. If you combine this with autogenic conditioning, you will get remarkable results.

To practice autogenic conditioning, which is best done first thing in the morning, sit down and relax. Progressive relaxation, in which you count down slowly from 50 to 1, taking deep breaths as you count, will set the stage for conditioning yourself. Once you achieve a state of deep relaxation, form a mental image of yourself with all the qualities you want to possess and hold that image for as long as you can.

> The most important thing you can do to achieve success is to continually act like the person you want to be.

Set for yourself the task of practicing this for the next 21 days. That is all it takes to build a completely new self-image. Throughout the day, practice affirmations and concentrate on behaving consistently with your ideal image. You will find that this will produce amazing results.

A WORD OF CAUTION

Be careful about which groups you belong to. David McClelland, who spent his professional life studying achievement, found that individuals who had been programming themselves for success would soon undo that programming if they participated in groups in which people had a very negative outlook. If you share your goals with people who have a

> Don't let unsuccessful people talk you out of success. If you share your goals with people who have a negative outlook, they will quickly put you down and tell you how unrealistic you are.

negative outlook, they will quickly put you down and tell you how unrealistic you are.

I remember once telling a cousin of mine that I was making $500 a day teaching seminars. She became indignant and told me I was aiming too high. I didn't bother to tell her that I was actually aiming for $1,000 a day. After all, the $500 a day fee was already a reality and had been for several years.

From this experience I learned to never tell anyone what I earned. Those who *have-not* often have difficulty accepting those who have. As Jesus said, "The poor we always have with us." These individuals believe that there is something morally wrong with making money and being successful. Strangely, they seem to have missed the fact that Jesus also said, "Herein is your Father glorified—that you bear fruit richly."

And I believe this very sincerely. There is no merit in failure or poverty. Money is not the root of all evil—it is an over-love of money that is. Putting money foremost in your mind is not right. Success can only exist if you place people first and practice the rules laid down by all of the world's great religions, the golden

Success can only exist if you place people first.

rule being first among them. In addition, if you earn a lot of money and hoard it, never contributing to worthy causes, you will eventually lose it. Everything that you have read in this chapter must be practiced with a spirit of doing good in the world. If you use any of these principles to cause harm to others, you will find that they backfire on you and leave you worse off than you were before you began using them.

Having said that, as long as you focus on doing good in the world, these laws and practices will support you in achieving more than you ever believed possible before you learned them! Finally, you may want to read the book by Hyrum Smith, founder of the Franklin Institute, entitled *The 10 Natural Laws of Time and Life Management* (1994). It helps a lot to get clear on what is really important to you, so that you don't fall into the delusion that money is everything.

APPENDIX: SCHEDULE COMPUTATIONS

Once a suitable network has been drawn, with durations assigned to all activities, it is necessary to perform computations to determine the longest path through the project. If start and finish dates have already been "dictated" for the project, these calculations will tell whether the required dates can be met. On the other hand, if a start date is given, the computations will provide the earliest completion date for the project.

The simplest computation that can be made for a network will determine total working time on the longest path through the project and will reveal whether any latitude exists on paths parallel to the longest path. The longest path is called the critical path, since a slip on the longest path will cause a corresponding slip in the completion of the project. This computation would specify how many weeks (or days or hours, depending on time units being used) it will take to complete the project if no holidays or vacation periods exist. Naturally, during certain parts of the year, holidays and/or vacations will intervene, so that the actual *calendar time* for the project is likely to exceed the *working time*.

It is also important to note that the conventional way to compute project working times is to ignore resources initially. In other words, activities are treated as though they have *fixed durations*, based on the assumption that certain levels of resources will be available when the work begins.

Further, these durations are estimated from historical data and are based on a person being available who possesses the skill level to do the required work. As was pointed out in previous chapters, if these conditions are not met the actual working times will deviate from estimated times, sometimes considerably.

NETWORK RULES

In order to compute project working times, two *universal* rules apply to defining how networks function. (The software you use may impose additional rules, which will be presented in the user manual.) These universal rules are:

Rule 1:   Before a task can begin, all tasks preceding it must be completed.

Rule 2:   Arrows denote logical precedence. Neither the length of the arrow nor its angular direction have any significance. (It is not a vector, but a scalar.)

BASIC SCHEDULING COMPUTATIONS

Although no one is likely to do manual network computations in this day of abundant scheduling software, it is important to understand how computations are made by the computer. Otherwise, it is easy to fall into the *garbage-in-garbage-out* problem. Further, the computer output is not easily understandable unless the computation method is understood. What does float really mean, for example?

The following material will explain how the basic computations are performed with no concern for resource limitations. That is, these computations all are based on the assumption that the required resources will indeed be available when time comes to do the work. This is equivalent to saying that the organization has an *unlimited* pool of people, which of course is never the case.

For this reason, a schedule which assumes unlimited resources is considered to be the *ideal* or *best-case* situation, and provides a starting point for resource-constrained project scheduling. Chapter 9 deals with the allocation of resources to yield a realistic working schedule.

We will use the network developed in Chapter 9 to prepare a meal to illustrate scheduling computations. That network is repeated in Figure A.1, using AON notation. A solution will be presented later using AOA notation. The numbers in the duration (DU) cells are working durations in minutes. Each activity contains cells in which we can enter the *earliest start* and *earliest finish* as well as the *latest start* and *latest finish* for the activity. Other notation schemes are used in other books and with various software packages, but this one seems to me to be very simple to understand.

In order to locate the critical path and compute earliest and latest start and finish times for noncritical project activities, two sets of computations are necessary. These are called *forward-pass* and *backward-pass* calculations.

Forward-Pass Computations

A forward pass is made through the network to calculate the earliest achievement times for each activity in the network. If we remember that each activity has a start and a finish, then we can talk about early start and early finish times, as mentioned above. This really amounts to having start and finish *events* for each activity, but they are not usually shown in activity-on-node diagrams. As was stated above, the durations for the activities in Figure A.1 are *working minutes*. The project is shown as starting at time T = 0. For schedules spanning several days or weeks, once activity start and finish times are determined they can be converted to calendar dates, but that step will be omitted in this chapter. For our simple project, we will compute the total project time in minutes and than convert to hours.

FIGURE A.1

AON Network for Preparing a Meal

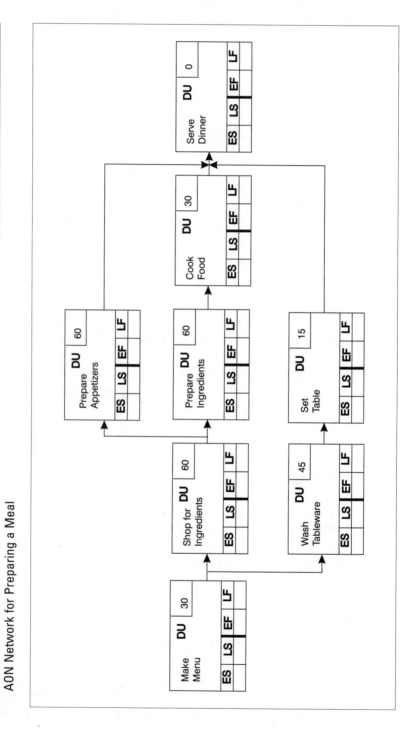

Figure A.2 shows the first steps in the forward-pass computation. "Make Menu" starts at time = zero. It takes 30 minutes. That means it has an early finish 30 minutes after it starts, or at t = 30. As soon as make menu is finished, two activities can start—"Shop" and "Wash Tableware." This means that the early finish for make menu becomes the early start for these two succeeding tasks.

It takes 60 minutes to do the shopping, so the early finish for that task is 90 minutes. You simply add its duration to its early start time to get its early finish. The same is done for wash tableware. Again, the early finish for each task becomes the early start for succeeding ones. We continue this process until we get to "Serve Dinner."

At this point, "Prepare Appetizers" has an early finish of 150 minutes, "Cook Meal" has an early finish of 180 minutes, and "Set Table" has 90 minutes for its early finish. Which one becomes the early start for serve dinner? Remember, Rule 1 presented above says that you can't start a task until all tasks preceding it have been completed. Since cook meal ends the latest (has the largest early finish time), then its early finish becomes the early start for the serving task.

Given the activity durations shown and the sequences detailed by the network, the project has a completion 180 minutes after it begins. Because we are usually trying to meet an imposed completion time for most projects, this working time can now be compared to the target to see if that target can be met, given an anticipated start date or time. If it cannot, then either the project must start earlier, the end date must slip out, or the network must be changed to compress (shorten) the critical path.

For our example, suppose we had planned to come home from work at 5 p.m. and have dinner prepared to serve at 7 p.m. Since we have found that it will take three hours to prepare the meal, this won't work. Either we will have to shorten the time of some tasks, start the process at 4 PM, or revise the network in

F I G U R E A.2

First Step, Forward-Pass Computation

some way. Naturally, we could shave 30 minutes off the project by preparing the menu the day before. For many projects, such a solution would not be an option, so we will say for now that this option is not available and see what our other approaches are.

In that case, the question is, "How will the network have to change in order to finish in two hours?" The answer to this question is never obvious in a complicated network (although it is fairly obvious in this one). As a general rule, in order to see what else in the network might have to change, more information is needed. Specifically, we need to know the *latest* times by which each activity can be achieved and still meet the 180-minute completion.

You might ask, "Why not use the 120-minute completion, since that is what is required?" The answer is that a *best-case* computation is made first, so that we can see which paths have latitude and which one(s) is critical. The best case is considered to be that 180 minutes is acceptable. A shorter time is a worse case because you will have to squeeze time out of something. A longer time is also a worse case, as you are stretching the project out unnecessarily.

For that reason, we assign a 180-minute late finish to serve dinner, which means that it has the same early finish and late finish times, and zero duration, making it actually an *event*. This is an example of the only kind of event actually shown in activity-on-node networks, and it is called a *milestone*.

Now that the late finish time has been set for serve dinner, we do a backward-pass computation to determine the latest event times on all activities, which will permit achievement of the 180-minute completion.

Backward-Pass Computations

Beginning with serve dinner, and assigning a late finish time of 180 to it, we subtract its duration of zero from that time to get its late start (see Figure A.3). Naturally, that gives a late start of 180.

FIGURE A.3

Backward Pass to Determine Latest Times

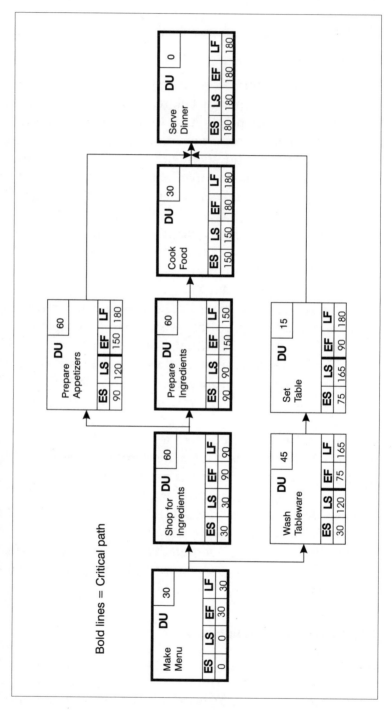

Bold lines = Critical path

This late start time must be the late finish for all predecessors to serve dinner, so that time is entered into the cells for each activity. In the case of prepare appetizers, we subtract its duration of 60 minutes from its late finish of 180, to get 120 minutes. This number becomes its late start time. For cook meal, we do the same and get a late start of 150. In turn, we use 150 as the late finish for prepare ingredients, subtract its duration, and get 90 minutes for its late start.

Notice the junction at the beginning of prepare appetizers and prepare ingredients. The late start for appetizers is 120 minutes, and for prepare ingredients it is 90 minutes. Which one of these should we use for the late finish of the predecessor, shop? If we allowed shopping to finish as late as 120 minutes, prepare ingredients could not start until that time; and if you work forward from there to the end of the project, you will see that this will push the end time out to 210 minutes instead of 180. We can now offer the following rules for assigning early and late times to activities that have multiple predecessors or successors.

Rule: When two or more activities follow a predecessor, the latest finish for the predecessor will be the earliest *late start* for the successors.

Rule: When two or more activities precede another, the earliest start for the successor will be the *latest* of the late finish times for the predecessors.

Continuing in this way, you arrive at the late activity times shown in Figure A.3.

Activity Maximum Float

Now examine prepare appetizers. Note that its early start is 90 and its late start is 120. The difference of 30 minutes is called the *activity float*. This float represents latitude for the activity. So long as it starts no later than 120 minutes and takes no longer than its duration of 60 minutes, the project can be finished within 180 minutes.

Note the activities that run through the center of the diagram. They all have the same early and late start and the same early and late finish times. These activities have no float and are called *critical*. The path containing those activities is, in turn, called the *critical path*. What we have done is apply the *critical path method* to locate that path. By making the final activity late finish the same as its early finish, we have forced one path to have no float. As you can see, it is the longest path.

> An activity is a critical activity any time it has no float.

The term float derives from the fact that prepare appetizers can start as early as 90 minutes and as late as 120 minutes, so we say it can float around for the difference of 30 minutes. Note that float is always calculated by taking the latest start minus the earliest start, or the latest finish minus the earliest finish. In equation form:

$$\text{Max. float} = LF - EF$$

or

$$\text{Max. float} = LS - ES$$

where LS means late start, LF means late finish, ES means early start, and EF means early finish.

The Value of Float

It is tempting to think that float is undesirable. The first suggestion people sometimes make is to finish a task that has float as early as possible and move resources onto the critical path to shorten it, so that you wind up with no float anywhere. To see why this is not a good idea, we must remember that the durations for all tasks are *estimates,* that they have 50-50 likelihoods if averages have been used, and that we often have made those estimates using poor history, so they are suspect to begin with. Given those facts, it is highly advisable to have float on all but the critical path to compensate for unforeseen problems, estimating errors, and so on.

> The best practice in managing projects is to do whatever is necessary to stay on schedule.

What about the critical path itself? That series of activities must be managed in such a way that all tasks are completed on time or the project will be delayed (unless lost time on one activity can be recovered on a later one). It is very risky to allow a critical path task to slip, under the assumption that you will recover the time later. Murphy's Law invariably prevails when you do this. In fact, the best working rule I know is *do whatever is necessary to stay on schedule.*

CALCULATIONS FOR AN AOA NETWORK

The calculations for AOA networks are done exactly the same as for AON networks. The only real problem is with notation. Figure A.4 is the same diagram for preparing a meal in AOA format. In the first edition of this book, I learned that people were confused by the notation, as I had split each node in half and placed an early time on the left side and a late time on the right. However, as was pointed out earlier, each node contains at least two events, and if several activities enter or leave there will be several events contained. I have looked at a number of systems of notation, and no single one is unambiguous. For that reason, I have placed the early and late times on each end of all arrows. On the left end will always be the early start and late start, and on the right end will be the early finish and late finish. Each node is simply numbered for easy reference. See Figure A.4.

CONSTRAINED END DATE SCHEDULING

As was mentioned above, the usual situation for most projects is that an end time (or date) has been imposed, either by contract with the customer or by management, based on business considerations. This end date may be earlier than the earliest completion date determined by the forward-pass computation, in which case the project must be started earlier or the schedule must be shortened somehow.

In many cases, as was mentioned previously, the start date for a project is also dictated by availability of resources or some other factor, so that the start date cannot be moved up. When this is true, the critical path must be shortened. When this is done, other paths may become problems as well.

For the network just analyzed, suppose the end time was established as 120 minutes (you want to serve dinner at 7 PM and start preparations at 5 PM). What would be the overall impact on the project? To answer that question, we will impose a late finish of 120 minutes on the project and do a new backward-pass calculation. Note that there is no need to do a new forward-pass computation yet, since the forward-pass only determines early times, and these will not change until an activity duration is changed or the network is redrawn.

Figure A.5 shows the network with the latest project completion constrained to 120 minutes. When the backward-pass computations have been completed, we find a strange thing. The float on the former critical path is now *negative!* When the float is negative, the activity or path is called *supercritical*. Note also that prepare appetizers now has negative 30 minutes of float, whereas before it had positive 30 minutes. Thus we have two supercritical paths. (Wash tableware and set table still have 30 minutes float, because originally this path had 90 minutes of float.)

AOA Diagram for Preparing a Meal

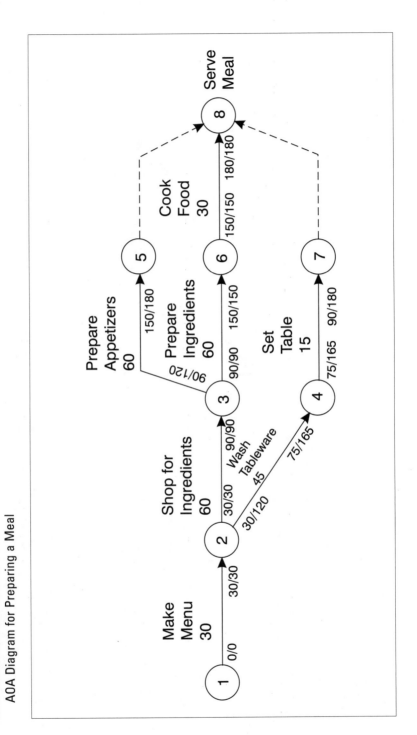

F I G U R E A.5

End Date Constrained

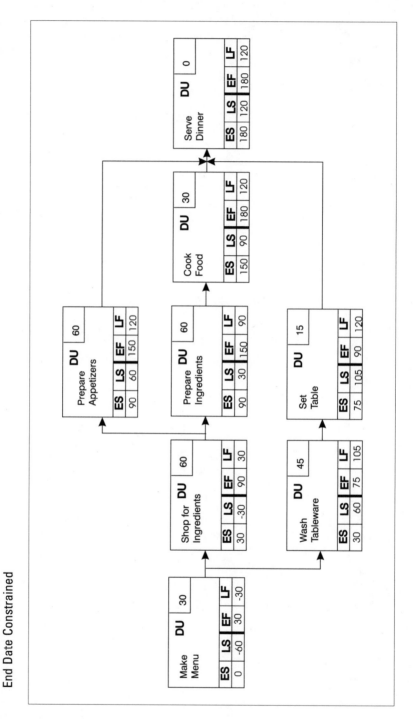

It is also interesting to examine the late times on make menu and shop. These times are now negative. In the case of make menu, this is telling us that the activity needs to start 60 minutes before it is planned to start, which we already knew.

If we cannot start the project early, we will have to shorten the critical path by at least 60 minutes to meet our deadline. Let's suppose we can do this by taking 30 minutes off the time to prepare ingredients and another 15 minutes out of make menu and shopping. We might get time out of prepare ingredients by buying frozen vegetables rather than fresh, so they don't have to be chopped. If these adjustments are made, we have the result shown in Figure A.6.

We now have a situation which is not desirable as a general rule. We have two critical paths. Prepare appetizers is critical, as are prepare ingredients and cook food. For this particular project we might not be concerned about having two critical paths, but most of the time this would be very undesirable. The reason is that when you have no float, anything that goes wrong with the task and increases its duration will cause your overall project finish time to slip by the amount of the increased duration (unless you can reduce the times taken by subsequent tasks). The presence of two critical paths increases risk.

For this reason, you should try to get rid of all but *one* critical path. This can only be done by changing the duration of one or more activities, allowing the end date to be extended, or redrawing the network into a new configuration.

The issue is how to decide which critical path to eliminate. There is no single answer to this problem. Float is only one kind of risk involved in a project. There are also risks from technical problems, poor estimates, weather and other uncontrollable factors, and so on. Table A.1 shows a list of some of the factors that should be considered in making a decision. The comments which follow each factor explain the rationale for deciding what to do.

Network with Times Reduced

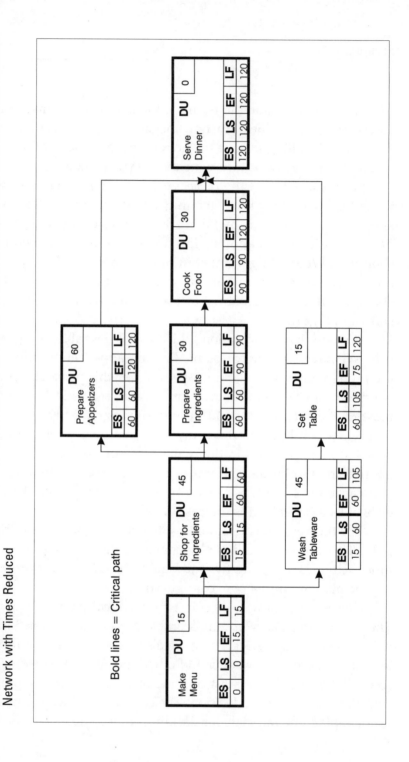

Bold lines = Critical path

T A B L E A.1

Factors to Consider in Eliminating a Dual Critical Path

Number of activities	Path with most activities might be most risky.
Skill level of people	Path with least-skilled people could be most risky.
Technical risk	Path with greatest technical risk should have float.
Weather/uncontrollable	Give float to activities with uncontrollable factors.
Cost	Give float to activities which cost most to do.
Historical data	Least historical data—give float; historically a problem—ditto.
Available backup plan	Give float to activities with no obvious backup.
Business cycle	If business tends to get hectic at certain times, give float to activities affected.
Difficulty	Float given to activities that are most difficult.

REDUCING ACTIVITY DURATIONS

When it is necessary to reduce the duration of a critical path, we usually try to reduce activity durations rather than redrawing the network. That is because we usually feel the logic is more or less sound, so changing sequences might not be an option. When it is, using techniques like lead-lag networks, for example, can be used first.

Whether activity durations can be reduced depends on three factors. Can the work be done faster by increasing *efficiency* (perhaps by using that more productive person mentioned previously)? Can the *scope* of the work be reduced? Can extra effort be applied to the job to get it done faster (by increasing resources)? It is not always possible to reduce activity time by adding more resources, since a point of *diminishing returns* is reached, often because people simply get in each other's way.

There are, of course, two ways to increase human resources applied to a project. One is by adding bodies. The other is by working the same number of people more hours per day, which we call working *overtime*. In both cases you tend to get diminishing returns very quickly. I know of one company that measured the impact on productivity of working overtime. They measured productivity for a normal 40-hour week, then again at the end of three weeks in which people worked 50 hours per week. Productivity after working overtime was back down to the normal 40-hour-per-week level, and errors had increased.

When productivity declines without errors increasing, it is often because people are pacing themselves. They think like a marathon runner who knows that if she runs too fast at the beginning and uses up her energy, she will be unable to finish the race. On the other hand, when error rates increase, it is usually because people are truly fatigued.

We also find that people doing knowledge work suffer the same kind of problems. One study found that when people put in 12 hours of overtime on knowledge work, you probably get an increase in output from them equivalent to what you would expect in 2 normal working hours!

CONVERTING ARROW DIAGRAMS TO BAR CHARTS

While an arrow diagram is essential to do a proper analysis of the relationships between the activities in a project, determine activity float, and identify the critical path, the best tool for the people actually doing the project work is the bar chart. People find it much easier to see when they are supposed to start and finish their jobs if given a bar chart. The schedule shown as an arrow diagram in Figure A.4 has been portrayed as a bar chart in Figure A.7, making use of what we've learned about the schedule from the network analysis.

In this figure, critical path activities are shown as solid bars, while those with float are shown as hollow bars with dots trailing to indicate the amount of float allowed each activity. Note that

F I G U R E A.7

Bar Chart for Project to Prepare a Meal

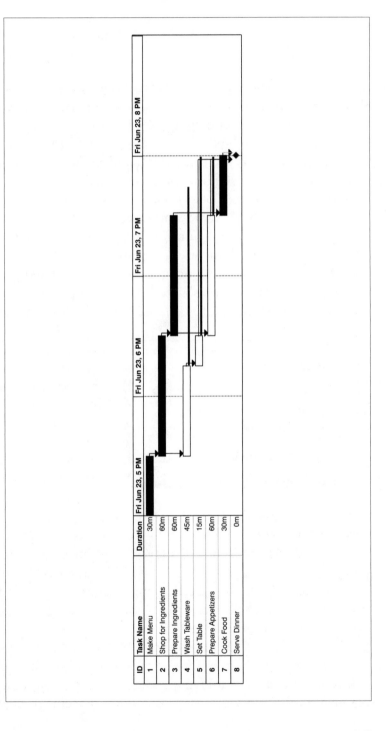

ID	Task Name	Duration	Fri Jun 23, 5 PM	Fri Jun 23, 6 PM	Fri Jun 23, 7 PM	Fri Jun 23, 8 PM
1	Make Menu	30m				
2	Shop for Ingredients	60m				
3	Prepare Ingredients	60m				
4	Wash Tableware	45m				
5	Set Table	15m				
6	Prepare Appetizers	60m				
7	Cook Food	30m				
8	Serve Dinner	0m				

each activity is shown starting at its earliest possible time, so that float is reserved to be used only if absolutely necessary. This is the conventional method of displaying bar charts.

Note that wash tableware has 90 minutes of float; so does set table. Naturally, it is the same float, and initially, before the project begins, there are 90 minutes of float available for each activity. However, if all of the float is used up on wash tableware, there will be none left for set table, and it would therefore be critical.

This illustrates a real pitfall of bar charts. Assume that different individuals are doing two sequential activities that share a common amount of float. Since the chart does not show interrelationships of activities, it is hard for the people performing the work to tell that the float is shared. They look at the chart and think that they each have the designated float. Then, if each tries to make use of the float, the project is in trouble.

In fact, Parkinson's Law can be applied to project float. Parkinson's Law says that work always expands to fit the time allowed. When applied to float, it means that *when you allow float, people will use it!* For this reason, some software can be set up so that float is not displayed. The implication of such a schedule is simply that the work should be done as shown.

Parkinson's Law

Work always expands to take the time allowed.

Lewis's Law for Float

If you give it to them, they'll take it!

I personally do not like this approach. I prefer to explain to team members that float is shared, and I encourage them to keep float in reserve to be used only if necessary. Indeed, it is always a good idea to keep float in reserve to be used if an estimate turns out to be wrong or if an unforeseen problem causes the work to be delayed. As someone told me recently, every project should be planned as if there will be at least some percentage of the total time when the entire city will have a power blackout and nothing will get done.

McGregor formulated a management model some years ago stating that some managers see workers as undependable, wanting only a paycheck from the job, and so on. He called this a *Theory-X* outlook, and postulated that a manager with such an outlook would tend to get the expected results.

The opposite outlook, which is more positive, he called a *Theory-Y* view. This would naturally be the more desired view, as a manager would tend to get the more positive result. It is easy to see Parkinson's Law and Lewis' Law for Float as *Theory-X* outlooks. However, I don't see them that way. In today's downsized, right-sized, understaffed organization, people simply have to do their work in priority order, and this leads to putting off things until they absolutely have to be done. Thus, if they have float they tend to take it, but unfortunately they may take it at the beginning of an assignment; if they encounter a problem with the work later on, no float is left to help get the work done on time.

LIMITATIONS OF CRITICAL PATH METHOD

It is important to remember that conventional critical path analysis, which has been illustrated for this network, assumes that unlimited resources exist in the organization, so that all activities can be done as planned. As the bar chart shows, however, a number of points exist at which activities are running in parallel. If those activities require the same resources, then there may not be enough to get the job done as shown, and the schedule cannot be met. This subject is addressed in Chapter 9.

Multiple Calendars

One final subject must be considered in doing basic network computations. Not all project activities can follow the same working schedule. Does everyone work Monday through Friday? Do some people only work weekends?

Some projects may include activities that require actual working days to complete; others do not. Pouring concrete must be done during the work week. However, that concrete may cure over a weekend. For this reason, it is important that multiple calendars be considered in scheduling.

For example, a situation in which one group works a conventional Monday–Friday schedule and another group only works weekends is shown in Figure A.8.

Now, suppose the two groups are scheduled to do two sequential tasks, with group 1 working exactly one week (M–F), followed by the people in group 2, who are supposed to finish their work over the weekend. However, group 1 gets behind on their work by one day. How much is the schedule impacted? As Figure A.9 shows, the work will slip an entire week because group 1 gets behind only one day!

This kind of problem highlights the occasional need for multiple calendars in scheduling. They are called calendars because holiday and overtime dates differ for the two groups. If the software

F I G U R E A.8

Multiple Calendar Network

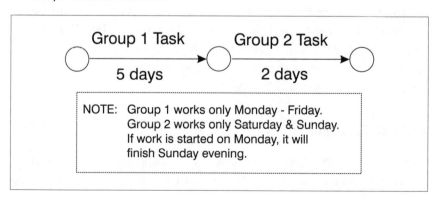

NOTE: Group 1 works only Monday - Friday.
Group 2 works only Saturday & Sunday.
If work is started on Monday, it will
finish Sunday evening.

FIGURE A.9

Slip One Week

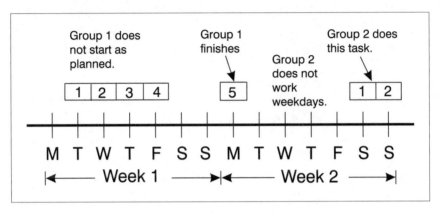

being used does not permit the use of multiple calendars, it may still be possible to "fake it" and force the schedule to reflect correct working dates, but it may be difficult to do. For this reason, software should be selected with this potential requirement in mind.

GLOSSARY

Activity   The work or effort needed to achieve a result. It consumes time and usually consumes resources.

Activity Description   A statement specifying what must be done to achieve a desired result.

Activity-on-Arrow   A network diagram showing sequence of activities, in which each activity is represented by an arrow, with a circle representing a node or event at each end.

Activity-on-Node   A network diagram showing sequence of activities, in which each activity is represented by a box or circle, (that is, a *node*) and these are interconnected with arrows to show precedence of work.

Authority   The legitimate power given to a person in an organization to use resources to reach an objective and to exercise discipline.

Backward-Pass Calculation   Calculations made working backward through a network from the latest event to the beginning event to calculate event late times. A forward pass calculation determines early times.

Calendars   The arrangement of normal working days, together with nonworking days, such as holidays and vacations, as well as special work days (overtime periods) used to determine dates on which project work will be completed.

Change Order   A document which authorizes a change in some aspect of a project.

Control   The practice of monitoring progress against a plan so that corrective steps can be taken when a deviation from plan occurs.

CPM   An acronym for critical path method. A network diagramming method which shows the longest series of activities in a project, thereby determining the earliest completion for the project.

Crashing   An attempt to reduce activity or total project duration, usually by adding resources.

Critical Path   The longest sequential path of activities which are absolutely essential for completion of the project.

Dependency   The next task or group of tasks cannot begin until preceding work has been completed, thus the word *dependent* or dependency.

Deviation   Any variation from planned performance. The deviation can be in terms of schedule, cost, performance, or scope of work. Deviation analysis is the heart of exercising project control.

Dummy Activity   A zero-duration element in a network showing a logic linkage. A dummy does not consume time or resources, but simply indicates precedence.

Duration   The time it takes to complete an activity.

Earliest Finish   The earliest time that an activity can be completed.

Earliest Start   The earliest time that an activity can be started.

Estimate   A forecast or guess about how long an activity will take, how many resources might be required, or how much it will cost.

Event   A point in time. An event is binary. It is either achieved or not, whereas an activity can be partially complete. An event can be the start or finish of an activity.

Feedback Information derived from observation of project activities which is used to analyze the status of the job and take corrective action if necessary.

Float A measure of how much an activity can be delayed before it begins to impact the project finish date.

Forward Pass Method The method used to calculate the earliest start time for each activity in a network diagram.

Free Float The amount of time that an activity can be delayed without affecting succeeding activities.

Gantt Chart A bar chart which indicates the time required to complete each activity in a project. It is named for Henry L. Gantt, who first developed a complete notational system for displaying progress with bar charts.

Hammock Activity A single activity which actually represents a group of activities. It "hangs" between two events and is used to report progress on the composite which it represents.

Histogram A vertical bar chart showing (usually) resource allocation levels over time in a project.

i-j Notation A system of numbering nodes in an activity-on-arrow network. The i-node is always the beginning of an activity, while the j-node is always the finish.

Inexcusable Delays Project delays that are attributable to negligence on the part of the contractor, which lead in many cases to penalty payments.

Latest Finish The latest time that an activity can be finished without extending the end date for a project.

Latest Start The latest time that an activity can start without extending the end date for a project.

Learning Curve The time it takes humans to learn an activity well enough to achieve optimum performance can be displayed by curves, which must be factored into estimates of activity durations in order to achieve planned completion dates.

Leveling   An attempt to smooth the use of resources, whether people, materials, or equipment, to avoid large peaks and valleys in their usage.

Life Cycle   The phases which a project goes through from concept through completion. The nature of the project changes during each phase.

Matrix Organization   A method of drawing people from functional departments within an organization for assignment to a project team, but without removing them from their physical location. The project manager in such a structure is said to have *dotted-line* authority over team members.

Milestone   An event of special importance, usually representing the completion of a major phase of project work. Reviews are often scheduled at milestones.

Most Likely Time   The most realistic time estimate for completing an activity under normal conditions.

Negative Float or Slack   A condition in a network in which the *earliest time* for an event is actually later than its *latest time*. This happens when the project has a constrained end date which is earlier than can be achieved, or when an activity uses up its float and is still delayed.

Node   A point in a network connected to other points by one or more arrows. In activity-on-arrow notation, the node contains at least one event. In activity-on-node notation, the node represents an activity, and the arrows show the sequence in which they must be performed.

PERT   An acronym which stands for program evaluation and review technique. PERT makes use of network diagrams as does CPM, but in addition applies statistics to activities to try and estimate the probabilities of completion of project work.

Pessimistic Time   Roughly speaking, this is the *worst-case* time to complete an activity. The term has a more precise meaning which is defined in the PERT literature.

Phase   A major component or segment of a project.

Precedence Diagram   An activity-on-node diagram.

Queue   Waiting time.

Resource Allocation   The assignment of people, equipment, facilities, or materials to a project. Unless adequate resources are provided, project work cannot be completed on schedule, and resource allocation is a significant component of project scheduling.

Resource Pool   A group of people who can generally do the same work, so that they can be chosen randomly for assignment to a project.

Risk   The possibility that something can go wrong and interfere with the completion of project work.

Scope   The magnitude of work which must be done to complete a project.

Subproject   A small project within a larger one.

Statement of Work   A description of work to be performed.

Time Now   The current calendar date from which a network analysis, report, or update is being made.

Time Standard   The time allowed for the completion of a task.

Variance   Any deviation of project work from what was planned. Variance can affect costs, time, performance, or project scope.

Work Breakdown Structure   A method of subdividing work into smaller and smaller increments to permit accurate estimates of durations, resource requirements, and costs.

RESOURCES FOR PROJECT MANAGERS

Following is a list of sources of information, books, and professional associations which may be helpful in managing projects. Not all are specifically aimed at project management, but you may find them helpful anyway.

CRM Learning: A good source of films for training, including "Mining Group Gold," "The Abilene Paradox," and many others. 2215 Faraday Avenue • Carlsbad, CA 92008 • Tel. (800) 421-0833.

The Lewis Institute, Inc.: Founded by the author, the Institute provides training in project management, team building, and related courses. The core program is Project Management: Tools, Principles, Practices, and has been attended by over 20,000 managers worldwide. 302 Chestnut Mountain Dr. • Vinton, VA 24179 • Tel. (540) 345-7850 • FAX: (540) 345-7844 • e-mail: jlewis@lewisinstitute.com • www.lewisinstitute.com.

McGraw-Hill Books: Source for other titles on project management. www.mcgraw-hill.com.

PBS Home Video: Source of the video "21st Century Jet." (800) 645-4727. www.shopPBS.com.

Pegasus Communications: Publishers of The Systems Thinker, a monthly newsletter. They also have videos by Russell Ackoff and Peter Senge, among others. P.O. Box 943 • Oxford, OH 45056-0943 • Tel. (800) 636-3796 • FAX: (905) 764-7983.

Pfeiffer & Company: A source of training programs, training materials, instruments, and books on management. 350 Sansome Street, 5th Floor • San Francisco, CA 94104 • Tel (800) 274-4434 • FAX: (800) 569-0443.

Pimsleur International: The most effective way to learn a language on your own is with the cassettes using a method developed by Dr. Paul Pimsleur. Learning is virtually painless. 30 Monument Square, Suite 135 • Concord, MA 01742 • Tel. (800) 222-5860 • FAX: (508) 371-2935.

Project Management Institute: The professional association for project managers. Over 100,000 members nationwide as of 2005. They have local chapters in most major U.S. cities and a number of countries. Tel. (610) 734-3330 • FAX: (610) 734-3266 • www.pmi.org.

REFERENCES AND READING LIST

Ackoff, Russell. *Ackoff's Fables: Irreverent Reflections on Business and Bureaucracy.* New York: Wiley, 1991.

Ackoff, Russell. *The Art of Problem Solving.* New York: Wiley, 1978.

Adams, James L. *Conceptual Blockbusting: A Guide to Better Ideas,* 2d ed. New York: W. W. Norton, 1979.

Adams, John D. (Editor) *Transforming Leadership: From Vision to Results.* Alexandria, VA: Miles River Press, 1986.

Ailes, Roger. *You Are the Message: Secrets of the Master Communicators.* Homewood, IL: Dow Jones-Irwin, 1988.

Albrecht, Karl. *The Northbound Train.* New York: AMACOM, 1994.

Archibald, R. D., and R. L. Villoria. *Network-Based Management Systems (PERT/CPM).* New York: Wiley, 1967.

Argyris, Chris. *Overcoming Organizational Defenses: Facilitating Organizational Learning.* Boston: Allyn and Bacon, 1990.

Axelrod, Robert. *The Evolution of Cooperation.* New York: Basic Books, 1984.

Barker, Joel A. *Future Edge.* New York: William Morrow, 1992.

Barker, Joel A. *Wealth, Innovation & Diversity.* Videotape. Carlsbad, CA: CRM Learning, 2000.

Bedi, Hari. *Understanding the Asian Manager.* Singapore: Heinemann Asia, 1992.

Beer, Stafford. *Brain of the Firm,* 2d ed. New York: Wiley, 1981.

Bennis, Warren G. *Managing the Dream: Reflections on Leadership and Change.* Cambridge, MA: Perseus, 2000.

Bennis, Warren G., and Burt Nanus. *Leaders: The Strategies for Taking Charge.* New York: Harper & Row, 1985.

Benveniste, Guy. *Mastering the Politics of Planning.* San Francisco: Jossey-Bass, 1989.

Barnhart, Robert K. *The Barnhart Concise Dictionary of Etymology: The Origins of American English Words.* New York: Harper Collins, 1995.

Blanchard, Benjamin S. *Engineering Organization and Management.* Englewood Cliffs, NJ: Prentice-Hall, 1976.

Block, Peter. *The Empowered Manager,* 2d ed. San Francisco: Jossey-Bass, 2000.

Brooks, F. P. *The Mythical Man-Month: Essays on Software Engineering.* Reading, MA: Addison-Wesley, 1975.

Bunker, Barbara Benedict, and Billie T. Alban. *Large Group Interventions: Engaging the Whole System for Rapid Change.* San Francisco: Jossey-Bass, 1997.

Burns, James McGregor. *Leadership.* New York: Harper & Row, 1978.

Buzan, Tony. *The Mind Map Book.* New York: NAL/Dutton, 1996.

Carlzon, Jan. *Moments of Truth.* New York: Perennial, 1987.

Chen, Yanping, and Francis N. Arko. *Principles of Contracting for Project Management.* Arlington, VA: UMT Press, 2003

Cialdini, Robert B. *Influence: The Power of Persuasion,* Revised Edition. New York: Quill, 1993.

Covey, Stephen. *The 7 Habits of Highly Effective People.* New York: Fireside Books, 1989.

Crosby, Philip. *Quality Is Free.* East Rutherford, NJ: Signet, 1980.

de Bono, Edward. *Serious Creativity.* New York: Harper, 1992.

de Bono, Edward. *Six Thinking Hats.* Boston: Little, Brown & Co., 1985.

Deming, Edwards. *Out of the Crisis.* Cambridge, MA: Massachusetts Institute of Technology, 1986.

Dimancescu, Dan. *The Seamless Enterprise. Making Cross-Functional Management Work.* New York: Harper, 1992.

Downs, Alan. *Corporate Executions: The Ugly Truth About Layoffs—How Corporate Greed Is Shattering Lives, Companies, and Communities.* New York: AMACOM, 1995.

Drucker, Peter F. *Management: Tasks, Responsibilities, Practices*. New York: Harper & Row, 1973, 1974.

Dyer, Wayne. *You'll See It When You Believe It*. New York: Avon Books, 1989.

Eisenstein, Paul A. "How Toyota's Kentucky Operations Mix People, Processes to Be Best." *Investor's Business Daily*, 12/4/2000.

Fleming, Q. W. *Cost/Schedule Control Systems Criteria*. Chicago: Probus, 1988.

Fleming, Quentin W., and Joel M. Koppelman. *Earned Value Project Management*. Upper Darbey, PA: Project Management Institute, 1996.

Fortune, Joyce, and Geoff Peters. *Learning from Failure: The Systems Approach*. Chichester, England: Wiley, 1998.

Frame, J. Davidson. *Managing Projects in Organizations*. San Francisco: Jossey-Bass, 1995.

Frame, J. Davidson. *The New Project Management*, 2d ed. San Francisco: Jossey-Bass, 2002.

Frame, J. Davidson. *Project Finance: Tools and Techniques*. Arlington, VA: UMT Press, 2003.

Frankl, Viktor. *Man's Search for Meaning*, 3d ed. New York: Touchstone, 1984.

Freiberg, Kevin, and Jackie Freiberg. *Nuts! Southwest Airlines' Crazy Recipe for Business and Personal Success*. New York: Broadway Books, 1996.

Gardner, Howard. *Frames of Mind: The Theory of Multiple Intelligences*. New York: Basic Books, 1993.

Garten, Jeffrey E. *The Mind of the C. E. O.* New York: Basic Books, 2001.

Gause, Donald, and Gerald Weinberg. *Exploring Requirements: Quality Before Design*. New York: Dorset House Publishing, 1989.

George, Michael. *Lean Six Sigma: Combining Six Sigma Quality with Lean Production Speed*. New York: McGraw-Hill, 2002.

George, Michael. *Lean Six Sigma for Service*. New York: McGraw-Hill, 2003.

Goldratt, Eliyahu M. *Critical Chain*. Great Barrington, MA: The North River Press, 1997.

Graham, Robert J. and Randall L. Englund. *Creating an Environment for Successful Projects*. San Francisco: Jossey-Bass, 1997.

Hammer, Michael, and James Champy. *Reengineering the Corporation.* New York: Harper Business, 1993.

Hampden-Turner, Charles, and Fons Trompenaars. *Building Cross-Cultural Competence.* New Haven: Yale University Press, 2000.

Hancock, Graham. *Fingerprints of the Gods.* New York: Crown, 1995.

Harry, Mikel, and Richard Schroeder. *Six Sigma: The Breakthrough Management Strategy Revolutionizing the World's Top Corporations.* New York: Currency, 2000.

Harvey, Jerry B. *The Abilene Paradox: And Other Meditations on Management.* San Diego: University Associates, 1988.

Heller, Robert. *Achieving Excellence.* New York: DK Publishing, 1999.

Heller, Robert, and Tim Hindle. *Essential Manager's Manual.* New York: DK Publishing, 1998.

Herrmann, Ned. *The Creative Brain.* Lake Lure, NC: Brain Books, 1995.

Herrmann, Ned. *The Whole Brain Business Book.* New York: McGraw-Hill, 1996.

Hersey, Paul, and Blanchard, Kenneth. *Management of Organizational Behavior: Utilizing Human Resources,* 4th ed. Englewood Cliffs, NJ: Prentice-Hall, 1981.

Highsmith, III, James A. *Adaptive Software Development.* New York: Dorset House, 2000.

Ittner, Christopher D., and David F. Larckner. "A Bigger Yardstick for Company Performance." London: *The Financial Times,* 10/16/2000.

Janis, Irving, and Leon Mann. *Decision Making.* New York: The Free Press, 1977.

Jones, Russel A. *Self-Fulfilling Prophecies.* Hillsdale, NJ: Lawrence Erlbaum, 1977.

Kaplan, Robert, and David Norton. *The Balanced Scorecard: Translating Strategy into Action.* Harvard Business School Press, 1996.

Kayser, Tom. *Mining Group Gold.* New York: McGraw-Hill, 1995.

Keane. *Productivity Management: Keane's Project Management Approach for Systems Development,* 2d ed. Boston: Keane Associates (800-239-0296).

Keirsey, David. *Please Understand Me II.* Del Mar, CA: Prometheus Nemesis Book Company, 1998.

Kepner, Charles H., and Benjamin B. Tregoe. *The Rational Manager.* Princeton, NJ: Kepner-Tregoe, Inc., 1965.

Kerzner, Harold. *In Search of Excellence in Project Management*. New York: Van Nostrand, 1998.

Kerzner, Harold. *Project Management: A Systems Approach to Planning, Scheduling, and Controlling*, 5th ed. New York: Van Nostrand, 1995.

Kiemele, Mark J., and Stephen R. Schmidt. *Basic Statistics. Tools for Continuous Improvement*, 3d ed. Colorado Springs, CO: Air Academy Press, 1993.

Knight, James A. *Value Based Management: Developing a Systematic Approach to Creating Shareholder Value*. New York: McGraw-Hill, 1998.

Koch, Richard. *The 80/20 Principle*. New York: Doubleday, 1998.

Kohn, Alfie. *Punished by Rewards*. Mariner Books, 1999.

Kouzes, James M., and Barry Z. Posner. *The Leadership Challenge: How to Get Extraordinary Things Done in Organizations*. San Francisco: Jossey-Bass, 1987.

Kuhn, Thomas. *The Structure of Scientific Revolutions*. Chicago: University of Chicago Press, 1970.

Leider, Richard J. *Life Skills: Taking Charge of Your Personal and Professional Growth*. Paramus, NJ: Prentice Hall, 1994.

Leider, Richard J. *The Power of Purpose: Creating Meaning in Your Life and Work*. San Francisco: Berrett Koehler, 1997.

Lerner, Michael. *The Politics of Meaning*. Reading, MA: Addison-Wesley, 1996.

Lewis, James. *Fundamentals of Project Management*, 2d ed. New York: AMACOM, 2001.

Lewis, James. *Mastering Project Management*. New York: McGraw-Hill, 1998.

Lewis, James. *Project Leadership*. New York: McGraw-Hill, 2002.

Lewis, James. *Project Planning, Scheduling and Control*, 3d ed. New York: McGraw-Hill, 2000.

Lewis, James. *The Project Manager's Desk Reference*, 2d ed. New York: McGraw-Hill, 2000.

Lewis, James. *The Project Manager's Pocket Survival Guide*. New York: McGraw-Hill, 2003.

Lewis, James. *Team-Based Project Management*. Baltimore, MD: Beard Books, 2004.

Lewis, James. *Working Together*. New York: McGraw-Hill, 2002.

Lewis, James, and Louis Wong. *Accelerated Project Management*. New York: McGraw-Hill, 2004.

Lewis, James, and Robert E. Dudley. *The McGraw-Hill Guide to the PMP Exam*. New York: McGraw-Hill, 2005.

Maidique, Modesto, and Billie Jo Zirger. *The New Product Learning Cycle*. Research Policy. (Cited in Peters, 1987).

Maier, Norman R. F. *Psychology in Industry*. Boston: Houghton Mifflin, 1955.

Maloney, Lawrence D. "For the Love of Flying." *Design News*, Vol. 51, Number 5, March 4, 1996.

March, James, and Herbert Simon. *Organizations*. New York: Wiley, 1966.

Maslow, Abraham. *Motivation and Personality*, 2d ed. New York: Harper & Row, 1970.

McCartney, Scott. "Out of the Blue. How Two Pacific Nations Became Oceanic Aces of Air-Traffic Control." *The Wall Street Journal*, Friday, December 29, 2000.

McClelland, David. *Power: The Inner Experience*. New York: Halsted Press, 1975.

McGraw, Phillip. *Life Strategies: Doing What Works, Doing What Matters*. New York, Hyperion, 1999.

Michalko, Michael. *Thinkertoys*. Berkeley, CA: Ten Speed Press, 1995.

Miller, William C. *The Creative Edge: Fostering Innovation Where You Work*. Reading, MA: Addison-Wesley, 1986.

Mintzberg, Henry. *Mintzberg on Management*. New York: The Free Press, 1989.

Moder, Joseph J., Cecil R. Phillips, and Edward W. Davis. *Project Management with CPM, PERT, and Precedence Diagraming*, 3d ed. New York: Van Nostrand, 1983.

Morrison, Terri; Wayne A. Conaway; and George A. Borden. *Kiss, Bow or Shake Hands*. Holbrook, MA: Adams Media Corporation, 1994.

Mouzelis, N. P. "Bureaucracy," *The New Encyclopaedia Britannica*. 15th ed., Macropaedia 3 (1974).

Nadler, Gerald, and Shozo Hibino. *Breakthrough Thinking*. Rocklin, CA: Prima Publishing, 1990.

NASA. *100 Rules for Project Managers*.

Nellore, Rajesh. "R&D Structures to Keep the Focus on Products." London: *Financial Times*, 12/11/2000.

von Oech, Roger. *A Whack on the Side of the Head*. New York: Warner, 1983.

von Oech, Roger. *A Kick in the Seat of the Pants*. New York: Warner, 1986.

Packard, Vance. *The Pyramid Climbers*. New York: McGraw-Hill, 1962.

Page, Rick. *Hope Is Not a Strategy*. New York: McGraw-Hill, 2003.

Pasmore, William. *Designing Effective Organizations: The Sociotechnical Systems Perspective*. New York: Wiley, 1988.

Patterson, Marvin. *Accelerating Innovation: Improving the Processes of Product Development*. New York: Van Nostrand Reinhold, 1993.

Peter, Lawrence J. *The Peter Principle*. New York: William Morrow & Co., 1969.

Peters, Tom. *Liberation Management*. New York: Knopf, 1992.

Peters, Tom. *Thriving on Chaos*. New York: Knopf, 1987.

Peters, Tom. "The WOW Project." *Fast Company* magazine, May 1999.

Peters, Tom, and Bob Waterman. *In Search of Excellence*. New York: Warner Books, 1988.

Pinto, Jeffrey K. *Power and Politics in Project Management*. Upper Darbey, PA: Project Management Institute, 1996.

Pinto, Jeffrey K., Editor. *The Project Management Institute Project Management Handbook*. San Francisco: Jossey-Bass, 1998.

Ray, M., and R. Myers. *Creativity in Business*. Garden City, NY: Doubleday, 1986.

Rickards, Tudor. *Problem Solving Through Creative Analysis*. Epping, Essex, England: Gower Press, 1975.

Rosen, Robert H. *Leading People: The 8 Proven Principles for Success in Business*. New York: Penguin Books, 1996.

Rosenthal, R., and L. Jacobson. *Pygmalion in the Classroom*. New Your: Holt, Rinehart, and Winston, 1968.

Saaty, Thomas L. *Decision Making for Leaders*. Pittsburgh: RWS Publications, 1995.

Sabbagh, Karl. *Twenty-First Century Jet*. New York: Scribner, 1996.

Schuster, John P., Jill Carpenter, and Patricia Kane. *The Power of Open-Book Management*. New York: Wiley, 1996.

Senge, Peter. *The Fifth Discipline*. New York: Doubleday, 1990.

Senge, Peter. Interview in *Fast Company*, May 1999.

Smith, Hyrum W. *The 10 Natural Laws of Successful Time and Life Management*. New York: Warner Books, 1994.

Smith, Preston G., and Donald G. Reinertsen. *Developing Products in Half the Time*. New York: Van Nostrand, 1995.

Stacey, Ralph D. *Complexity and Creativity in Organizations*. San Francisco: Berrett-Koehler, 1996.

Steiner, Claude. *Scripts People Live By*, 2d ed. New York: Grove Weidenfeld, 1990.

Sugimoto, T. *Estimation on the Project Management Workload*. In Proceedings of the International Conference on Project Management, Singapore, 31 July to 2 August, 2002.

Sykes, Charles. *A Nation of Victims: The Decay of the American Character*. New York: St. Martin's Press, 1992.

Sykes, Charles. *Dumbing Down Our Kids*. New York: St. Martin's Press, 1995.

Treacy, Michael, and Fred Wiersema. *The Discipline of Market Leaders*. Reading, MA: Addison-Wesley, 1995.

Vroom, Victor, and Arthur Jago. *The New Leadership*. Englewood Cliffs, NJ: 1988.

Vroom, Victor, and Phillip Yetton. *Leadership and Decision Making*. Pittsburgh: University of Pittsburgh Press, 1973.

Walpole, Ronald E. *Introduction to Statistics*, 2d ed. New York: Macmillan, 1974.

Watzlawick, Paul, John Weakland, and Richard Fisch. *Change: Principles of Problem Formulation and Problem Resolution*. New York: Norton, 1974.

Weisbord, Marvin. *Productive Workplaces*. San Francisco: Jossey-Bass, 1987.

Weisbord, Marvin, editor. *Discovering Common Ground: How Future Search Conferences Bring People Together to Achieve Breakthrough Innovation, Empowerment, Shared Vision, and Collaborative Action*. San Francisco: Berrett-Koehler, 1992.

Weisbord, Marvin, and Sandra Janoff. *Future Search: An Action Guide to Finding Common Ground in Organizations and Communities*. San Francisco: Berrett-Koehler, 1995.

Wheatley, Margaret. *Leadership and New Science.* San Francisco: Berrett-Koehler, 1992.

White, Gregory L. "In Order to Grow, GM Finds That the Order of the Day Is Cutbacks." *The Wall Street Journal,* Monday, December 18, 2000.

Wilson, Larry. *Changing the Game.* New York: Fireside, 1988.

Wing, R. L. *The Tao of Power.* New York: Doubleday, 1986.

Wysocki, Robert K. *Effective Project Management,* 2d ed. New York: Wiley, 2000.

Wysocki, Robert K., and James P. Lewis. *The World-Class Project Manager.* Boston: Perseus Books, 2000.

Young, S. David, and Stephen F. O'Byrne. *EVA® and Value-Based Management.* New York: McGraw-Hill, 2001.

Zander, Rosamund Stone, and Benjamin Zander. *The Art of Possibility.* Boston: Harvard Business School Press, 2000.

INDEX

ABOUT THE AUTHOR

James P. Lewis, Ph.D. is an experienced project manager who now teaches seminars on the subject throughout the United States, England, and the Far East. His solid, no-nonsense approach is largely the result of the 15 years he spent in industry, working as an electrical engineer engaged in the design and development of communication equipment. He held various positions, including Project Manager, Product Engineering Manager, and Chief Engineer, for Aerotron, Inc. and ITT Telecommunications, both of Raleigh, NC. He also was a Quality Manager for ITT Telecom, managing a department of 63 quality engineers, line inspectors, and test technicians.

While he was an engineering manager, he began working on a doctorate in organizational psychology, because of his conviction that a manager can only succeed by developing good interpersonal skills.

Since 1980, Dr. Lewis has trained over 30,000 supervisors and managers in Argentina, Canada, England, Germany, India, Indonesia, Malaysia, Mexico, Singapore, Sweden, Thailand, and the United States. He has written articles for *Training and Development Journal, Apparel Industry Magazine,* and *Transportation and Distribution Magazine,* and is the author of *Mastering Project Management,*

The Project Manager's Desk Reference, Second Edition, Working Together: The 12 Principles Employed by Boeing Commercial Aircraft to Manage Projects, Teams, and the Organization, Project Leadership, and *The Project Manager's Survival Guide,* and co-author with Louis Wong of *Accelerated Project Management,* published by McGraw-Hill, and *Fundamentals of Project Management, Second Edition; How to Build and Manage a Winning Project Team;* and *Team-Based Project Management,* published by the American Management Association. He is co-author, with Bob Wysocki, of *The World-Class Project Manager,* published by Perseus in 2001. The first edition of *Project Planning, Scheduling and Control* has been published in a Spanish edition, and the AMACOM book *Fundamentals of Project Management* has been published in Portuguese and Latvian. Several of his books have also been published in Chinese, and *Project Leadership* has been translated into Spanish and Russian.

He has a B.S. in Electrical Engineering and a Ph.D. in Psychology, both from NC State University in Raleigh. He is a member of the Project Management Institute. He is also a certified Herrmann Brain Dominance Instrument practitioner.

He is president of The Lewis Institute, Inc., a training and consulting company specializing in project management, which he founded in 1981. He is a member of the Project Management Institute and the American Society for Training and Development.

Jim is married to the former Lea Ann McDowell, and they live in Vinton, Virginia.